The Creation
of the
BOOK OF MORMON

The Prophet Joseph Smith

The Creation
of the
BOOK OF MORMON

A Historical Inquiry

LaMar Petersen

𝕱𝖗𝖊𝖊𝖙𝖍𝖎𝖓𝖐𝖊𝖗 𝕻𝖗𝖊𝖘𝖘
Salt Lake City

∞ *The Creation of the Book of Mormon:*
A Historical Inquiry
was printed on acid-free paper,
and meets the permanence of paper requirements
of the American National Standard for Information Sciences.
This book was printed in the United States of America.

The frontispiece of Joseph Smith is reproduced
from Edward W. Tullidge's 1878 *Life of Joseph the Prophet.*

03 02 01 00   6 5 4 3 2

———————

Library of Congress Cataloging-in-Publication Data

Petersen, LaMar, 1910-.
The creation of the Book of Mormon :
a historical inquiry
/ LaMar Petersen.
p. cm.
Includes bibliographical references and index.
ISBN 1-890686-04-2 (alk. paper)
1. Book of Mormon--Criticism, interpretation, etc.
2. Church of Jesus Christ of Latter-day Saints
--History--19th century.
3. Smith, Joseph, 1805-1844.
I. Title.
BX8627.P435 2000
289.3'22--dc20   98-11620
CIP
www.freethinkerpress.com

"I told the brethren
that the Book of Mormon was
the most correct of any book on earth,
and the keystone of our religion,
and a man would get nearer to God
by abiding by its precepts,
than by any other book."

The Prophet Joseph Smith

Contents

Illustrations

Foreword

To explain my own background let me mention that when I was twelve, I was employed at the Associated Newspapers as mailing clerk and errand boy. My father, Adam L. Petersen, was general manager for the LDS foreign newspapers: *Bikuben* (Danish), *Beobachter* (German), *Utah-Posten* (Swedish), and *Der Nederlander* (Dutch). Our office functioned under the Seven Presidents of the Seventy with Apostle John A. Widtsoe as supervisor. My pleasant task from 1923 to 1930 was gofer between offices and I was proud to serve the good men in charge. I came to admire B. H. Roberts, Levi Edgar Young, J. Golden Kimball, and the other members of the Seventy. Sometime in 1929 Elder Roberts gave a lecture at the old Granite Tabernacle on State Street. Tracy Y. Cannon, organist at the Tabernacle on Temple Square, was to assist at the Estey Pipe Organ. He became indisposed and sent me, his pupil. It was exciting for me to be on the program with the great B. H. Roberts. I noted how firm he stood with his cane at the podium, despite physical problems. His oratory was fiery, memorable, and compelling.

In June 1934 I was returning from music study in New York and had arranged to spend two days at the Joseph Smith home in Palmyra. A quarterly conference was being held, with Willard Bean and his family in charge. At the dinner table Apostle George Albert Smith suggested that I be the privileged one to occupy the "Vision Room." Next morning I encountered him on the path to the "Sacred Grove." He was very knowledgeable about the area and benevolent toward me. We had a long and, for me, rewarding conversation. Three years later he would perform the marriage ceremony for me and my bride in the Salt Lake Temple.

As I was seeking information in the years that followed, I had several visits with some of the General Authorities (David O. McKay; J. Reuben Clark, Jr.; James E. Talmage; John A. Widtsoe; Richard L. Evans; Joseph Wirthlin; Milton R. Hunter; and Hartman Rector, Jr.)—some more memorable than others. The most noteworthy were six sessions in which my wife and I spent with Levi Edgar Young in 1952. He was forthright in discussing Mormon problems in history and theology, but always in loyal church terms. He told us that he had been defended before the First Presidency by his "buffers"—Apostles Merrill, Callis, and Widtsoe. He told us of a "strange account" (Young's own term) of the First Vision, which he thought was written in Joseph's own hand and which had been concealed for 120 years in a locked vault. He declined to tell us details, but stated that it did not agree entirely with the official version. Jesus was the center of the vision, but God was not mentioned. I respected Young's wish that the information be withheld until after his death.

Introduction

God spoke to Joseph Smith on 1 November 1831, at Hiram, Ohio, and declared that the church[1] Joseph had recently founded was "the only true and living church upon the face of the whole earth, with which I, the Lord, am well pleased" (D&C 1:30).

In the hundred and sixty-eight years since the Lord voiced his approval of the church, millions of believing Mormons have accepted this pronouncement at face value. Their assurance as to the divinity of the church has not been lessened with the knowledge that many billions of people have never heard of the gospel. This has served merely to intensify their spirit of dedication in the cause of truth and to quicken their missionary zeal in behalf of both the living and the dead.

The Latter-day Saints believe that only two churches lay claim to divine sanction—their own and the Roman Catholic, the one just and the other spurious. "Behold there are save two churches only; the one is the church of the Lamb of God, and the other is the church of the devil" (1 Ne. 14:10). The world's thousand other churches are not categorized but it is believed that they are somewhere in outer spiritual darkness.

---

[1]Throughout the text the words "church," "Mormon Church," "LDS Church," "Utah Church," "Mormons," "saints," and "Latter-day Saints" refer to the Church of Jesus Christ of Latter-Day Saints and its members. Also, the word "church," when used in connection with events after the death of Joseph Smith, refers to the one with headquarters at Salt Lake City and not to the Reorganized Church of Jesus Christ of Latter Day Saints in Independence, Missouri, or to any of the smaller factions.

LAMAR PETERSEN

Because of their security in the realm of absolute truth, Mormons seldom question its claims. If the gospel is analyzed, weighed, or compared, it is on the scales of foreknowledge whereby it is known at the outset that the weight of evidences will prove its divinity. "If ye shall ask with a sincere heart, with real intent, having faith in Christ, he will manifest the truth of it unto you, by the power of the Holy Ghost" (Moro. 10:4). Their authority to act in God's name comes directly from Jesus Christ himself and from angelic beings who bestowed the priesthood upon Joseph Smith and Oliver Cowdery by the laying on of hands. Thus the restoration, effected by physical contact between mortals and immortals, is not less a reality than the promise of the establishment of Zion in definite locale, the return of the Lost Ten Tribes from the north, or the second coming of Christ, which is imminent—even at our doors. Being Bible literalists the Latter-day Saints avoid the heresy of metaphysicians to whom the kingdom of God is only a mental concept. The restoration of all things must be more than abstract peace of mind; it is to include the tangible realities of temples where Christ can lay his head, of saints gathered from the four corners of the earth, and of an earth which will receive its paradisiacal glory.

Material evidences have sustained the saints since the beginning of their history in 1830. As ancient Israel had its sacred implements in the Ark of the Covenant and the Rod of Aaron so modern Israel has a counterpart in the Urim and Thummim and the Golden Plates. The latter of these were seen, handled, and examined by those favored of God, and carried with them the same threats of destruction for those who viewed unworthily as did the awful relics of the past. This emphasis on the physical, coupled with unique doctrinal exposition in matters spiritual, has placed the Mormons in an ethnocentric position in regards to their fellows.[2] Being a chosen people has made them a peculiar people, and great pride is taken in those refinements which distinguish them from the Gentiles: being of the blood of Ephraim, having a knowledge of a personal God, enjoying the privileges and responsibilities of the Aaronic and Melchizedek Priesthoods, and marrying for time and eternity. To the people of the nineteenth century these differences were largely academic; it was the doctrine of polygamy that inflamed the public mind to the extent that nothing the Mormons did could possibly have any value. But persecution often breeds respectability. The twentieth century church has sought, in some ways at least, to conform to world opinion. It is relentless in denunciation of the modern polygamist, its early communitarianism is looked upon as too Utopian for the people of today, speaking in tongues is a forgotten practice, bringing the saints to Zion is no longer earnestly recommended, the temple garment has been modified according to the dictates of fashion, and even the temple ceremony has been revamped and shortened. Pressures from within the church as well as from without account for certain of these changes but all were effected with a minimum of embarrassment owing to the doctrine of progressive revelation.

While it is true some principles have undergone modification, there has never been a recession in those arts for which the Mormons are justly famed: home-making and the building of strong family ties. Historically Mormonism was largely an agrarian empire with cheerful villages dotting western valleys from Canada south along the Rockies into Mexico. Formerly, the bulk of population centered in Utah, Idaho, and California, but now over half of its membership is found in other coun-

---

[2]Ethnocentrism is defined by William Graham Sumner, *The Folkways: A Study of the Sociological Importance of Usages, Manners, Customs, Mores, and Morals* (Boston: Ginn and Co., 1940), 13, as the "view of things in which one's own group is the center of everything and all others are sealed and rated with reference to it."

tries. Community life is built around the church building, where are conducted the sacrament meetings, the rites of ordination, choir rehearsals, and young people's activities. Prayers and plays, blessings and basketball, funerals and frolics all take place under the same roof but in separate departments, each sacrosanct and officially dedicated unto the Lord for its specific purpose. Here the Mormon bears his testimony. He knows this is the only true church, he knows that Jesus is the Christ, and that Joseph Smith is a prophet of the Lord. His testimony is sincere and unshakable. If he is an orthodox member reared in the church, he knows these things as he knows the sun, the light, and the air. If he is a convert, he knows them with emotional conviction "beyond a shadow of doubt," for he may have given up native land and even friends and family to embrace the gospel. His testimony may have been gained through study of the four standard works of the church, viz., the Bible, the Book of Mormon, the Doctrine and Covenants, and the Pearl of Great Price, or it may have come as a gift of grace, a direct flash of knowledge imparted through the power of the Holy Ghost. This most-prized possession makes him invulnerable in argument and he will brook no criticism of his faith.

Adherents of a creed sometimes preserve a *status quo* through lack of introspection. In the Mormon Church it is particularly difficult to adopt an analytical viewpoint, because members are admonished to respect authority, obey the covenants, and above all to guard their testimony of the gospel.

In 1854 Heber C. Kimball, counselor to Brigham Young in the First Presidency, proclaimed:

> Now a man will be condemned for not obeying the person properly appointed to preside over him, . . .; and the people will be as much condemned if they do not obey brother Brigham, as they would if they should disobey the Lord God were He here in person.[3]

---

[3] *Journal of Discourses* 3 (1856): 110.

INTRODUCTION

John A. Widtsoe, a member of the Quorum of the Twelve Apostles, said:

> These various groups who are subjected to the ever present temptation to depart from the truth, under the caption of "outgrowing" Mormonism, should examine, carefully, the processes which are leading them astray. They should do some hard, straight thinking. If they will do so earnestly, honestly, intelligently, and prayerfully, they will soon discover, to their full satisfaction, that no man can "outgrow" the gospel. They will learn that those who "outgrow" Mormonism are not happy. Happiness comes to those only who cling to truth.[4]

In examining the claims of Mormonism, many early critics used scorn in place of scholarship and watched in surprise as the church grew not into a hydra-headed monster intent on ruling the world but a benevolent theocracy dedicated to the temporal and spiritual betterment of its members and supported by such organizations as the women's Relief Society and the Young Men's and Young Women's Mutual Improvement Associations. The church easily withstood the onslaughts of ministers who ridiculed and apostates who exposed, but it remains to be seen what direction the church will take in view of the objective studies being advanced by scholars from within the church itself. Excommunication does not necessarily stop objective appraisals. Archaeologists, philosophers, sociologists, and historians are turning a penetrating gaze upon the claims of Mormonism, not with the intent of undermining, but evaluating and understanding. Is the church to be explained as a social phenomenon—a prime example of pragmatism; is it a snare and a delusion as contended by ardent critics; or is it God's own plan of life and salvation as claimed by sincere believers? There seems to be no middle ground for the individual who accepts the social program of the church but

---

[4]John A. Widtsoe, *Gospel Interpretations: Aids to Faith in a Modern Day* (Salt Lake City: Bookcraft, 1947), 33.

cannot subscribe to all of its Articles of Faith. In appraising itself the church has long since crystallized an all-or-nothing criterion which invites the inquiring mind to believe or perish.

Jesus declared:

> Therefore, repent all ye ends of the earth, and come unto me, and believe in my gospel, and be baptized in my name; for he that believeth and is baptized shall be saved; but he that believeth not shall be damned (Ether 4:18; cf. Mark 16:15-16).

The Lord revealed to Joseph Smith:

> Hearken and hear, O ye my people, saith the Lord and your God, ye whom I delight to bless with the greatest of all blessings, ye that hear me; and ye that hear me not will I curse, that have professed my name, with the heaviest of all cursings (D&C 41:1).

The Prophet Joseph Smith, speaking to the Twelve Apostles, explained:

> You need an endowment, brethren, in order that you may be prepared and able to overcome all things; and those that reject your testimony will be damned.[5]

Heber C. Kimball told William E. McLellin:

> I tell you Mormonism is true, and Joseph is a true prophet of the living God; and you with all others that turn therefrom will be damned and go to hell, and Judas will rule over you.[6]

Orson Pratt, a member of the Quorum of the Twelve, warned the person who rejects the Book of Mormon:

---

[5]B. H. Roberts, ed., *History of the Church of Jesus Christ of Latter-day Saints, Period I: History of Joseph Smith, the Prophet by Himself* (Salt Lake City: Deseret News, 1902), 2:309.

[6]Orson F. Whitney, *Life of Heber C. Kimball, an Apostle, the Father and Founder of the British Mission* (Salt Lake City: The Kimball Family, 1888), 218.

He is cursed of God, and will die and go to hell, unless he repents, notwithstanding his apparent honesty. Therefore, no man, . . . can be justified, for one moment, in rejecting God's revealed will, contained in the Book of Mormon, . . .[7]

These judgments seem severe to the unbeliever and in truth they are not emphasized as much today as in former times; nevertheless, the LDS Church has no wish to erase the more extreme pronouncements of its leaders. The assurance of the past is the testimony of the present and these utterances form an unyielding catechism along with the irrevocable scriptures. The church points the way to ultimate exaltation of man and there can be no compromise.

Brigham Young explained:

We ask where Christ's Church is. My conclusive answer is, if the Latter-day Saints do not constitute the Kingdom of God on the earth, the Church of Jesus Christ, it is no where to be found upon it.[8]

John Taylor, an apostle who later became the third president of the LDS Church, laid out the options:

There is one of two things true. We are either laboring under one of the greatest delusions that ever afflicted the human race, or we are under the direction of the great God. There is no half-way business about it.[9]

Joseph Fielding Smith, tenth president of the church, stressed the importance of seeking the truth:

To record as truth that which is false, and to palm off as facts that which is fiction degrades [the writer], insults his readers, and outrages his profession.[10]

---

[7]Orson Pratt, "Repentance," *The Seer* 2 (March 1854): 235.

[8]*Journal of Discourses* 2 (1855): 179.

[9]*Journal of Discourses* 9 (1862): 342.

[10]Leonard J. Arrington, "Joseph Fielding Smith: Faithful Historian," *Dialogue: A Journal of Mormon Thought* 7 (Spring 1972): 21.

Likewise, B. H. Roberts, member of the First Council of Seventy, said:

> The facts in which Mormonism had its origin are of such a character that they cannot be resolved into delusion or mistake. Either they were truth or conscious, Simon-pure invention. It is not possible to place the matter on middle ground. Joseph Smith was either a true prophet or a conscious fraud or villain.[11]

In contrast to the vindictive spirit of some of the above quotations, this sober appraisal was made by E. E. Ericksen, professor of philosophy at the University of Utah:

> There are many reasons why it is extremely difficult for the Mormon doctrines to be harmonized with the new scientific and democratic conceptions. The more basic doctrines of Mormonism center around such questions as the creation of man, the literal interpretation of the Bible, the authority of the priesthood, the divine and eternal nature of Mormon institutions, God's commandments as absolute moral laws, and revelation through the prophet as the only source of all religious truth. All these questions create friction between the present educational spirit and Mormon orthodoxy. . . . The dogmatic opponent of Mormonism regards all of its institutions as positively bad and as directly hindering progress. To him the solution of the problem is the elimination of all that is Mormon. The orthodox Mormon, on the other hand, believes that all the institutions of his church are divine and essential to the great plan of human salvation. His solution of the problem is the silencing of critics and heretics. The ideal situation, in his mind, is for every member of the church to accept with implicit faith every word that falls from the lips of the prophet and obey unhesitatingly the authority of the priesthood. Or as one of the apostles of the church expressed it: "I would that the faith of all Israel increased to the point that every man, woman, and child would say, 'I know not save the Lord commandeth.'" To the

---

[11]B. H. Roberts, *Defense of the Faith and the Saints* (Salt Lake City: The Deseret News, 1907), 1:59.

unprejudiced mind neither of these attitudes points the way to progress. . . . To overcome the present maladjustment two concessions must be made. On the one hand every institution of Mormonism must be subjected to the searchlight of science, and scientific truths, in so far as they provide human welfare, must be considered as sacred as religious truths. On the other hand the educators of Utah must be willing to analyze the Mormon institutions with the true impartial attitude and recognize the desirable as well as the undesirable qualities. In short, prejudice must be removed from both sides before real progress can be attained. The ideal situation will be more fully realized when the church will make more frequent use of scientific experts to aid in its many educational enterprises, and when the college graduate will regard the church, of which he is a member, as an organization through which he can render social and moral service.[12]

The late Ray R. Canning, former professor of sociology at both Brigham Young University and the University of Utah, reminded us that in any study of the Book of Mormon we must not forget the key role played by Joseph Smith:

He was surrounded by simple and fervently believing people. . . . They wanted to believe; he easily helped them to do so—step by step—from digging for treasure, to locating treasure, to treasure being ever more grand, to a golden record which was an addendum to the Bible yet local in its application, to a book of potential profitability once the record was translated and printed.[13]

Church leaders are not oblivious to the fact that they live in a changing world. The Apostle Albert E. Bowen sought to reassure the saints against the barbs of skeptics:

You may put it down that the scoffer is of too small calibre to make his opinion worth bothering about

---

[12]E. E. Ericksen, *Psychological and Ethical Aspects of Mormon Group Life* (Salt Lake City: University of Utah Press, 1975), 62-63, 96-97.

[13]Ray R. Canning, *My Continuing Quest: Sociological Perspectives on Mormonism* (Salt Lake City: Freethinker Press, 1996), 52.

anyway. You need never quarrel with established facts, but neither need you be bondsman to speculative conclusions assumed to flow from those facts, nor yield your own beliefs to such conclusions.[14]

Some philosophers, in contrast to most theologians, hold that the absolute cannot be defined and that truth is relative. "Truth is that which serves us best in expressing our lives. A rotting log is truth to a bed of violets, while sand is truth to a cactus."[15] If this aphorism is tenable, it may be that Mormonism has passed the point of no return, for it insists there is but one road to the Celestial Kingdom and to find it all men must embrace the gospel. By its own yardstick the church is a healthy, flowering organism, highly adaptable to the needs of the individual, and an unfailing guide to the best in his life. The words of Jesus are often quoted by defenders of the faith as a proof of its efficacy: "Ye shall know them by their fruits. Do men gather grapes of thorns, or figs of thistles?" (Matt. 7:16). The apologist can point to the thousands of Mormon homes where harmony reigns, or to the American Medical Association's report on the harmful effects of cigarette smoking which verifies the Lord's Word of Wisdom to Joseph Smith in 1833. Few will deny that Mormonism has contributed color and expansiveness to the American scene, nor that Joseph Smith's ideas were often legitimate and helpful, irrespective of how he obtained them.

Despite the zeal of the saints' activity throughout life, there is a growing awareness in some quarters that enthusiasm alone can not determine truth or falsity. Scholars are demanding more information on the origin of Mormonism and are impatient with the admonition to "leave the mysteries alone."

---

[14]Albert E. Bowen, *Constancy amid Change* (Salt Lake City: The Deseret News Press, 1944), 72.

[15]Elbert Hubbard, "Aristotle," in *Little Journeys to the Homes of Great Philosophers* (East Aurora, NY: The Roycrofters, 1904), 1:77.

Discussion of the miraculous coming forth of the Book of Mormon is being superseded by examination of its intrinsic worth. One member has suggested that readers adopt a better touchstone of authenticity—not "Was it inspired?" but "Is it inspiring?"[16]

We must also keep in mind the counsel of Joseph Campbell, an authority on world mythologies:

> In the later stages of many mythologies, the key images hide like needles in the great haystacks of secondary anecdote and rationalization; . . . Furthermore, it is never difficult to demonstrate that as a science and history mythology is absurd.[17]

Restudy of the Book of Mormon will either emphasize its place in the lives of readers as a great moral guide and bona fide history or a magnificent curiosity. Scholarly B. H. Roberts seems to have anticipated a departure from the age of dogmatic assertion into a day of liberal opinion:

> The disciples of "Mormonism," growing discontented with the necessarily primitive methods which have hitherto prevailed in sustaining the doctrine, will yet take profounder and broader views of the great doctrines committed to the Church; and, departing from mere repetition, will cast them in new formulas; cooperating in the works of the Spirit, until they help to give to the truths received a more forceful expression, and carry it beyond the earlier and cruder stages of its development.[18]

In the following pages an attempt has been made to ex-

---

[16]William Mulder, "Mormonism and Literature," *The Western Humanities Review* 9 (Winter 1954-1955): 88.

[17]Joseph Campbell, *The Hero with a Thousand Faces* (Princeton, NJ: Princeton University Press, 1973), 249.

[18]B. H. Roberts, "Book of Mormon Translation: Interesting Correspondence on the Subject of the Manual Theory," *Improvement Era* 9 (July 1906): 713; reprinted in B. H. Roberts, "The Disciples of Mormonism," *Dialogue: A Journal of Mormon Thought* 1 (Winter 1966): 134.

plore, and possibly to illumine, the origin of the Book of Mormon. Particular attention has been paid to the statements of those who were instrumental in building the church and to those who were interested spectators. The personal bias of each individual must, of course, be considered and also the time and circumstance under which his information was given. Some statements are uttered in retrospect so that faulty memory may have taken its toll. It is not to be supposed that the information presented is final or conclusive.

In studying the provenance of the Book of Mormon one should consider the following questions: Did the young Joseph Smith find golden plates with an ancient history in a nearby hill? Does the Book of Mormon reflect its gold foundation or does it resemble Rumpelstiltskin's gold, spun from straw? Will those who seek Bountiful, Moronihah, and Zarahemla—great cities of Book-of-Mormon lands—be more successful than those who seek Atlantis, Lilliput, and Shangri-la—the famous habitats of storyland? Does fantasy sometimes supercede reality? The mythologist believes that "myth is more potent than history . . . dreams are more powerful than facts."[19] However, the realist favors a more precise appraisal.

In the final analysis the reader must decide whether the Book of Mormon is a valid history, an imaginative fable, or perhaps a nineteenth-century expression of religious belief. Whether one is friend or foe of Mormonism, Francis Bacon's advice might well be heeded:

> Read not to contradict and confute; nor to believe and take for granted; nor to find talk and discourse; but to weigh and consider.[20]

---

[19]Robert Fulghum, *All I Really Need to Know I Learned in Kindergarten: Uncommon Thoughts on Common Things* (New York: Villard Books, 1990), viii.

[20]"Of Studies," Essay 50, in Francis Bacon, *Essays*, ed. Michael J. Hawkins (London: Everyman, 1994), 129.

Acknowledgments

D uring the last sixty-five years I have studied Mormon history and theology. In this activity I have been aided by a host of friends and colleagues, who helped me clarify my concerns—sometimes in agreement and sometimes in dispute.

At the top of the list I place my wife Faye; our six children: Tracy, Calvin, Linda, Becky, Brian, and Dana; and also our eight grandchildren: Michelle, Christopher, Dane Paul, Peter, Britt, Anna, Devin, and Mason—all of whom gave constant support.

I have also received counsel from the following diverse sources: Jack H. Adamson, Lowell L. Bennion, Mary L. Bradford, Fawn M. Brodie, Juanita Brooks, Will Brooks, Ray R. Canning, Tracy Y. Cannon, Ralph V. Chamberlin, Horace Christensen, Ezra and Geri Clark, Everett L. Cooley, J. Allan Crockett, Richard and Joan Cummings, E. E. Ericksen, John W. Fitzgerald, Heber Q. Hale, Gordon and Alta Howard, H. Grant Ivins, Stanley S. Ivins, Francis W. Kirkham, A. C. Lambert, Andrew Karl Larson, Gustive O. Larson, Stan Larson, William J. Luttrell, Brigham D. Madsen, H. Michael Marquardt, Bill and Olive Moran, Dale L. Morgan, Sterling M. McMurrin, Herman Oliekan, Irene Oliekan, A. Russell Mortensen, Arlen and Chris Petereit, M. Wilford Poulson, Ross and Lola Ramsey, Waldemer P. Read, W. B. Robins, L. Max Rogers, Alexander Schreiner, Helen Sheffield, George D. Smith, Richard Smoot, Heber C. Snell, Albert Southwick, Justin and Martha Stewart, Omer C. Stewart, Jerald and Sandra Tanner, Obert C. Tanner,

LAMAR PETERSEN

Frank Van West, Kent L. Walgren, John Walker, Wesley P. Walters, James D. Wardle, and Angus and Grace Woodbury.

In the mid-1920s I began my career as an organist at the old Salt Lake Eleventh Ward. Lewis A. Ramsey, noted painter of Western canyons and landscapes, had been chosen to portray the boy Joseph receiving the gold plates from the Angel Moroni. Ramsey had built a huge scaffold to reach the entire surface where the canvas was attached to the wall in the ward building. It took Ramsey several months to complete the painting. During this time I practiced every day at the ward and was able to watch his progress. About twenty-five years later the ward building was to be demolished in favor of a new one nearby. The Ramseys had moved to California and I was no longer a resident of the Eleventh Ward. However, I was concerned over the fate of the painting and checked with Bishop Thomas Montgomery, who informed me that the painting could not be extricated from the wall and would be destroyed along with the building. I suggested that he call Horace Sorenson, owner and builder of Pioneer Village on Connor Street. Sorenson with his crew of men, heavy equipment, and a flatbed truck transported the entire wall to a storage repository on Redwood Road. There it was kept until it was finally installed at the new chapel, where it still reposes. During his lifetime Lewis A. Ramsey retained copyright to this painting, and Charles Ramsey and Ross L. Ramsey have granted permission to reproduce this painting on the dust jacket.

Britt Petersen designed the monogram located in the top-left corner at the beginning of each section throughout the book. Abbreviations used in the text are the standardized ones used by the Church of Jesus Christ of Latter-day Saints.

I take full responsibility for this work, but I would be remiss if I did not acknowledge the influence of the individuals mentioned on my efforts to write this study on the Book of Mormon.

CHAPTER 1

The Early Visions

> That becomes the hinge pin on which this whole cause turns. If the First Vision was true, if it actually happened, then the Book of Mormon is true. Then we have the priesthood. Then we have the Church organization and all of the other keys and blessings of authority which we say we have. If the First Vision did not occur, then we are involved in a great sham. It is just that simple (Gordon B. Hinckley, *Teachings of Gordon B. Hinckley*, 226).

The "official" and consequently the most well-known account of the First Vision of Joseph Smith was dictated in 1838 and recopied in 1839. Three years later, on Friday, 1 April 1842, in Nauvoo, the largest city in the state of Illinois (and not long since reclaimed from a parcel of swamp), the *Times and Seasons*, a miniature newspaper devoted to the interests of the Mormon people, made its semi-monthly appearance. There was nothing on the cover page to suggest the thunderbolt that lay obscurely on page 748: God, the Creator of the Universe, had visited the earth and in company with his Son, Jesus Christ, the Redeemer of the World! This plain announcement, set in lower case, and without fanfare, was one of the most astounding items ever to appear in an American publication. Transcending the limits of the word "news," it became history in this 1842 publication.

However, examination of the sources in which Joseph

Smith himself recounted or referred to the First Vision shows a dramatic evolution in the story. There are five such accounts by Joseph Smith, as follows: (1) Joseph's 1832 account, (2) Joseph's 1835 account to Robert Matthews, (3) Joseph's 1835 account to Erastus Holmes, (4) Joseph's 1839 account (which became part of the Pearl of Great Price), and (5) Joseph's 1842 account to John Wentworth.

The following is a transcript of the earliest known account, which has been dated to 1832, and happens also to be the only account written in Joseph Smith's own hand.[1] Its extreme importance justifies its being quoted at length:

> I was born in the town of Charon [Sharon] in the <State> of Vermont, North America on the twenty third day of December AD 1805 of goodly Parents who spared no pains to instructing me in <the> christian religion.
>
> At the age of about ten years my Father Joseph Smith Siegnior [Senior] moved to Palmyra Ontario County in the State of New York and being in indigent circumstances [we] were obliged to labour hard for the support of a large Family having nine children and as it required the exertions of all that were able to render any assistance for the support of the Family therefore we were deprived of the bennifit of an education suffice it to say I was mearly instructid in reading and writing and the ground <rules> of Arithmatic which const[it]uted my whole literary acquirements.
>
> At about the age of twelve years my mind become seriously imprest with regard to the all important concerns for the wellfare of my immortal Soul which led me to searching the scriptures believeing as I was

---

[1]Milton V. Backman, Jr., *Joseph Smith's First Vision: Confirming Evidences and Contemporary Accounts*, 2d ed., rev. and enl. (Salt Lake City: Bookcraft, 1980), 155, states that this account is in the handwriting of the scribe—not Joseph Smith. For some reason, Backman has retained this error in the second edition of his book even though it was pointed out in the review of the first edition by Dean C. Jessee, "How Lovely was the Morning," review of *Joseph Smith's First Vision* by Milton V. Backman, in *Dialogue: A Journal of Mormon Thought* 6 (Spring 1971): 86.

taught, that they contained the word of God thus applying myself to them and my intimate acquaintance with
those of different denominations led me to marvel excedingly for I discovered that <they did not ~~adorn~~>
~~instead~~ of adorning their profession by a holy walk and
Godly conversation agreeable to what I found contained
in that sacred depository this was a grief to my Soul.

Thus from the age of twelve years to fifteen I pondered many things in my heart concerning the sittuation
of the world of mankind the contentions and divi[si]ons
the wicke[d]ness and abominations and the darkness
which pervaded the ~~of the~~ minds of mankind my mind
become excedingly distressed for I become convicted of
my sins and by searching the scriptures I found that
~~mand~~ <mankind> did not come unto the Lord but that
they had apostatised from the true and liveing faith and
there was no society or denomination that built upon
the gospel of Jesus Christ as recorded in the new
testament and I felt to mourn for my own sins and for
the sins of the world.

For I learned in the scriptures that God was the
same yesterday to day and forever [and] that he was no
respecter to [of] persons for he was God for I looked
upon the sun the glorious luminary of the earth and also
the moon rolling in their magesty through the heavens
and also the stars shining in their courses and the earth
also upon which I stood and the beast of the field and
the fowls of heaven and the fish of the waters and also
man walking forth upon the face of the earth in magesty
and in the strength of beauty whose power and intili-
gence in governing the things which are so exceding
great and marvilous even in the likeness of him who
created ~~him~~ <them>.

And when I considered upon these things my
heart exclaimed well hath the wise man said ~~the~~ <it is
a> fool <that> saith in his heart there is no God my
heart exclaimed all all these bear testimony and bespeak
an omnipotent and omnipreasant power a being who
makith Laws and decreeeth and bindeth all things in
their bounds who filleth Eternity who was and is and
will be from all Eternity to Eternity and when I considered all these things and that <that> being seeketh
such to worship him as worship him in spirit and in
truth therefore I cried unto the Lord for mercy for
there was none else to whom I could go and ~~to~~ obtain

mercy the Lord heard my cry in the wilderness and while in <the> attitude of calling upon the Lord <in the 16th year of my age>[2] a piller of fire light above the brightness of the sun at noon day come down from above and rested upon me and I was filled with the spirit of god and the <Lord> opened the heavens upon me and I saw the Lord.

And he spake unto me saying Joseph <my son> thy sins are forgiven thee. go thy <way> walk in my statutes and keep my commandments behold I am the Lord of glory I was crucifyed for the world that all those who believe on my name may have Eternal life <behold> the world lieth in sin and at this time and none doeth good no not one they have turned asside from the gospel and keep not <my> commandments they draw near to me with their lips while their hearts are far from me and mine anger is kindling against the inhabitants of the earth to visit them acording to th[e]ir ungodliness and to bring to pass that which <hath> been spoken by the mouth of the prophets and Ap[o]s-tles behold and lo I come quickly as it [is] written of me in the cloud <clothed> in the glory of my Father.

And my soul was filled with love and for many days I could rejoice with great Joy and the Lord was with me but [I] could find none that would believe the hevnly vision nevertheless I pondered these things in my heart. . . .[3]

In the second account, on 9 November 1835, Joseph Smith had a long conversation with Robert Matthews, also

---

[2]The phrase "16th year of my age" probably meant "sixteen years old" (which would be the spring of 1822), but technically refers to being "fifteen years old" (which would be the spring of 1821).

[3]Dean C. Jessee, ed., *The Papers of Joseph Smith* (Salt Lake City: Deseret Book Co., 1989), 1:3-7. Cf. Scott H. Faulring, ed., *An American Prophet's Record: The Diaries and Journals of Joseph Smith*, 2d ed. (Salt Lake City: Signature Books in association with Smith Research Associates, 1989), 4-6. Paragraph divisions have been added for clarity. Three kinds of typographical devices are used throughout this book: (1) square brackets enclose editorial comments or additions, e.g., [ ]; (2) angle brackets enclose above-the-line insertions made in the original manuscript; and (3) words with a horizontal line through them indicate words that are crossed out in the original manuscript.

known as Robert Matthias and Joshua, the Jewish minister. Joseph explained that when he was "about 14 years old" (which would be the spring of 1820) he prayed to the Lord. He was startled by the sound of someone walking and jumped up but saw no one. He again prayed and then a fiery pillar appeared above his head. He saw an unidentified personage in this flame. A short time later another personage appeared, who told him (a) "thy sins are forgiven thee" and then this personage (b) "testifyed unto me that Jesus Christ is the Son of God." The angelic personage refers to Jesus Christ in the third person and offers testimony that Jesus is "the Son of God." Joseph explained: "I saw many angels in this vision." The next item mentioned in this account is that three years later—when Joseph was "about 17 years old"—he saw "another vision of angels," though this time it was during the night after going to bed. Joseph related that "an angel appeared before me." The same angel repeated his message twice that night. This angel is not identified.[4]

In the third account, just five days later, Erastus Holmes, who lived in Newbury, Ohio, asked Joseph Smith about the establishment of the church. Joseph related to Holmes his experiences as a youth—"from 6 years old up to the time I received the first visitation of Angels which was when I was about 14 years old."[5] It may seem unusual for Joseph Smith to say that he "received the first visitation of Angels" in the year 1820.[6] It fits with the angels mentioned in the account to

[4]Jessee, *Papers of Joseph Smith*, 2:68-70. Cf. Faulring, *American Prophet's Record*, 50-52. The entire account of Joseph's early visions as related to Robert Matthews is deleted in the *History of the Church*, 2:304, and replaced by the misleading words "as recorded in the former part of this history."

[5]Jessee, *Papers of Joseph Smith*, 2:79. Cf. Faulring, *American Prophet's Record*, 59.

[6]In order to solve the problem of Joseph Smith's referring to his 1820 vision as receiving "the first visitation of Angels"—and not specifically having a vision of God the Father and his son Jesus Christ—the *History of*

Robert Matthews, but is difficult to reconcile with the 1832 account, which refers only to a vision of Jesus.

The fourth account was dictated in 1838 (and then recopied in an 1839 manuscript), published on 15 March 1842 in the *Times and Seasons*, and now part of Mormon canon in the Pearl of Great Price (see JS-H 1:5-26). In this familiar version Joseph at the age of fourteen in the spring of 1820 and in the midst of a religious revival went to a woods to pray to God for answer to his questions. Joseph described what then happened:

> I saw a pillar <of> light exactly over my head above the brightness of the sun, which descended ~~gracefully~~ gradually until it fell upon me. . . . When the light rested upon me I saw two personages (whose brightness and glory defy all description) standing above me in the air. One of <them> spake to me calling me by name and said (pointing to the other) "This is my beloved Son, Hear him." My object in going to inquire of the Lord was to know which of all the sects was right, that I might know which to join. No sooner therefore did I get possession of myself so as to be able to speak, than I asked the personages who stood above me in the light, which of all the sects was right, (for at this time it had never entered into my heart that all were wrong) and which I should join. I was answered that I must join none of them, for they were all wrong. . . .[7]

In 1839 Joseph Smith was certain that two Personages[8] had addressed him; nevertheless, he amended the assertion with "or one of them did."[9] Because he had wondered if all the churches were wrong, Joseph sought enlightenment from the Personages

---

the Church, 2:312, simply changed his words to receiving "my first vision."

[7]Jessee, *Papers of Joseph Smith*, 1:272-73; cf. JS-H 1:16-19.

[8]Probably based on the 1839 manuscript, references to unidentified dual beings who resembled each other and who appeared to the boy Joseph were first published in Orson Pratt, *An Interesting Account of Several Remarkable Visions and of the Late Discovery of Ancient American Records* (Edinburgh: Ballantyne and Hughes, 1840).

[9]This phrase, deemed contradictory, was deleted from the official *History of the Church*, which was edited by B. H. Roberts in 1902.

and was told that their creeds were abominable and he was to join none of them.

In the last account Joseph Smith summarized his early life for John Wentworth, editor of the *Chicago Democrat*. Joseph wrote that when he was "about fourteen" years old (again, the spring of 1820) he began to think seriously about religious questions. He felt that all the diverse religious groups could not be right and, having confidence in the promise in James 1:5, he "retired to a secret place in a grove" and prayed to the Lord. Joseph saw a vision in which "two glorious personages who exactly resembled each other in features, and likeness" told him that none of the various denominational groups "was acknowledged of God as his church and kingdom."[10] Notice that the two personages are not identified.

The First Vision of the young Joseph is certainly an important topic to research.[11] The most astounding difference between the earliest account and the traditional account (written in 1838-1839 and published in 1842) is that only the Lord Jesus Christ appeared in 1832, while the well-known version has both the Father and the Son appearing. Another difference is that the 1832 account relates a vision of Jesus who forgives his sins, while the later account "introduces a revival before his vision and creates a chronologically implausible picture."[12]

The 1832 account and the other recitations of the First Vision have stimulated comparative studies by LDS historians

---

[10]Joseph Smith, "Church History," *Times and Seasons* 3 (1 March 1842): 706-10.

[11]Gregory A. Prince, *Power from on High: The Development of Mormon Priesthood* (Salt Lake City: Signature Books, 1995), 1, explained that "despite the importance attached to the first vision by subsequent generations of Latter-day Saints, it did not serve as Smith's call to the ministry or claim to divine authorization."

[12]H. Michael Marquardt and Wesley P. Walters, *Inventing Mormonism: Tradition and the Historical Record*, 2d ed. ([Salt Lake City]: Smith Research Associates, 1998), 56.

and as a result "considerable controversy has been generated."[13] Several studies provide analysis of the variations in the different accounts of Joseph Smith's First Vision.[14] One LDS researcher has suggested that when Joseph Smith dictated the Book of Mormon translation, he "apparently envisioned God as modalists did: he accepted Christ and Christ's father as one God. In his first written account of his 'first vision' in 1832 Smith told of seeing 'the Lord'—one being."[15] After comparing several First Vision accounts, an RLDS historian commented: "Neither Joseph Smith nor any other Latter Day Saint analyst has satisfactorily accounted for the discrepancies among the ... accounts on the point of the number and identity of the personage(s) appearing to him in the First Vision."[16] Marvin S. Hill, professor of history at Brigham Young University, suggested a radical new way to look at these accounts of the First Vision:

> It seems to me that everybody has approached the issue from the wrong end, by starting with the 1838 [1839] official version when the account they should be considering is that of 1832. Merely on the face of it, the 1832 version stands a better chance of being more accurate and unembellished than the 1838 account which was intended as a public statement, streamlined for publication. When Joseph dictated his 1838 version (if he did

---

[13]Marvin S. Hill, *Quest for Refuge: The Mormon Flight from American Pluralism* (Salt Lake City: Signature Books, 1989), 10.

[14]For comparative studies of how the 1832 account relates to the other versions of the First Vision, see James B. Allen, "Eight Contemporary Accounts of Joseph Smith's First Vision: What Do We Learn from Them?" *The Improvement Era* 73 (April 1970): 4-13; and Paul R. Cheesman, *The Keystone of Mormonism: Early Vision of the Prophet Joseph Smith* (Provo, UT: Eagle Systems International, 1988).

[15]Melodie Moench Charles, "Book of Mormon Christology," in *New Approaches to the Book of Mormon: Explorations in Critical Methodology*, ed. Brent Lee Metcalfe (Salt Lake City: Signature Books, 1993), 103.

[16]Richard P. Howard, "An Analysis of Six Contemporary Accounts Touching Joseph Smith's First Vision," in *Restoration Studies I: Sesquicentennial Edition*, ed. Maurice L. Draper (Independence, MO: Herald Publishing House, 1980), 112.

in fact actually dictate it), he was aware of what had been previously published by Oliver Cowdery and aware of his stature as the prophet of a new and important religious movement. It would be natural for him to have smoothed out the story, making it more logical and compelling than perhaps it first seemed in 1820.[17]

The initial visit had occurred in the early 1820s—either 1820 or 1823—in a quiet grove not far south of Palmyra, an ordinary American village in western New York. The event had been witnessed by a lad, one Joseph Smith, the fourth child of humble parents, destined to become the famous American prophet. Joseph had carried the glorious vision in memory these many years, saying little even to intimates within the church he had founded in 1830. His reticence may have stemmed from the bitter persecution he claimed to have suffered at the hands of professors of religion, neighbors, and men of high standing to whom he had related the vision soon after it occurred. He had felt like Paul when he made his defense before King Agrippa and was reviled for saying he had seen a light and heard a voice, no amount of persecution inducing him to gainsay it (JS-H 1:24). So it was with Joseph.

Visions of God, Jesus, and/or angels occurred to a number of religious believers in early nineteenth-century America. Some of these visionaries published accounts of their experiences. Richard L. Bushman, professor of history at Columbia University, located thirty-two such pamphlets, and ten of them described visions of "God or Christ or both."[18] For example, Bushman quoted Norris Stearns' 1815 account of his vision of God the Father and his Son Jesus Christ:

... I saw two spirits, which I knew at the first sight. But

---

[17]Marvin S. Hill, "The First Vision Controversy: A Critique and Reconciliation," *Dialogue: A Journal of Mormon Thought* 15 (Summer 1982): 39.

[18]Richard L. Bushman, "The Visionary World of Joseph Smith," *Brigham Young University Studies* 37, no. 1 (1997-1998): 202n24.

if I had the tongue of an Angel I could not describe their glory, for they brought the joys of heaven with them. One was God, my Maker, almost in bodily shape like a man. His face was, as it were a flame of Fire, and his body, as it had been a Pillar and a Cloud. In looking steadfastly to discern features, I could see none, but a small glimpse would appear in some other place. Below him stood Jesus Christ my Redeemer, in perfect shape like a man—His face was not ablaze, but had the countenance of fire, being bright and shining. His Father's will appeared to be his! All was condescension, peace, and love.[19]

During the years following his audience with the Deities, Joseph, candid in his admissions of frailty, succumbed to the "corruption" of his human nature, and to the "gratification of many appetites" offensive in the sight of God.[20] On the evening of 21 September 1823 Joseph went to his room to ask God to forgive him for his sins and follies and to obtain a divine manifestation. A personage appeared at his bedside, announcing (according to the 1842 published "History of Joseph Smith") that his name was Nephi, and that God had a great work for him to do.[21] Nephi quoted some of the prophesies of

---

[19]Norris Stearns, *The Religious Experience of Norris Stearns* (Greenfield, [MA], 1815), quoted in Bushman, "Visionary World," 191.

[20]Such candor was thought unnecessary by redactors. The offensive words were deleted from the official history of 1902, and the following explanation (which is a note in the manuscript history and goes back to Joseph Smith) was inserted: "In making this confession, no one need suppose me guilty of any great or malignant sins. A disposition to commit such was never in my nature. But I was guilty of levity, and sometimes associated with jovial company, etc., not consistent with that character which ought to be maintained by one who was called of God as I had been. But this will not seem very strange to any one who recollects my youth, and is acquainted with my native cheery temperament." See *History of the Church*, 1:9-10.

[21]The name "Nephi" appeared in reprints of the story for several years, including the *Millennial Star*, August 1842, the first edition of the *Pearl of Great Price* (1851), Lucy Mack Smith's *Biographical Sketches of Joseph Smith the Prophet, and His Progenitors for Many Generations* (Liverpool, England: Published for Orson Pratt by S. W. Richards, 1853), and the *History of the*

Malachi, but with variation from the Bible text. Although many years had now elapsed since his encounter with the angel, Joseph, in recording the interview, remembered the exact words that Nephi used on that memorable September night of 1823 (JS-H 1:37-39), noting perhaps as he wrote them that not only did they vary from the King James Bible (Mal. 4:1-6), but also from his own Inspired Translation of the Scriptures (which in 1842 was still a manuscript), as well as the Savior's quotes from Malachi in the Book of Mormon (3 Ne. 25:1-6), and a revelation from God to Joseph dated 3 November 1831 (D&C 133:64). Nephi spoke of the priesthood which was soon to be restored by the hand of Elijah, but for reasons unknown Joseph had failed to record these portentous words, among the most important in all Latter-day Saint scripture, in any of the published revelations.[22]

The *Times and Seasons'* story of Nephi's visit appeared in the 15 April 1842 issue, being a part of the third installment of the "History of Joseph Smith," which might well have been entitled "The Story of the Birth of Mormonism." It was not the first time the story had been told. Seven and a half years earlier Oliver Cowdery, with Joseph Smith's assistance, had written eight articles in the form of letters to W. W. Phelps, which appeared in the *Messenger and Advocate*, the official church publication at Kirtland, Ohio, beginning with the October 1834 issue. The reader was informed that "we have thought that a full history of the rise of the church of Latter Day Saints,

---

[Reorganized] *Church of Jesus Christ of Latter Day Saints* (1897). According to Andrew Jenson, "The Eight Witnesses," *The Historical Record* 7 (October 1888): 621, John C. Whitmer, nephew of David Whitmer, said that he often heard his grandmother, Mary M. Whitmer, say that she was shown the plates of the Book of Mormon by an holy angel "whom she always called Brother Nephi." Cf. Cheesman, *Keystone of Mormonism*, 57-60.

[22]This important omission was corrected by church officials thirty-two years after Joseph's death when it became Section 2 of the 1876 edition of the Doctrine and Covenants.

and the most interesting parts of its progress, to the present time, would be worthy the perusal of the Saints. . . . That our narrative may be correct, and particularly the introduction, it is proper to inform our patrons, that our brother J. Smith jr. has offered to assist us." The promise was made that it would be "founded upon facts" and would be "particular."[23] The third letter offered an additional promise of accuracy:

> Since, then, our opposers have been thus kind to introduce our cause before the public, it is no more than just that a correct account should be given; and since they have invariably sought to cast a shade over the truth, and hinder its influence from gaining ascendency, it is also proper that it should be vindicated, by laying before the world a correct statement of events as they have transpired from time to time.[24]

In Cowdery's version, thousands of words were used to relate the dramatic story of Joseph's early quest for guidance after partaking of the excitement of a religious revival, his prayer asking to know which church to join, the resultant visit of a personage—all of which occurred, it was said, in 1823 when Joseph was seventeen.[25] Cowdery has not a single word

---

[23]*Latter Day Saints' Messenger and Advocate* 1 (October 1834): 13.

[24]*Latter Day Saints' Messenger and Advocate* 1 (December 1834): 42.

[25]Oliver Cowdery, Letter III to W. W. Phelps, *Latter Day Saints' Messenger and Advocate* 1 (December 1834): 42-43, stated that Joseph's age was "the 15th year of his life." However, two months later Cowdery, Letter IV to W. W. Phelps, *Latter Day Saints' Messenger and Advocate* 1 (February 1835): 78, corrected it to the "17th" year, adding that "this would bring the date down to the year 1823." Hill, "First Vision Controversy," 42, explained about Cowdery's account: "Giving priority to the 1832 account also makes it more understandable why Oliver Cowdery got his story tangled. He started out telling of Joseph's 1820 vision, perhaps along the lines of the 1832 version with one personage involved. It seems apparent that Joseph must have said something to him in December after he published the story of George Lane and the revival to the effect that the Lane revival was not until 1823. Rather than admitting that his details about the revival were wrong, Oliver decided to jump ahead and tell of Moroni's coming."

about a First Vision in 1820.[26] The reader might become confused at certain obvious discrepancies. Did Joseph's spiritual excitation occur in 1820 or in 1823? Was he fourteen or seventeen when the personage answered his appeal, and was this personage single or were there two personages?

There is also the question of whether the 1823 experience was a dream or a vision. The earliest accounts, based on Mormon sources in 1829 and 1830, state that it was in fact a dream during the night. A Palmyra newspaper in August 1829 stated: "In the fall of 1827, a person by the name of Joseph Smith, of Manchester, Ontario county, reported that he had been visited in a dream by the spirit of the Almighty."[27] In September 1829 a Rochester newspaper reported that Martin Harris declared: Joseph Smith "had been visited by the spirit of the Almighty in a dream, and . . . after the third visit from the same spirit in a dream he proceeded to the spot."[28] Being aware of this early newspaper evidence, D. Michael Quinn concluded: "The earliest Mormon accounts state that Smith's 1823 epiphany was the nocturnal visit of a spirit three times in a dream."[29] Another

---

[26]Cowdery single account of the revival leading to the vision of an angel is physically cut into two separate parts by Francis W. Kirkham, *A New Witness for Christ in America: The Book of Mormon*, enl. 3d ed. (Salt Lake City: Utah Printing Co., 1959),1:85, 447-48, in order to make it appear to the reader that Cowdery describes an 1820 revival (1:443) as well as an 1823 vision of an angel.

[27]"The Golden Bible," *Rochester Advertiser and Telegraph*, 31 August 1829, printed in Kirkham, *New Witness for Christ*, 2:31.

[28]"A Golden Bible," *The Gem*, Rochester, NY, 5 September 1829, printed in Kirkham, *New Witness for Christ*, 2:32.

[29]D. Michael Quinn, *Early Mormonism and the Magic World View* (Salt Lake City: Signature Books, 1987), 114. On the next page Quinn discusses the biblical and nineteenth century evidence equating the term *dream* and *vision*. He could also have added Lehi's statement: "Behold, I have dreamed a dream; or, in other words, I have seen a vision" (1 Ne. 8:2). Richard L. Bushman, *Joseph Smith and the Beginnings of Mormonism* (Urbana, IL: University of Illinois Press, 1984), 50, cited a comparative use of the terms *vision* and *dream* in the Smith family, for Lucy Mack Smith, in relating one of Joseph Sr.'s visions, "reported that her husband fell asleep one night 'and

factor to consider is that Joseph Smith shared his bedroom with his brothers and they seem not to have been disturbed by the visitation.[30]

Due to the real possibility of getting an inside glimpse into Joseph's early activities, it is important to examine the accounts given directly by members of the Smith family. The Smith family's continuing religious activities during the 1820s may be instructive, since it is known that Lucy and her sons, Hyrum and Samuel, were active members of the Western Presbyterian Church in Palmyra, until they stopped attending in September 1828.[31] Notice how the Prophet's mother, Lucy Mack Smith, told Joseph's story in 1845:

> One evening [in 1823] we were sitting till quite late conversing upon the subject of the diversity of churches that had risen up in the world and the many thousand opinions in existence as to the truths contained in scripture Joseph ~~who~~ never said many words upon any subject but always seemed to reflect more deeply than common persons of his age upon everything of a religious nature.
>
> ~~This~~ After we ceased conversation he went to bed <and was pondering in his mind which of the churches were the true one> ~~and~~ but he had not laid there long till <he saw> a bright <light> ~~entered~~ the room where he lay he looked up and saw an angel of the Lord ~~stood~~ <standing> by him
>
> The angel spoke I perceive that you are enquiring in your mind which is the true church there is not a true church on Earth No not one ~~Nor~~ <and> has not been since Peter took the Keys <of the Melchesidec priesthood after the order of God> into the Kingdom of Heaven The churches that are now upon the Earth are all man made churches. ~~Joseph there is a record for~~

---

before waking had the following vision. . . .'"

[30]Oliver Cowdery, Letter IV to W. W. Phelps, *Latter Day Saints' Messenger and Advocate* 1 (February 1835): 79, stated that Joseph prayed while "slumber had spread her refreshing hand over others beside him."

[31]Marquardt and Walters, *Inventing Mormonism*, 31-33.

14

~~you and you must get it one day get it~~ There is a record for you and Joseph ~~when you have learned to keep the commandments of God~~ but you cannot get it untill you learn to keep the commandments of God <For it is not to get gain> But it is to bring forth that light and intelligence which has been long lost in the Earth Now Joseph beware <or> when you go to get the plates your mind will be filled with darkness and all maner of evil will rush into your mind To ~~keep~~ <prevent> you from keeping the commandments of God <that you may not succe[e]d in doing his work> and you must tell your father of this for he will believe every word you say the record is on a side hill on the Hill of cumorah 3 miles from this place remove the Grass and moss and you will find a large flat stone pry that up and you will find the record under it laying on 4 pillars <of cement>—then the angel left him.[32]

Another family member, William Smith, Joseph's younger brother, stated in an 1841 interview with Rev. James Murdock that "About the year 1823, there was a revival of religion in that region, and Joseph was one of several hopeful converts."[33] According to William Smith, a visit from an angel was Joseph's first heavenly ministration and this occurred in 1823.[34] William's 1841 interview is important because it provides an in-

---

[32]Lucy Mack Smith, 1845 "Preliminary Manuscript," in the handwriting of Howard Coray, quoted in Dan Vogel, comp. and ed., *Early Mormon Documents* (Salt Lake City: Signature Books, 1996), 1:289-91. A photocopy of the "Preliminary Manuscript" is located in Accession 989, Manuscripts Division, J. Willard Marriott Library, University of Utah, Salt Lake City. Eight years later when Orson Pratt published her manuscript as *Biographical Sketches*, this account is replaced with the account of Joseph Smith's First Vision printed in the 1842 *Times and Seasons*.

[33]Letter of Rev. James Murdock, 19 June 1841, to the Hartford, Connecticut, *Congregational Observer* 2 (3 July 1841): 1, quoted in Marquardt and Walters, *Inventing Mormonism*, 19, 36n14.

[34]Hill, *Quest for Refuge*, 193n49, citing William Smith's account as printed in the July 1841 *New-York Observer*. Hill's reference to this publication may be because Murdock's letter was reprinted in the *New-York Observer* or it may be a transcriptional error for the *Congregational Observer*.

sight into the Smith family's understanding of Joseph's experience's before there was any published record by Joseph himself. Four decades later William reaffirmed that his brother's
First Vision was an unnamed angel in 1823:

> In 1822 and 1823, the people in our neighborhood were
> very much stirred up with regard to religious matters by
> the preaching of a Mr. [George] Lane, an Elder of the
> Methodist Church, . . .
>   . . . The consequence [of this growing religious
> revival] was that my mother, my brothers Hyrum and
> Samuel, older than I, joined the Presbyterian Church.
> Joseph, then about seventeen years of age [1823], had
> become seriously inclined, though not "brought out," as
> the phrase was, began to reflect and inquire, which of all
> these sects was right. . . . He continued in secret to call
> upon the Lord for a full manifestation of his will, the
> assurance that he was accepted of him, and that he
> might have an understanding of the path of obedience.
>   At length he determined to call upon the Lord
> until he should get a manifestation from him. He
> accordingly went out into the woods and falling upon
> his knees called for a long time upon the Lord for
> wisdom and knowledge. While engaged in prayer a light
> appeared in the heavens, and descended until it rested
> upon the trees where he was. It appeared like fire. But
> to his great astonishment, did not burn the trees. An
> angel then appeared to him and conversed with him
> upon many things. He told him that none of the sects
> were right; but that if he was faithful in keeping the
> commandments he should receive, the true way should
> be made known to him; that his sins were forgiven, etc.
> A more elaborate and accurate description of his vision,
> however, will be found in his own history.
>   The next day I was at work in the field together
> with Joseph and my eldest brother Alvin. Joseph
> looked pale and unwell, so that Alvin told him if he was
> sick he need not work; he then went and sat down by
> the fence, when the angel again appeared to him, and
> told him to call his father's house together and commu-
> nicate to them the visions he had received, which he had
> not yet told to any one; and promised him that if he
> would do so, they would believe it. He accordingly
> asked us to come to the house, as he had something to

tell us. After we were all gathered, he arose and told us how the angel appeared to him; what he had told him as written above; and that the angel had also given him a short account of the inhabitants who formerly resided upon this continent, a full history of whom he said was engraved on some plates which were hidden, and which the angel promised to show him. . . . The whole family . . . believed all he said.[35]

It is important to point out that Oliver Cowdery's account confirms the role of Rev. George Lane in preaching on a scriptural text that led to Joseph's First Vision in 1823.[36] Though the presence of Rev. Lane is supported by William Smith and Oliver Cowdery, the date is a problem because Lane was not made the presiding elder of the Methodist circuit that includes Palmyra until July 1824.[37]

Was the identity of the custodian of the plates known to Joseph at the Hill Cumorah in 1827? His 1839 story tells that the angel revealed his identity at the time of the first visitation to his bedroom the night of 21 September 1823. If Joseph was making an honest report of an actual occurrence, then he knew the angel's identity at each of the dozen or more[38] subsequent meetings with the heavenly messenger at Cumorah and elsewhere. Oddly enough there is no reference to the angel *by name* in any account prior to 1835. The earliest letters and newspapers refer only to an unnamed spirit, an angel, a person-

---

[35]William Smith, *William Smith on Mormonism* (Lamoni, IA: Herald Steam Book and Job Office, 1883), 5-8, quoted in Vogel, *Early Mormon Documents*, 1:494-96. A decade later William Smith told the same story of Rev. Lane's preaching leading to Joseph's prayer and first vision of an angel. See E. C. Briggs' interview with William Smith in November 1893, printed in *Zion's Ensign* 5 (13 January 1894): 6 and *Deseret Evening News* 27 (20 January 1894): 11, which is quoted in Kirkham, *New Witness for God*, 1:43-44.

[36]*Latter Day Saints' Messenger and Advocate* 1 (December 1834): 42.

[37]Marquardt and Walters, *Inventing Mormonism*, 21, 38n25.

[38]Kirkham, *New Witness for Christ*, 1:404, counted seventeen visits with the angel.

age, or a heavenly messenger. Joseph Smith's 1832 account refers to an unnamed "angel," who tells him about golden plates that had "engravings which was engraven by Maroni."[39] Notice that the angel did not say, "engravings which was engraven by me" or "I, Moroni, engraved these plates." Also, the 1833 Book of Commandments speaks only of "an holy angel" (24:7; cf. D&C 20:6).

Even more revealing is the revelation of 4 September 1830, which was printed in the 1833 Book of Commandments:

> Listen to the voice of Jesus Christ, your Lord, your God and your Redeemer, whose word is quick and powerful. ... Behold this is wisdom in me, wherefore marvel not, for the hour cometh that I will drink of the fruit of the vine with you, on the earth, and with all those whom my Father hath given me out of the world (Book of Commandments 28:1, 6).

This same revelation is printed in the 1835 Doctrine and Covenants as follows:

> Listen to the voice of Jesus Christ, your Lord, your God, and your Redeemer, whose word is quick and powerful. ... Behold this is wisdom in me: wherefore marvel not for the hour cometh that I will drink of the fruit of the vine with you on the earth, and with Moroni, whom I have sent unto you to reveal the book of Mormon, containing the fulness of my everlasting gospel; to whom I have committed the keys of the record of the stick of Ephraim (1835 D&C 50:1-2; D&C 27:1, 5).[40]

There is some confusion in official church records and publications regarding the identity of the angel even after 1835 —some books declaring he was Moroni, others that he was Nephi. The first edition of the Doctrine and Covenants in

---

[39] Jessee, *Papers of Joseph Smith*, 1:8. Cf. Faulring, *American Prophet's Record*, 6.

[40] Also, the modern edition of the Doctrine and Covenants has changed the date to August 1830.

1835, Oliver Cowdery in the 1835 *Messenger and Advocate*, and the *Elders' Journal* in 1838 call him Moroni, but the 1839 manuscript "History of Joseph Smith," the 1842 *Times and Seasons*, the 1842 *Millennial Star*, and the first edition of the Pearl of Great Price in 1851 refer to him as Nephi. Historians of the church have deemed the last group of references as errors, but as Joseph Smith was editor of the *Times and Seasons* and author of the article which carried the Nephi designation there is reason to wonder why the error went uncorrected in later issues and why it was sustained in two other publications.

In the Book of Mormon story Nephi and Moroni are distinctive characters living a thousand years apart. To insist that the angel of western New York in the 1820s was one or the other may seem of little consequence to the outsider—a distinction without a difference. But to the devout Mormon the angel is an historical figure of such stature and importance to the modern world that there can be no uncertainty as to his reality or identity. Moroni is the embodiment of the ideal, the link between Christ's two American churches—the Nephite and the Latter-day Saint, the one of whom John said, "And I saw another angel fly in the midst of heaven, having the everlasting gospel to preach unto them that dwell on the earth, and to every nation, and kindred, and tongue, and people" (Rev. 14:6). Moroni, the lone survivor of the Nephite debacle, buried the record in the Hill Cumorah, and as a resurrected being revealed them to Joseph Smith fourteen hundred years later. For over a century the large Moroni statue has adorned the top of the Salt Lake temple, a symbol of truth for all the world to see. The historical importance of Moroni was noted in an 1854 Independence Day speech by Orson Hyde, who declared that the same angel that revealed the Book of Mormon plates to Joseph Smith also accompanied Columbus on his voyage to the New World.[41] In the Wentworth letter Joseph

---

[41]*Journal of Discourses* 6 (1859): 368.

declared that prior to 1827 he had had "many visits from the angels of God."[42] So possibly Joseph confused the identities of two of the angels that visited him, or perhaps one is a clerical error.

In 1839 Joseph, writing in retrospect of the events of 1823, gives us this description of the angel:

> While I was thus in the act of calling upon God, I discovered a light appearing in my room, which continued to increase until the room was lighter than at noonday, when immediately a personage appeared at my bedside, standing in the air, for his feet did not touch the floor. He had on a loose robe of most exquisite whiteness. It was a whiteness beyond anything earthly I had ever seen; nor do I believe that any earthly thing could be made to appear so exceedingly white and brilliant. His hands were naked, and his arms also, a little above the wrist; so, also, were his feet naked, as were his legs, a little above the ankles. His head and neck were also bare. I could discover that he had no other clothing on but this robe, as it was open, so that I could see into his bosom. Not only was his robe exceedingly white, but his whole person was glorious beyond description, and his countenance truly like lightning. The room was exceedingly bright as immediately around his person. When I first looked upon him, I was afraid; but the fear soon left me (JS-H 1:30-32).

In stark contrast we have the testimony of one of Joseph's contemporaries—Abner Cole:

> At a time when the money digging ardor was somewhat abated, the elder Smith declared that his son Joe had seen the *spirit*, (which he then described as a little old man with a long beard,). . . .[43]

---

[42]*Times and Seasons* 3 (1 March 1842): 707. Cf. *History of the Church*, 4:537.

[43]Abner Cole, using the penname Obadiah Dogberry, "Gold Bible," Palmyra *Reflector*, 14 February 1831, with emphasis in original, printed in Kirkham, *New Witness for Christ*, 1:289.

There are many stories from non-Mormon sources that could be quoted, but they are often preposterous. Believers in the Book of Mormon might well argue that they are utterly fictitious so far as having originated with the Prophet, for if he had told such tales in 1827 would not his book two years later be in like vein? Yet whether they were made from whole cloth or embroidered from thin air there may be some who will find in them a common thread, with Joseph as tailor, and even proclaim that the angel of Cumorah may be but a pale imitation of the avenger in chapter nine of Third Nephi.

It is perplexing—even disturbing—to modern Latter-day Saint readers who have heard the First Vision and Moroni story from the cradle to find radically different accounts of the First Vision and allusions to unnamed angels, or the angel Nephi, or the angel Moroni in the writings of early Mormon chroniclers. Exposure to these accounts may significantly affect them. One Mormon scholar was devastated by the "strange accounts" of the First Vision and dramatically exclaimed: "They had plucked all the feathers out of the bird and shot it, and there it lies 'dead and naked on the ground.'"[44]

Most Mormons consider the traditional account of Joseph Smith's First Vision as canonized in the Pearl of Great Price to be one of the cornerstones of the LDS Church. Usually there is very little discussion of the historical development —which can be shown by the dateable sources—of the early visions of Joseph Smith. The most traditional approach is simply to bear a testimony to its truthfulness. For example, Gordon B. Hinckley expressed his conviction: "I add my own witness, given me by the Spirit, that the Prophet's description of that marvelous event is true, that God the Eternal Father and

---

[44]Thomas Stuart Ferguson, quoted in Stan Larson, *Quest for the Gold Plates: Thomas Stuart Ferguson's Archaeological Search for the Book of Mormon* (Salt Lake City: Freethinker Press in association with Smith Research Associates, 1996), 142.

the risen Lord Jesus Christ spoke with him on that occasion in a conversation as real and personal and intimate as are our conversations today."[45]

---

[45]Gordon B. Hinckley, *Be Thou an Example* (Salt Lake City: Deseret Book Co., 1981), 10.

CHAPTER 2

The Seer Stone

And the Lord said: I will prepare unto my servant Gaze-lem[1] a stone, which shall shine forth in darkness unto light, that I may discover unto my people who serve me, that I may discover unto them the works of their brethren, yea, their secret works, their works of darkness, and their wickedness and abominations (Alma 37:23).

When Joseph Smith began dictating his history in 1838 he told that an angel had appeared to him fifteen years earlier and directed him to golden plates and Urim and Thummim hid in a nearby hill. After a four-year interval in which he received spiritual guidance from the angel, these sacred articles were entrusted to his keeping on 22 September 1827, thus setting in motion the chain of events which was to re-establish Christ's church on earth and usher in the Last Dispensation of the Fulness of Times, a period of preparation for the Millennium. On the actuality of these events hinges the further study

---

[1] In editions of the Doctrine and Covenants before 1981, the term "Ga-zelam" (derived from the spelling "Gazelem" in Alma 37:23) was printed at D&C 78:9; 82:11; 104:26, 43, 45-46. However, in the 1981 edition this code-name was eliminated and replaced by the identification "Joseph Smith, Jun." See David J. Whittaker, "Substituted Names in the Published Revelations of Joseph Smith," *Brigham Young University Studies* 23 (Winter 1983): 103-12, where the remaining four code-names are identified.

of Mormonism as the only church on earth to which God has set his seal of approval.

It is the purpose of this chapter to examine the statements made by those who surrounded Joseph at this early period of his prophetic career and also the statements of some later writers. While testimony relating to these experiences is often sharply divided into two camps, the one to defame and the other to vindicate, it will be noted that there are numerous meeting points between the traducers and disciples. The stories of Joseph's use of media to translate the Book of Mormon are placed in juxtaposition with stories of his divination of things unseen which preceded his finding of Urim and Thummim in 1827. This subject has never been fully explored by church writers owing to a belief that some matters are impenetrable; also to the belief that it was the province of the Prophet to withhold information if he chose to do so.

There has been an understandable reluctance to accept the uncomplimentary stories from residents of Palmyra, New York and vicinity as to the character and pursuits of the Smith family even though these same deponents claimed to be eyewitnesses to Joseph's use of a seer stone prior to the above date. There is a dearth of detail from the Prophet himself regarding his activities of this period and he left no reference to his use of any media apart from the Urim and Thummim either for translating or for any other purpose. Regarding the statements of key figures such as Martin Harris and David Whitmer, it should be remembered that the church does not recognize the validity of testimony by disaffected members or apostates unless it agrees with the official church history.

Joseph Smith simply stated that "through the medium of the Urim and Thummim I translated the record by the gift and power of God."[2] This succinct statement by Joseph is corroborated by Oliver Cowdery after his return to the church in 1848:

---

[2]*History of the Church*, 4:537.

I wrote with my own pen the entire Book of Mormon (save a few pages) as it fell from the lips of the Prophet, ... I beheld with my eyes, and handled with my hands, the gold plates from which it was translated. I also beheld the Interpreters."[3]

The next two statements are somewhat at variance with the above two unless it develops that the Urim and Thummim and the seer stone were one and the same article. This possibility is not admitted by church historians.

Emma Smith, wife of the Prophet, speaking to her son, Joseph Smith III, said:

In writing for your father, I frequently wrote day after day, often sitting at the table close to him, he sitting with his face buried in his hat, with the stone in it, and dictating hour after hour with nothing between us.[4]

Edward Stevenson, member of the First Council of Seventy, stated:

Martin Harris related an incident that occurred during the time that he wrote that portion of the translation of the Book of Mormon which he was favored to write direct from the mouth of the Prophet Joseph Smith. He said that the Prophet possessed a seer stone, by which he was enabled to translate as well as from the Urim and Thummim, and for convenience he then used the seer stone. Martin explained the translation as follows: By aid of the seer stone, sentences would appear and were read by the Prophet and written by Martin, and when finished he would say, "Written," and if correctly written, that sentence would disappear and another appear in its place, but if not written correctly it remained until corrected. ...[5]

---

[3]Reuben Miller, Journal, 21 October 1848, quoted in Richard L. Anderson, "Reuben Miller, Recorder of Oliver Cowdery's Reaffirmations," *Brigham Young University Studies* 8 (Spring 1968): 278.

[4]Joseph Smith III, "Last Testimony of Sister Emma [Smith]," *The Saints' Herald* 26 (1 October 1879): 289.

[5]*The Latter-day Saints' Millennial Star* 44 (6 February 1882): 86-87.

That these statements are disconcerting to the orthodox mind is attested by the following response of B. H. Roberts:

> I care very little, comparatively, for what Messrs. Whitmer and Harris have said about the subject. . . . I wish Messrs. Whitmer and Harris, and those who have worked out theories based upon their statements, had left the whole matter where the Prophet Joseph left it; but this they failed to do.[6]

Perhaps the reason for concern is that the use of the stone in the hat brings the Prophet's seership perilously close to magical arts, as described by Joseph's father-in-law, Isaac Hale:

> The manner in which he [Joseph] pretended to read and interpret, was the same as when he looked for the money-diggers, with the stone in his hat, and his hat over his face, while the Book of Plates were at the same time hid in the woods![7]

The two following statements, one from a skeptic and the other from a believer, agree that Joseph found a stone while digging a well for Willard Chase, son of Clark Chase, to which he attached some importance.

Willard Chase said:

> I became acquainted with the Smith family, known as the authors of the Mormon Bible, in the year 1820. At that time, they were engaged in the money digging business, which they followed until the latter part of the season of 1827. In the year 1822, I was digging a well. I employed Alvin and Joseph Smith to assist me; the latter of whom is now known as the Mormon prophet. After digging about twenty feet below the surface of the earth, we discovered a singularly appearing stone, which excited my curiosity. I brought it to the top of the well,

---

[6]Roberts, *Defense of the Faith*, 1:284-86.

[7]Eber D. Howe, *Mormonism Unvailed; or, A Faithful Account of that Singular Imposition and Delusion, from Its Rise to the Present Time* (Painesville, OH, 1834), 265.

and as we were examining it, Joseph put it into his hat, and then his face into the top of his hat. It has been said by Smith, that *he* brought the stone from the well; but this is false. There was no one in the well but myself. The next morning he came to me, and wished to obtain the stone, alleging that he could see in it; but I told him I did not wish to part with it on account of its being a curiosity, but would lend it. After obtaining the stone, he began to publish abroad what wonders he could discover by looking in it, and made so much disturbance among the credulous part of the community, that I ordered the stone to be returned to me again. He had it in his possession about two years. I believe, some time in 1825, Hiram Smith (brother of Joseph Smith) came to me, and wished to borrow the same stone, alleging that they wanted to accomplish some business of importance, which could not very well be done without the aid of the stone. I told him it was of no particular worth to me, but merely wished to keep it as a curiosity, and if he would pledge me his word and honor, that I should have it when called for, he might take it; which he did and took the stone. . . .

In the fall of 1826, a friend called upon me and wished to see that stone, about which so much had been said; and I told him if he would go with me to Smith's, (a distance of about half a mile) he might see it. But to my surprise, on going to Smith's, and asking him for the stone, he said, "you cannot have it;" I told him it belonged to me, repeated to him the promise he made me, at the time of obtaining the stone: upon which he faced me with a malignant look and said, "I don't care who in the Devil it belongs to, *you* shall not have it."[8]

Martin Harris stated in an 1859 interview:

Joseph had a stone which was dug from the well of Mason Chase, twenty-four feet from the surface. In this stone he could see many things to my certain knowledge.[9]

---

[8]Ibid., 240-42, with emphasis in original.

[9]*Tiffany's Monthly* 5, no. 4 (August 1859): 163. For a reprint of the entire Harris interview, see Appendix A, below.

Probably the earliest printed mention of divination by means of a stone to appear in a Palmyra newspaper is the following item from the *Wayne Sentinel* in December 1825. The seer is not identified:

WONDERFUL DISCOVERY—A few days since was discovered in this town [Albion], by help of a mineral stone, which becomes transparent when placed in a hat and the light excluded by the face of him who looks into it, provided he is fortune's favorite, a monstrous POT-ASH KETTLE in the bowels of Mother Earth, filled with the purest bullion. Some attempts have been made to dig it up, but without success. His Satanic Majesty, or some other unseen agent, appears to keep it under marching orders, for no sooner is it dug onto in one place, than it moves off like "false delusive hope" only to re-appear in some remote place. But its pursuers are now sanguine of success. They have entrenched the kettle all around, and driven a steel ramrod into the ground immediately over it, to break the enchantment. Nothing now remains but to raise its ponderous weight and establish a mint that it may be coined into federal money. Good news indeed for these hard times. . . .[10]

The Prophet's mother, Lucy Mack Smith, contributed this interesting item regarding her son's seership, while camouflaging his use of a seer stone with the ambiguous term "certain means":

A short time before the house was completed [1825], a man by the name of Josiah Stoal came from Chenango county, New York, with the view of getting Joseph to assist him in digging for a silver mine. He came for Joseph on account of having heard that he possessed certain means by which he could discern things invisible to the natural eye.[11]

---

[10]*Wayne Sentinel*, 27 December 1825, printed in Willard Bean, *A. B. C. History of Palmyra and the Beginning of "Mormonism"* (Palmyra, NY: Palmyra Courier Co., 1938), 38.

[11]L. M. Smith, *Biographical Sketches*, 91.

Lucy provided an even more revealing glimpse into the Smith family's involvement in magical abracadabra and other aspects of folk magic:

> Let not the reader suppose that because I shall pursue another topic for a season that we stopt our labor and went at trying to win the faculty of Abrac[,] drawing Magic circles or sooth saying [*sic*] to the neglect of all kinds of buisness [W]e never during our lives suffered one important interest to swallow up every other obligation but whilst we worked with our hands we endeavored to remmember the service of & the welfare of our souls.[12]

As a young man Joseph Smith not only labored on his family's farm, but he also worked "in blessing crops, finding lost articles, predicting future events or prophesying, and using divine rods and seer stones."[13]

One of the most detailed accounts of Joseph's use of a seer stone for purposes other than translation is recorded in a pre-trial examination by justice Albert Neely at Bainbridge, New York, in March 1826, where Joseph was charged with being a disorderly person[14] and an imposter. One author who studied this episode felt that charge and decision of the court was not significant, but rather "what is important is the evidence adduced, and its bearing on the life of Joseph Smith

---

[12]Lucy Mack Smith, "Preliminary Manuscript," 46, quoted in Quinn, *Magic World View*, 54. This passage was eliminated from the manuscript tradition by the time her memoirs were printed by Pratt in 1853.

[13]Ronald W. Walker, "Martin Harris: Mormonism's Early Convert," *Dialogue: A Journal of Mormon Thought* 19 (Winter 1986):41.

[14]Marquardt and Walters, *Inventing Mormonism*, 71, 83*n*40, quoted New York law at that time to the effect that the terminology *Disorderly Persons* "included, along with beggars, prostitutes, and those who neglect their wives and children, 'all persons pretending to have skill in physiognomy, palmistry, or like crafty science, or pretending to tell fortunes, or to discover where lost good may be found."

before he announced his claim to be a prophet of God."[15] LDS Church writers were extremely reluctant to recognize its authenticity as it seems that such examinations before a justice of the peace were not usually recorded. Also, the fact that it was published through the instrumentality of Episcopal Bishop Daniel S. Tuttle did not enhance its value. In 1961 Hugh W. Nibley, professor of history and religion at Brigham Young University, explained the seriousness of the alleged trial:

> You knew its immense value as a weapon against Joseph Smith *if* its authenticity could be established.... *If* this court record is authentic, it is the most damning evidence in existence against Joseph Smith.[16]

Another LDS researcher, Francis W. Kirkham, recognizing the disturbing implications of the report, said:

> If any evidence had been in existence that Joseph Smith had used a seer stone for fraud and deception, and especially had he made this confession in a court of law as early as 1826, or four years before the Book of Mormon was printed, and this confession was in a court record, it would have been impossible for him to have organized the restored Church.[17]

Thomas Stuart Ferguson, a lawyer and an amateur Mormon archaeologist, was startled by the evidence for the 1826 examination and tried to put it in context:

---

[15]John Phillip Walker, ed., *Dale Morgan on Early Mormonism: Correspondence and a New History* (Salt Lake City: Signature Books, 1986), 373n44.

[16]Hugh Nibley, *Tinkling Cymbals and Sounding Brass: The Art of Telling Tales about Joseph Smith and Brigham Young,* The Collected Works of Hugh Nibley: Volume 11, ed. David J. Whittaker (Salt Lake City: Deseret Book Co., 1991; Provo, UT: Foundation for Ancient Research and Mormon Studies, 1991), 246, with emphasis in original. Nibley used the second person to rhetorically speak to Bishop Tuttle of Salt Lake City in the nineteenth century.

[17]Kirkham, *New Witness for Christ,* 1:387.

In 1826 Joseph Smith was 21 [20] and at this point was midway between the *First Vision* and 1830. What a strange time to be convicted of fraud—fraudulently getting money after convincing the victim that he could detect the whereabouts of hidden treasure on the victim's land. Wow. . . . It is as genuine and sound as can be—published right in Joseph Smith's own camp.[18]

That Joseph did appear as defendant in a court of law four years before the Book of Mormon was printed is verified by Abram W. Benton's 1831 statement that Joseph had to face a court for using a seer stone to locate lost good and buried treasure "four or five years ago."[19] This is also confirmed by Oliver Cowdery's statement:

> Some very officious person complained of him [Joseph Smith] as a disorderly person, and brought him before the authorities of the county; but there being no cause of action, he was honorably acquitted.[20]

The first part and conclusion of the alleged court record published by Bishop Tuttle is here reproduced, which indicates that young Joseph admitted to using his seer stone to search for lost property, buried coins, hidden treasures, and gold mines:

> People of State of New York *vs.* Joseph Smith. Warrant issued upon oath of Peter G. Bridgman, who informed that one Joseph Smith of Bainbridge was a disorderly person and an imposter. Prisoner brought into court March 20 (1826). Prisoner examined. Says that he came from town of Palmyra, and had been at the house of Josiah Stowell in Bainbridge most of time since; had small part of time been employed in looking for mines, but the major part had been employed by said Stowell

---

[18]Thomas Stuart Ferguson, Letter to James Boyack, 13 March 1971, with emphasis in original, quoted in Larson, *Quest for the Gold Plates*, 142.

[19]A[bram] W. B[enton], "Mormonites," *Evangelical Magazine and Gospel Advocate* 2 (9 April 1831): 120.

[20]*Latter Day Saints' Messenger and Advocate* 2 (October 1835): 201.

on his farm, and going to school; that he had a certain stone, which he had occasionally looked at to determine where hidden treasures in the bowels of the earth were; that he professed to tell in this manner where gold-mines were a distance under ground, and had looked for Mr. Stowell several times, and informed him where he could find those treasures, and Mr. Stowell had been engaged in digging for them; that at Palmyra he pretended to tell, by looking at this stone, where coined money was buried in Pennsylvania, and while at Palmyra he had frequently ascertained in that way where lost property was, of various kinds; that he has occasionally been in the habit of looking through this stone to find lost property for three years, but of late had pretty much given it up on account its injuring his health, especially his eyes—made them sore; that he did not solicit business of this kind, and had always rather declined having anything to do with this business. . . .

And thereupon the Court finds the defendant guilty.[21]

Recent discoveries have confirmed the reality of the 1826 pre-trial examination of "Joseph Smith The Glass looker" before Albert Neely, a justice of the peace.[22]

Additional evidences of Joseph's use of the stone are not lacking. Either one of two conclusions is forced upon the reviewer who probes this period of the Prophet's life: he was indeed a practitioner of necromantic arts far afield from true religion or he was, and is, a victim of colossal collusion between his neighbors and acquaintances at Palmyra, Manchester, and Bainbridge in New York, and Harmony in Pennsylvania. If the

---

[21]"Mormonism," *New Schaff-Herzog Encyclopedia of Religious Knowledge* (New York, 1883), 2:1576, omitting the sworn statements by Josiah Stowell, Horace Stowell, Arad Stowell, McMaster, and Jonathan Thompson. The whole document is reprinted in Kirkham, *New Witness for Christ*, 2:359-362, and in Fawn M. Brodie, No *Man Knows My History: The Life of Joseph Smith, The Mormon Prophet*, 2d ed., rev. and enl. (New York: Vintage Books, a division of Random House, Inc., 1995), 427-29.

[22]Marquardt and Walters, *Inventing Mormonism*, xxix, 71-75, 222-30. Cf. Gordon A. Madsen, "Joseph Smith's 1826 Trial: The Legal Setting," *Brigham Young University Studies* 30 (Spring 1990): 91-108.

latter view is held then one must ponder Martin Harris' role in this drama of an American religion being born. Was he a modern Judas seeking to betray a once-beloved leader, or was he a proud yet credulous participant in those miraculous events which preceded the restoration of Christ's Church? A third view is possible: Joseph's sincere practice of religion included many magical elements. Martin Harris explained:

> In the first place, he [Joseph] told me of this stone, and proposed to bind it on his eyes, and run a race with me in the woods. A few days after this, I was at the house of his father in Manchester, two miles south of Palmyra village, and was picking my teeth with a pin while sitting on the bars. The pin caught in my teeth, and dropped from my fingers into shavings and straw. I jumped from the bars and looked for it. Joseph and Northrop Sweet also did the same. We could not find it. I then took Joseph on surprise, and said to him—I said, "Take your stone." I had never seen it, and did not know that he had it with him. He had it in his pocket. He took it and placed it in his hat—the old white hat—and placed his face in his hat. I watched him closely to see that he did not look one side; he reached out his hand beyond me on the right, and moved a little stick, and there I saw the pin, which he picked up and gave to me. I know he did not look out of the hat until after he had picked up the pin.
>
> Joseph had had this stone for some time. There was a company there in that neighborhood, who were digging for money supposed to have been hidden by the ancients. Of this company were old Mr. Stowell—I think his name was Josiah—also old Mr. Beman, also Samuel Lawrence, George Proper, Joseph Smith, Jr., and his father, and his brother Hiram Smith. They dug for money in Palmyra, Manchester, also in Pennsylvania, and other places. When Joseph found this stone, there was a company digging in Harmony, Pa., and they took Joseph to look in the stone for them, and he did so for a while, and then he told them the enchantment was so strong that he could not see, and they gave it up.[23]

---

[23] *Tiffany's Monthly* 5, no. 4 (August 1859): 164.

Major John H. Gilbert of Palmyra, New York, the type-setter of the Book of Mormon, recalled:

> He was the discoverer of a magic stone which he used to carry around in his hat. Holding it carefully laid in the bottom of his hat he would bring his eye to bear on it at an angle of about 45 degrees and forthwith discover the whereabout of hidden treasures. He would draw a circle on the ground and say to the awe struck bystanders, "dig deep enough within this circle and you will find a pot of gold," but he never dug himself.[24]

Thurlow Weed said:

> About 1829 a stout, round smooth-faced young man, between twenty-five and thirty, with the air and manners of a person without occupation, came into the *Rochester Telegraph* office and said he wanted a book printed, and added that he had been directed in a vision to a place in the woods near Palmyra, where he resided, and that he found a "golden Bible," from which he was directed to copy the book which he wanted published. He then placed what he called a "tablet" in his hat, from which he read a chapter of the "Book of Mormon," a chapter which seemed so senseless that I thought the man either crazed or a very shallow imposter, and therefore declined to become a publisher, thus depriving myself of whatever notoriety might have been achieved by having my name imprinted upon the title-page of the first Mormon Bible.[25]

What were Joseph Smith's reactions to the face-in-the-hat stories, many of which were prevalent during his lifetime? It can not be supposed that they escaped his attention, yet he accorded them only the dignity of silence. In a public letter to Oliver Cowdery in 1834 he admitted to "a light, and too often,

---

[24]"Joe Smith," *The Post and Tribune* (Detroit, MI), 3 December 1877, printed in Kirkham, *New Witness for Christ*, 2:370-71.

[25]Thurlow Weed, *Autobiography of Thurlow Weed*, ed. Harriet A. Weed (Boston: Houghton, Mifflin and Co., 1883), 358-59.

vain mind, exhibiting a foolish and trifling conversation,"[26] but he insisted that was all his accusers could substantiate against him. It may not be of great moment whether Joseph dictated from a hat or received his inspiration from a more exalted source, for as one early pragmatist put it, we have his work and "whether it was concocted in a sunbeam, or in the mud" it speaks for itself.[27] His title of "Seer" is well established in the hearts of the faithful and his fame epitomized forever in a poetic tribute by John Taylor:

> The Seer, the Seer, Joseph, the Seer!
> I'll sing of the Prophet ever dear, the Prophet ever dear;
> His equal now cannot be found
> By searching the wide world around.
> With Gods he soared in the realms of day,
> And men he taught the heav'nly way.
> The earthly Seer! The heav'nly Seer!
> I love to dwell on his memory dear;
> The chosen of God and the friend of man,
> He brought the priesthood back again.

Was Joseph the Seer forthright in the telling of the Cumorah story? If so, erroneous beliefs concerning those miraculous events have sometimes persisted in the minds of defenders as well as critics. Martin Harris explained:

> Joseph . . . described the manner of his finding the plates. He found them by looking in the stone found in the well of Mason Chase. The family had likewise told me the same thing.[28]

Hosea Stout, an early stalwart of Mormonism closely associated with both Joseph Smith and Brigham Young, recorded a meeting of the regents of the University of Deseret:

---

[26]*Latter Day Saints' Messenger and Advocate* 1 (December 1834): 40.

[27]Jonathan B. Turner, *Mormonism in All Ages; or, The Rise, Progress, and Causes of Mormonism, with the Biography of Its Author and Founder, Joseph Smith, Junior* (New York: Platt and Peters, 1842), 221.

[28]*Tiffany's Monthly* 5, no. 4 (August 1859): 169.

> President Young exhibited the Seer's stone with which
> The Prophet Joseph discovered the plates of the Book
> of Mormon, to the Regents this evening.[29]

There is the following further evidence that the translation of the Book of Mormon was accomplished by means of the stone and not the Urim and Thummim. Emma Smith, who was an eyewitness, affirmed:

> Now the first that my husband translated by the use of
> the Urim and Thummim, and that was the part that
> Martin Harris lost, after that he used a small stone, not
> exactly black, but was rather a dark color. . . .[30]

David Whitmer explained about the seer stone:

> With this stone all the present book was translated. The
> prophet would place the stone in a hat, then put his face
> in the hat and read the words that appeared thereon.[31]

The premise has sometimes been adopted that the stone and the Urim and Thummim were one and the same, but it is difficult to reconcile some of the statements that describe the Urim and Thummim as unique. These descriptions, however, vary to such a degree that the accuracy of the observations is open to question, and it may be that some can be attributed to hearsay rather than knowledge.

Joseph Smith explained:

---

[29]Juanita Brooks, ed., *On the Mormon Frontier: The Diary of Hosea Stout, 1844-1861* (Salt Lake City: University of Utah Press and Utah State Historical Society, 1982), 2:593.

[30]Emma Smith Bidamon, Letter to Emma Pilgrim, 27 March 1870, quoted in Richard S. Van Wagoner and Steven C. Walker, "Joseph Smith: 'The Gift of Seeing,'" *Dialogue: A Journal of Mormon Thought* 15 (Summer 1982): 62. This article is marred by twice quoting the fraudulent Oliver Cowdery *Defense in a Rehearsal of My Grounds for Separating Myself from the Latter Day Saints* at 51, 58, 64n15, and 66n50.

[31]Lyndon W. Cook, ed., *David Whitmer Interviews: A Restoration Witness* (Orem, UT: Grandin Book Co., 1991), 230.

Having removed the earth, I obtained a lever, which I got fixed under the edge of the stone, and with a little exertion raised it up. I looked in, and there indeed did I behold the plates, the Urim and Thummim, and the breastplate, as stated by the messenger (JS-H 1:52).

The Rev. Henry Caswall in 1842 reported a statement made by Lucy Mack Smith, the Prophet's mother:

I have seen and felt also the Urim and Thummim. They resemble two large bright diamonds set in a bow like a pair of spectacles. My son puts these over his eyes when he reads unknown languages, and they enable him to interpret them in English.[32]

Lucy Mack Smith herself stated:

I . . . found that it [the Urim and Thummim] consisted of two smooth three-cornered diamonds set in glass, and the glasses were set in silver bows, which were connected with each other in much the same way as old fashioned spectacles.[33]

Edward Stevenson relayed information he received from Martin Harris:

I have conversed with Martin Harris, who handled them, and he said he had placed them as he would a pair of spectacles, but they were too large for him, as if they had been made for a larger race of people than the present generation.[34]

Professor Charles Anthon of Columbia University wrote in 1834 concerning information allegedly obtained from Martin Harris six years earlier:

---

[32]Henry Caswall, *The City of the Mormons; or, Three Days at Nauvoo, in 1842* (London: J. G. F. and J. Rivington, 1842), 27.

[33]L. M. Smith, *Biographical Sketches*, 101.

[34]Edward Stevenson, *Reminiscences of Joseph, the Prophet, and the Coming Forth of the Book of Mormon* (Salt Lake City, 1893), 31.

These spectacles were so large, that, if a person attempted to look through them, his two eyes would have to be turned towards one of the glasses merely, the spectacles in question being altogether too large for the breadth of the human face.[35]

Martin Harris stated in an interview:

The two stones set in a bow of silver were about two inches in diameter, perfectly round, and about five-eighths of an inch thick at the centre; but not so thick at the edges where they came into the bow. They were joined by a round bar of silver, about three-eighths of an inch in diameter, and about four inches long, which, with the two stones, would make eight inches.

The stones were white, like polished marble, with a few gray streaks. I never dared to look into them by placing them in the hat, because Moses said that "no man could see God and live," and we could see anything we wished by looking into them; and I could not keep the desire to see God out of my mind.[36]

William Smith, brother of Joseph Smith, in an interview by J. W. Peterson on 4 July 1890 explained how the stones in the Urim and Thummim were set in the two rims of a bow:

A silver bow ran over one stone, under the other, around over that one and under the first in the shape of a horizontal figure 8 much like a pair of spectacles. That they were much too large for Joseph and he could only see through one at a time using sometimes one and sometimes the other. By putting his head in a hat or some dark object it was not necessary to close one eye while looking through the stone with the other. In that way sometimes when his eyes grew tired he releaved [*sic*] them of the strain. He also said the Urim and Thummim was attached to the breastplate and to the end of the silver bow. This rod was just the right length so that when the Urim and Thummim was removed

---

[35]Charles Anthon, Letter to E. D. Howe, 17 February 1834, printed in Howe, *Mormonism Unvailed*, 270.

[36]*Tiffany's Monthly* 5, no. 4 (August 1859): 165-66.

from before the eyes it would reach to a pocket on the left side of the breastplate where the instrument was kept when not in use by the Seer. I was not informed whether it was detachable from the breastplate or not. From the fact that Joseph often had it with him and sometimes when at work, I am of the opinion that it could be detached. He also informed us that the rod served to hold it before the eyes of the Seer.[37]

The term "Urim and Thummim" does not occur in the Book of Mormon, although there are numerous references to "stone," "stones," and "interpreters" (see Mosiah 8:13, 19; 28:13, 20; Alma 37:21, 23, 24; Ether 3:23; 4:5). Neither does it occur in Joseph's first printed revelations in 1833, yet two years later the term was inserted in the corresponding place. In May 1829 the Lord reproved Joseph for entrusting certain pages to Martin Harris:

> Now, behold I say unto you, that because you delivered up so many writings, which you had power to translate, into the hands of a wicked man, you have lost them (Book of Commandments 9:1).

> Now, behold, I say unto you, that because you delivered up those writings which you had power given unto you to translate, by the means of the Urim and Thummim, into the hands of a wicked man, you have lost them (1835 D&C 36:1; cf. current D&C 10:1).[38]

Another reference to the Urim and Thummim in the Doctrine and Covenants is not to be found in the Book of Commandments. The Lord said to Cowdery, Harris, and Whitmer in June 1829:

---

[37]MSS Collection, Library, Reorganized Church of Jesus Christ of Latter Day Saints, Independence, MO.

[38]The current edition of D&C 10 has the incorrect date of "summer 1828," instead of the correct date of May 1829, which was printed in the chronologically arranged sections in the 1833 Book of Commandments.

> . . . you shall have a view of . . . the Urim and
> Thummim, which were given to the brother of Jared
> upon the mount, when he talked with the Lord face to
> face (1835 D&C 42:1; current D&C 17:1).

The lack of reference to the Urim and Thummim in the
Book of Commandments in 1833 is curious but consistent with
other contemporary documents. A very early reference to the
Urim and Thummim in connection with Mormon history is
found in W. W. Phelps' 1833 comment in *The Evening and the
Morning Star*, where he referred to "a pair of Interpreters, or
spectacles" and then adds the parenthetical suggestion—
"known, perhaps, in ancient days as Teraphim, or Urim and
Thummim."[39] Consistently, the earliest reports refer to "spectacles"[40] or "glasses."[41]

Again, the significant question persists. Did Joseph
Smith receive a unique instrument through angelic interposition in 1827—known to the ancients as Urim and Thummim
and likewise known to Joseph from the time he removed it
from Cumorah—or did the stone found in the well of Willard
Chase become a Urim and Thummim to him several years after
the founding of the church? The following quotations would
indicate that the curious spectacles may have been either one or
two stones used in the manner previously described by skeptics.

---

[39]*The Evening and the Morning Star* 1 (January 1833): 2. Cf. Brent Lee
Metcalfe, "Apologetic and Critical Assumptions about Book of Mormon
Historicity," *Dialogue: A Journal of Mormon Thought* 26 (Fall 1993):
159*n*20.

[40]Joseph Smith's 1832 account, in Jessee, *Papers of Joseph Smith*, 1:9,
and Faulring, *American Prophet's Record*, 7. Also, Rev. Willers's 1830 letter,
in D. Michael Quinn, trans. and ed., "The First Months of Mormonism: A
Contemporary View by Rev. Diedrich Willers," *New York History* 54
(1973): 326.

[41]Dean C. Jessee, "Joseph Knight's Recollection of Early Mormon History," *Brigham Young University Studies* 17 (Autumn 1976): 33.

By placing the spectacles in a hat, and looking into it, Smith could (he said so at least) interpret these characters.[42]

David Whitmer, interviewed by a *Chicago Times* correspondent in October 1881, said:

The tablets or plates were translated by Smith, who used a small oval or kidney-shaped stone, called Urim and Thummim.[43]

William Smith, younger brother of the Prophet Joseph, said:

The manner in which this [the translation] was done was by looking into the Urim and Thummim, which was placed in a hat to exclude the light, (the plates lying near by covered up), and reading off the translation, which appeared in the stone by the power of God. He was engaged in this business as he had opportunity for about two years and a half.[44]

If the reader finds the stories of this chapter in conflict, his puzzlement is likely to grow in the examination of testimony regarding the existence or absence of the Urim and Thummim in the post-Book-of-Mormon period. Its mystery deepened as presidents and leaders of the church made reference to it as a legitimate means of learning the mind and will of God yet could not agree on its availability. Instead of it becoming a symbol of the quest for knowledge it became more than ever a tangible, albeit elusive, pawn to be used in religious argument and exhortation.

Joseph Smith said:

---

[42]Rochester *Daily Advertiser and Telegraph*, 31 August 1829, printed in Kirkham, *New Witness for Christ*, 1:151.

[43]Cook, *David Whitmer Interviews*, 76.

[44]Smith, *William Smith on Mormonism*, 11-12, printed in Vogel, *Early Mormon Documents*, 1:497.

But by the wisdom of God, they [the golden plates and the Urim and Thummim] remained safe in my hands, until I had accomplished by them what was required at my hand. When, according to arrangements, the messenger called for them, I delivered them up to him; and he has them in his charge until this day, being the second day of May, one thousand eight hundred and thirty-eight.[45]

E. Cecil McGavin concluded:

The Urim and Thummim were returned with the plates. Joseph had found a seerstone by means of which he could get inspiration much as he did through the sacred stones he found with the plates. He retained the seerstone, but he surely gave the Urim and Thummim back to the angel. . . . There are a few references in history to the Urim and Thummim which Joseph retained, but the term was used incorrectly. On such occasions they had reference to the seerstone.[46]

Joseph Smith, speaking of the *Book of Martyrs* at the home of Edward Stevenson, stated in 1834:

I have, by the aid of the Urim and Thummim, seen those martyrs and they were honest, devoted followers of Christ, according to the light they possessed, and they will be saved.[47]

William Clayton, Joseph's scribe, spoke of the revelation concerning polygamy on 12 July 1843:

Hyrum very urgently requested Joseph to write the revelation by means of the Urim and Thummim but Joseph, in reply, said he did not need to, for he knew the revelation perfectly from beginning to end.[48]

---

[45] *History of the Church*, 1:18-19.

[46] E. Cecil McGavin, *The Historical Background of the Doctrine and Covenants* (Salt Lake City: Paragon Printing Co., 1949), 77.

[47] Stevenson, *Reminiscences of Joseph*, 6.

[48] William Clayton, notarized statement, 16 February 1874, printed in George D. Smith, ed., *An Intimate Chronicle: The Journals of William Clayton* (Salt Lake City: Signature Books in association with Smith Research

Joseph Smith gave the following instruction in 1843:

The place where God resides is a great Urim and Thummim. This earth, in its sanctified and immortal state, will be made like unto crystal and will be a Urim and Thummim to the inhabitants who dwell thereon, whereby all things pertaining to an inferior kingdom, or all kingdoms of a lower order, will be manifest to those who dwell on it; and this earth will be Christ's. Then the white stone mentioned in Revelation 2:17, will become a Urim and Thummim to each individual who receives one, whereby things pertaining to a higher order of kingdoms will be made known; And a white stone is given to each of those who come into the celestial kingdom, whereon is a new name written, which no man knoweth save he that receiveth it. The new name is the key word (D&C 130:8-11).

Significant information about the seer stone and the Urim and Thummim comes from two men who were to become, respectively, the second and fourth presidents of the church. Making an important distinction between the seer stone and the Urim and Thummim found with the plates, Brigham Young recorded in his history on 27 December 1841:

I met with the Twelve at brother Joseph's. He conversed with us in a familiar manner on a variety of subjects, and explained to us the Urim and Thummim which he found with the plates, called in the Book of Mormon the Interpreters. He said that every man who lived on the earth was entitled to a seer stone, and should have one, but they are kept from them in consequence of their wickedness, and most of those who do find one make an evil use of it; he showed us his seer stone.[49]

Probably misunderstanding this distinction, Wilford Woodruff, an apostle in 1841, said about the same episode:

Associates, 1995), 558.

[49]Elden Jay Watson, ed., *Manuscript History of Brigham Young, 1801-1844* (Salt Lake City, 1968), 112.

I had the privilege of seeing for the first time in my day
the Urim and Thummim.[50]

The elusiveness of the stone in the nineteenth century is
consistent with its appearance and disappearance in Book of
Mormon itself (see Ether 1, 3, and 4 and Mosiah 8, and 28).
After the confusion of tongues at the tower of Babel, Jesus,
then in the "body of his spirit," commands the brother of Jared
to record certain precious information on plates. Then, in order to thwart the interpretation of the writing until after he
(Jesus) has been lifted up upon the cross, he commands that
the stones, or interpreters, be sealed up with the record. The
brother of Jared does as bidden, presumably "sealing them up"
in the Old World before departing for the New. Some two
thousand years later forty-three people depart from a region
somewhere in the New World in search of Zarahemla. Failing
in this, and apparently by-passing the object of their search,
they discover the Jaredite record in a land where the Jaredites
had exterminated several millions of themselves in battle at the
hill Ramah later known as Cumorah.

Oddly enough the stones are not with the twenty-four
gold plates containing the history of the extinct people and so
the record is summarily dispatched to Mosiah, king over Zarahemla, who has "wherewith that he can look." This "wherewith" proves to be the stone interpreters, now set into two
rims of a bow, which have been handed down from one generation to another from the days of Lehi who evidently brought
them from Jerusalem to the New World in 600 B.C. (but failed
to mention them among other sacred articles of the exodus).
Although the crucifixion is still more than one hundred years
distant, Mosiah, contrary to the injunction forbidding interpretation, proceeds with the translation of the plates and gives the
account to the people who alternately mourn and rejoice ex-

---

[50]Scott G. Kenney, ed., *Wilford Woodruff's Journal:1833-1898, Typescript* (Midvale, Utah: Signature Books, 1983), 2:144, at 27 December 1841.

ceedingly.

A puzzling aspect of the chronology is the assertion in all the early editions of the Book of Mormon that king Benjamin, who had died before the forty-three scouts found the gold plates, is nevertheless keeping the plates in custody "that they should not come unto the world until after Christ should show himself unto his people" (Ether 4:1). This anachronism went undetected during Joseph Smith's lifetime, finally being changed in the 1849 edition to read "king Mosiah."[51] The premature disclosure of the interpretation is not adequately explained. Eventually Moroni, the last of the Nephite prophets, deposits the stones in the hill Cumorah where Joseph Smith finds them some fourteen hundred years later. The Doctrine and Covenants assures us they are the stones used by the brother of Jared (D&C 17:1). That the statement is not altogether satisfying is indicated in one of the official church magazines:

> It seems from the reference in Mosiah 8:13 that the Nephite prophets were the custodians of a Urim and Thummim of their own, which had been handed down from generation to generation long before the finding of Jaredite records, so it seems not improbable that for a period, at least, they had two of those instruments in their possession.[52]

Joseph Fielding Smith, president of the Quorum of the Twelve and Church Historian, said:

> The history concerning the Urim and Thummim, or "Interpreters" as they are called in the Book of Mor-

---

[51]Sidney B. Sperry, *Problems of the Book of Mormon* (Salt Lake City: Bookcraft, 1964): 203, frankly stated that "the reading 'king Benjamin' [at both Mosiah 21:28 and Ether 4:1 in the original edition of the Book of Mormon] is an out-and-out error, because the king had been dead for some time."

[52]Joel Ricks, "Urim and Thummim," *Improvement Era* 18 (May 1915): 612.

mon, is not very clear. . . . We have no record of Lehi bringing with him to America the Urim and Thummim. . . . How Mosiah came into possession of these "two stones" or Urim and Thummim, the record does not tell us, more than to say that it was a "gift from God."[53]

Perhaps the number of stones and the problem of transmitting them from one seer to another is not of consequence in light of the fact that the Lord had other media for guiding his prophets. If Lehi had the Urim and Thummim, it seems to have been rendered superfluous by the magic ball which, according to Nephi, was both a compass and a means of divination:

> And it came to pass that the voice of the Lord said unto him: Look upon the ball [Liahona], and behold the things which are written. And it came to pass that when my father beheld the things which were written upon the ball, he did fear and tremble exceedingly, and also my brethren and the sons of Ishmael and our wives. And it came to pass that I, Nephi, beheld the pointers which were in the ball, that they did work according to the faith and diligence and heed which we did give unto them. And there was also written upon them a new writing, which was plain to be read, which did give us understanding concerning the ways of the Lord; and it was written and changed from time to time, according to the faith and diligence which we gave unto it. And thus we see that by small means the Lord can bring about great things (1 Ne. 16:26-29).

The reference to the propensities of the ball as "small means" hardly seems applicable to the awful power of the Urim and Thummim used by Mosiah and Joseph Smith. Notwithstanding the assertion of David Whitmer that he had frequently placed it to his eyes but could see nothing through it, the peril to the uncommissioned viewer is emphatically stated.

---

[53]Joseph Fielding Smith, "Urim and Thummim," *The Improvement Era* 57 (June 1954): 382-83.

And the things are called interpreters, and no man can look in them except he be commanded, lest he should look for that he ought not and he should perish (Mosiah 8:13).

Joseph Smith said:

I should not show them to any person; neither the breastplate with the Urim and Thummim; only to those whom I should be commanded to show them; if I did I should be destroyed (JS-H 1:42).

Martin Harris said:

I never dared to look into them by placing them in the hat. . . . We had a command to let no man look into them, except by the command of God, lest he should "look aught and perish."[54]

At this juncture the student must ponder again: Was Joseph Smith a product of an age of superstition and credulity which prepared him for the role of a seer with a peepstone, or was he the much-maligned instrument in God's hands to restore something of infinite value to the world? Is the mass of testimony against him the result of gossip and misinformation supplied by those who were incapable of accepting sober truth or is it the result of his own adventures in the field of vivid imagination? To members of the church Joseph emerges unscathed from the welter of bad opinion concerning his activities and they point to the fulfillment of his prophecy as proof of vindication: ". . . my name should be had for good and evil among all nations, kindreds, and tongues, or that it should be both good and evil spoken of among all people" (JS-H 1:33). The fact that such a generalized prophecy is easy of fulfillment does not bother faithful Mormons, even though the prediction was already largely realized when it was first published in Nauvoo in 1842. The Prophet may have lived at a time when fool-

---

[54]*Tiffany's Monthly* 5, no. 4 (August 1859): 166.

ish minds and weak reeds were being influenced by subversive spirits but Joseph stood aloof from such unworthy pursuits as crystal gazing and fortune telling which were being practiced so abundantly in his village.

Abner Cole, speaking of activities in Palmyra in the 1820s, wrote:

> Mineral rods and balls, (as they were called by the imposter who made use of them,) were supposed to be infallible guides to these sources of wealth–"PEEP STONES" or pebbles, taken promiscuously from the brook or field, were placed in a hat or other situation excluded from the light, when some WIZARD or WITCH (for these performances were not confined to either sex) applied their eyes, and nearly starting their balls from their sockets, declared they saw all the wonders of nature, including of course, ample stores of silver and gold.[55]

Joseph Smith said:

> To our great grief, however, we soon found that Satan had been lying in wait to deceive, and seeking whom he might devour. Brother Hiram Page [one of the eight witnesses to the Book of Mormon plates] had in his possession a certain stone, by which he had obtained certain "revelations" concerning the upbuilding of Zion. ... Finding, however, that ... the Whitmer family and Oliver Cowdery were believing much in the things set forth by this stone, we thought best to inquire of the Lord concerning so important a matter; and before conference convened, we received the following: ... "And again, thou shalt take thy brother, Hiram Page, between him and thee alone, and tell him that those things which he hath written from that stone are not of me, and that Satan deceiveth him" (D&C 28:11).[56]

E. Cecil McGavin said:

---

[55] Abner Cole, using the pseudonym of Obadiah Dogberry, "Golden Bible, No. 3," *Palmyra Reflector*, 1 February 1831, with emphasis in original, printed in Kirkham, *New Witness for Christ*, 2:69.

[56] *History of the Church*, 1:109-111.

A few years before the hiding place of the gold plates was revealed, there had been a mania for "peepstones" and magic crystal balls in the neighborhood of Palmyra. Many people became obsessed with the desire to use some peculiar stone as a means of gaining supernatural information and guidance. It seems as if a spurious agency were rampant in the community—the adversary working overtime with his cunning schemes of counterfeiting.

Every person who possessed a "peepstone" used it for the purpose of finding hidden treasure. Amid the haze of nonsense and error there may have been enough truth to keep the curious people believing in the "magic stones" but they were always associated with treasure hunting.[57]

Martin Harris said:

He [the angel] told him [Joseph] to go and look in the spectacles, and he would show him the man that would assist him. That he did so, and he saw myself, Martin Harris, standing before him. That struck me with surprise. I told him I wished him to be very careful about these things. "Well," said he, "I saw you standing before me as plainly as I do now." I said, if it is the devil's work I will have nothing to do with it; but if it is the Lord's, you can have all the money necessary to bring it before the world. He said the angel told him, that the plates must be translated, printed and sent before the world. I said, Joseph, you know my doctrine, that cursed is every one that putteth his trust in man, and maketh flesh his arm; and we know that the devil is to have great power in the latter days to deceive if possible the very elect; and I don't know that you are one of the elect. Now you must not blame me for not taking your word. If the Lord will show me that it is his work, you can have all the money you want.[58]

The peepstone craze evidently did not die out with the founding of the church in 1830. Heber C. Kimball of the

---

[57]McGavin, *Historical Background*, 11.
[58]*Tiffany's Monthly* 5, no. 4 (August 1859): 169.

Council of the Twelve reported that after he returned from his mission to England there was a small faction seeking to guide the church at Kirtland by means of a peepstone.

After analyzing the various eyewitness accounts of Joseph Smith's use of the seerstone, it has been concluded that the translation of the Book of Mormon "was accomplished through a single seer stone from the time of the loss of the 116 pages until the completion of the book."[59] At the turn of the century, John A. Widtsoe frankly stated that "there are men among us, holding the Holy Priesthood, who in events of their lives would rather stare into a bit of flint-glass that enterprising dealers name a seer-stone, for the solution of their troubles, than to go with the power and authority of their Priesthood to the Almighty Father in prayer."[60]

Brent Lee Metcalfe discussed the dilemma brought about by Joseph Smith's use of a seer stone:

> Antagonists typically condemn Smith as a slavish plagiarist, while apologists exonerate him as an inspired marionette. Both models envision an unimaginative rustic parroting his sources or his God. . . . The evidence invites a critical reappraisal of Smith's role in the formation of the Book of Mormon. . . . Engaging in the reinterpretive task promises to disclose a charismatic seer who was more than a mere copier or puppet but an imaginative prophetic author.[61]

Today the LDS Church is silent regarding the whereabouts or use of Joseph's seer stone, though it is reported to be in the First Presidency's vault. It seems somehow beneath the dignity of a prophet to have ever placed a seer stone in his hat.

---

[59]Van Wagoner and Walker, "Gift of Seeing," 53.

[60]John A. Widtsoe, "The Folly of Astrology," *Improvement Era* 4 (February 1901): 290, quoted in Quinn, *Magic World View*, 204.

[61]Brent Lee Metcalfe, "The Priority of Mosiah: A Prelude to Book of Mormon Exegesis," in *New Approaches to the Book of Mormon: Explorations in Critical Methodology*, ed. Brent Lee Metcalfe (Salt Lake City: Signature Books, 1993), 434.

CHAPTER 3

Buried
Treasures

In the month of October, 1825, I hired with an old gentleman by the name of Josiah Stoal, who lived in Chenango county, State of New York. He had heard something of a silver mine having been opened by the Spaniards in Harmony, Susquehanna county, State of Pennsylvania; and had, previous to my hiring to him, been digging, in order, if possible, to discover the mine. After I went to live with him, he took me, with the rest of his hands, to dig for the silver mine, at which I continued to work for nearly a month, without success in our undertaking, and finally I prevailed with the old gentleman to cease digging after it. Hence arose the very prevalent story of my having been a money-digger (JS-H 1:56).

Joseph Smith in the 1832 account of his early experiences admitted that when he first saw the golden plates he was "tempted of the advisary and saught the Plates to obtain riches."[1] However, he was not usually given to explanations, apologies, or alibis for his conduct and, though he often denounced his enemies, he seldom answered specific charges. The statement quoted at the top of this page comes as close to a denial of treasure-seeking as he ever made and were it not for

---

[1] Jessee, *Papers of Joseph Smith*, 1:8. Cf. Faulring, *American Prophet's Record*, 7.

much contrary testimony the matter might well be forgotten. An assumption has grown within the church that one Philastus Hurlbut was chiefly responsible for the malicious stories directed against the Prophet and that, if his endeavor be exposed as revenge and character assassination, then the matter would be disposed of. For example, Francis M. Gibbons, secretary to the First Presidency, in denying that Isaac Hale was opposed to Joseph's marriage to his daughter Emma because of his treasure-seeking activities, stated that Hurlbut wrote Hale's affidavit.[2] It has been shown, however, that E. D. Howe simply reprinted Hale's statement from its printing in a newspaper.[3]

Apostle John A. Widtsoe affirmed concerning Hurlbut:

> These affidavits were collected by one P. Hurlburt [Hurlbut], of unsavory fame, who had been cast out from the Church for adultery. In revenge he proceeded to write a book against the Mormons, in which these affidavits were included. . . . Honest historians cannot safely make the charge that Joseph Smith was a professional money digger.[4]

In April 1834 Joseph Smith uttered a prophecy concerning the fate of Philastus Hurlbut:

> The Lord shall destroy him who has lifted his heel against me even that wicked man Docter P. H[u]rlbut he <will> deliver him to the fowls of heaven and his bones shall be cast to the blast of the wind <for> he lifted his <arm> against the Almity therefore the Lord shall destroy him.[5]

---

[2]Francis M. Gibbons, *Joseph Smith: Martyr, Prophet of God* (Salt Lake City: Deseret Book Co., 1977), 44.

[3]Quinn, *Magic World View*, 140n12.

[4]Widtsoe, *Gospel Interpretations*, 123-24. For a recent examination of the Hurlbut affidavits, see Rodger I. Anderson, *Joseph Smith's New York Reputation Reexamined* (Salt Lake City: Signature Books, 1990), 27-62.

[5]Jessee, *Papers of Joseph Smith*, 2:28, with this passage being in Joseph Smith's own handwriting. Cf. Faulring, *American Prophet's Record*, 25.

Evidently the curse did not immediately overtake Mr. Hurlbut for Ellen Dickinson, who visited him forty-six years later at Gibsonburg, Ohio, found him in tolerable health, even though doddering with age.[6] While it is true his exposé sought to undermine the Prophet's character, he was not alone in his accusations. If the affidavits and the eighty or more signatures that he obtained are ignored, the remaining accounts of Joseph's interest in mystic arts still form a formidable challenge to church history. Even if true, however, they may not be a crippling indictment; they do not obviate his right or his ability to establish a church, but they do make his claims to divine guidance suspect.

Corroboration of much of the material contained in the Hurlbut affidavits printed by Eber D. Howe in *Mormonism Unvailed* comes (as it did in stories relating to the Urim and Thummim) from diverse sources: contemporary newspapers, residents of Palmyra, Manchester, Bainbridge (later known as Afton), and Harmony, and some, surprisingly, from church members. Nearly all have a common ingredient: that certain treasures in the earth were about to be obtained when some enchantment pulled them deeper into the earth out of reach of the seekers.

Brigham Young told the members at Farmington, Utah, in 1877:

> These treasures that are in the earth are carefully watched, they can be removed from place to place according to the good pleasure of Him who made them and owns them. He has his messengers at his service, and it is just as easy for an angel to remove the minerals from any part of one of these mountains to another, as it is for you and me to walk up and down this hall. . . . Orrin P. Rockwell is an eye-witness to some powers of removing the treasures of the earth. He was with cer-

---

[6]Ellen E. Dickinson, *New Light on Mormonism* (New York: Funk and Wagnalls, 1885), 62-72.

tain parties that lived near by where the plates were found that contain the records of the Book of Mormon. There were a great many treasures hid up by the Nephites. Porter was with them one night where there were treasures, and they could find them easy enough, but they could not obtain them it.[7]

In 1831 Abner Cole, editor of the *Palmyra Reflector*, said:

We are not able to determine whether the elder Smith was ever concerned in money digging transactions previous to his emigration from Vermont, or not, but it is a well authenticated fact that soon after his arrival here he evinced a firm belief in the existence of hidden treasures, and that this section of country abounded in them. He also revived, or in other words propagated the vulgar, yet popular belief that these treasures were held in charge of some EVIL spirit, which was supposed to be either the *Devil* himself, or some one of his most trusty favorites. . . .[8]

Martin Harris explained the following about money-digging activities:

Mr. Stowell was at this time at old Mr. Smith's, digging for money. It was reported by these money-diggers, that they had found boxes, but before they could secure them, they would sink into the earth. A candid old Presbyterian told me, that on the Susquehannah flats he dug down to an iron chest, that he scraped the dirt off with his shovel, but had nothing with him to open the chest; that he went away to get help, and when they came to it, it moved away two or three rods into the earth, and they could not get it. There were a great many strange sights. One time the old log school-house south of Palmyra, was suddenly lighted up, and frightened them away. Samuel Lawrence told me that while they were digging, a large man who appeared to be eight or nine feet high, came and sat on the ridge of the barn,

---

[7] *Journal of Discourses* 19 (1878): 36-38.

[8] Abner Cole, using the pseudonym of Obadiah Dogberry, "Golden Bible, No. 3," *Palmyra Reflector*, 1 February 1831, with emphasis in original, printed in Kirkham, *New Witness for Christ*, 2:68-69.

and motioned to them that they must leave. They motioned back that they would not; but that they afterwards became frightened and did leave. At another time while they were digging, a company of horsemen came and frightened them away. These things were real to them, I believe, because they were told to me in confidence, and told by different ones, and their stories agreed, and they seemed to be in earnest—I knew they were in earnest.[9]

Rev. Jesse Townsend in an 1833 letter to Phineas Stiles of Palmyra stated:

Smith flattered a few of his peculiar fraternity to engage with him in digging for money. After a while, many of these got out of patience with his false pretensions and repeated failures; and, finally, to avoid the sneers of those who had been deceived by him, he pretended that he had found, in digging alone, a wonderful curiosity, which he kept closely secreted. After telling different stories about it, and applying to it different names, he at length called it *the golden plates of the Book of Mormon.*[10]

The two statements following are from persons who claim to have been acquainted with Joseph Smith's activities while he was a resident of Harmony, Pennsylvania. Emily Austin, a reluctant convert to the church and a sister-in-law of Newel Knight, the first member to have a devil cast from him, stated that she moved with the saints during their peregrinations from New York to Nauvoo:

Six months had elapsed, and we hear a rumor going around that Joe Smith, of whom we had often heard as a fortune teller, was at this time in Colesville, preaching a very strange doctrine, and that our sister and her husband [Newell Knight] were attentive listeners to his fanaticism. This rumor staggered our wits to compre-

---

[9]*Tiffany's Monthly* 5, no. 4 (August 1859): 165.

[10]Pomeroy Tucker, *Origin, Rise, and Progress of Mormonism: Biography of Its Founders and History of Its Church* (New York: D. Appleton and Co., 1867), 288-89, with emphasis in original.

hend. The story was repeated in our ears almost daily.
. . . He [Joseph Smith] also told his friends that he
could see money in pots, under the ground. He pretended to foretell people's future destiny, and, according to his prognostication, his friends agreed to suspend
their avocations and dig for the treasures, which were
hidden in the earth; a great share of which, he said, was
on Joseph Knight's farm.

    . . . in the time of their digging for money and not
finding it attainable, Joe Smith told them there was a
charm on the pots of money.[11]

Hiel Lewis and Joseph Lewis, cousins of Joseph Smith's
wife, Emma Hale, stated in a letter to James T. Cobb in 1879:

Their digging in several places was in compliance with
"Peeper" Smith's revelations, who would attend *with his
peepstone in his hat, and his hat drawn over his face*, and
tell them how deep they would have to go; and when
they found no trace of the chest of money, he would
peep again and *weep like a child*, and tell them that the
enchantment had removed it on account of some sin, or
thoughtless word, and finally the enchantment became
so strong that he could not see, and the business was
finally abandoned.[12]

The money-digging stories continued to plague Joseph's
name for over half a century. After the removal of the church
from Nauvoo to Salt Lake Valley there were still many inquir-
ers among both saints and Gentiles regarding the veracity of
the treasure-hunting reports—some hoping they could be disproved, others that they could be sustained. Elderly residents
from the cradle of Mormonism were questioned and reexamined concerning their earlier testimonies but if they were guilty

---

[11]Emily M. Austin, *Mormonism; or, Life among the Mormons, Being an
Autobiographical Sketch, Including an Experience of Fourteen Years of Mormon Life* (Madison, WI: M. J. Cantwell, 1882), 31-33.

    [12]Wilhelm Ritter von Wymetal, using the pseudonym of W. Wyl, *Mor-
mon Portraits; or, The Truth about Mormon Leaders from 1830 to 1886* (Salt
Lake City: Tribune Printing and Publishing Co., 1886), 79, with emphasis
in original.

of perjury it did not come to light.

John Stafford, a resident of Rochester, at the age of seventy-six stated:

> The Smiths, with others, were digging for money before Joe got the plates. My father [William Stafford] had a stone, which some thought they could look through, and old Mrs. Smith came there for it one day, but never got it. Saw them digging one time for money; (this was three or four years before the Book of Mormon was found) the Smiths and others. The old man and Hyrum were there, I think, but Joseph was not there.[13]

William Law, a member of the First Presidency at Nauvoo, stated in an interview in 1887 with Wilhelm Ritter von Wymetal, who used the pseudonym of W. Wyl:

> Hyrum told me once that Joseph, in his younger years, *used to hunt for hidden treasures with his peepstone.*[14]

Some commentators have been heretical enough to suggest that Joseph's interest in buried treasure did not wane after the church was established. They point to a section of the Doctrine and Covenants as evidence that his burning dream of sudden wealth was still smoldering at the time of his visit to Salem, Massachusetts, in the summer of 1836.

> I, the Lord your God, am not displeased with your coming this journey, notwithstanding your follies. I have much treasure in this city for you, for the benefit of Zion. . . . I will give this city into your hands, that you shall have power over it, insomuch that they shall not discover your secret parts; and its wealth pertaining to gold and silver shall be yours (D&C 111:1-2, 4).

---

[13]George Reynolds, *The Myth of the "Manuscript Found," or the Absurdities of the "Spaulding Story"* (Salt Lake City: Juvenile Instructor Office, 1883), 59-60.

[14]Lyndon W. Cook, ed., *William Law: Biographical Essay, Nauvoo Diary, Correspondence, Interview* (Orem, UT: Grandin Book Co., 1994), 122, with emphasis in original.

By the time the saints were ensconced at Nauvoo interest in treasure-seeking had abated but was not altogether quelled. Hosea Stout stated in September 1845:

> I ... went with Br [Jessie P.] Harmon and [Alvin] Horr to see a boy look in a "peep Stone" for some money which he said he could see hid up in the ground, he would look and we would dig but he found no money he said it would move as we approached it, I came home about ten oclock at night.[15]

Donna Hill, in her biography of Joseph Smith, concluded that "Joseph had searched for treasure, [and] that to some extent he had accepted the myths which often accompanied belief in buried treasure."[16] Today the thought of Joseph Smith having been a money-digger is repulsive to the saints and the charge is often vociferously denied. Some have been aware that such dark rumors existed but inasmuch as the church did not consider them worth an evaluation the members have been willing to accept the Prophet's explanation of how he came to be incriminated. Nevertheless, there was a time when the charges were not strenuously denied. Brigham Young stated:

> Ten years ago, it was called heresy for Joseph Smith to be a money digger, and receive revelations; ... and now I see hundreds of reverend gentlemen going to dig money [Rev. G. B. Day and others on their way to the California mines]. I despise a man who wont dig for gold; he is a lazy man, and intends to sponge on others. Do not think I blame you; all I have to say is that you have to follow in the wake of "Old Joe Smith," and paddle away to dig gold; it is a comic, novel thing to me.[17]

George Reynolds explained:

> Again, he [Joseph Smith] is charged with the grave offense of being a "money-digger." In one sense this is

---

[15]Brooks, *Diary of Hosea Stout*, 1:61-62.

[16]Donna Hill, *Joseph Smith: The First Mormon* (Garden City, NY: Doubleday and Co., 1977), 66.

[17]*Deseret News* 1, no. 3 (29 June 1850): 20.

true. The whole country round about western New York was in those days affected with a mania to discover hidden treasures in the earth. Most marvelous stories are told of the interposition of unseen beings when some of these treasure were disturbed. The public mind was greatly troubled on this subject, and Joseph Smith was employed by a man at one time to dig for him in the hope of discovering some of these buried riches, or an ancient Spanish mine. Joseph worked for him as he would for any other man, or for the same man if he engaged him to plant potatoes or hoe corn. From this grew the story of Joseph being a money-digger. Even if he dug for treasure on his own responsibility, we do not know that there is anything degrading, dishonest or criminal in such an action.[18]

If Joseph Smith was not really guilty of conjuring, crystal-gazing, and using a peepstone to search for buried treasure, then it is unfortunate for his case that these charges are preserved by both friends and foes.

---

[18]Reynolds, *Myth of the "Manuscript Found,"* 57.

Figure 2

The Hill Cumorah

Reproduced from
John W. Barber and Henry Howe's 1841
Historical Collections of the State of New York

Figure 3

Joseph Smith Receiving the Plates

Reproduced from
Pomeroy Tucker's 1867
Origin, Rise, and Progress of Mormonism

Figure 4

Joseph Smith Translating the Plates

Reproduced from
Drawing by Michael Clane Graves
in *Dialogue* 15 (Summer 1982)
Courtesy of the Dialogue Foundation

CHAPTER 4

The Golden Plates

> Convenient to the village of Manchester, Ontario county, New York, stands a hill of considerable size, and the most elevated of any in the neighborhood. On the west side of this hill, not far from the top, under a stone of considerable size, lay the plates, deposited in a stone box. . . . Having removed the earth [from the edge of the stone], I obtained a lever, which I got fixed under the edge of the stone, and with a little exertion raised it up. I looked in, and there indeed did I behold the plates, . . . (JS-H 1:51-52).

There are two significant differences between the official story Joseph Smith dictated in 1838 (and which eventually became the *History of the Church*) regarding his discovery of golden plates at Cumorah in 1823 and Joseph's earlier account (dictated in 1832) as well as the stories of others who claimed to know some of the details of the miraculous find: (1) Joseph does not admit any mercenary temptations in viewing his unusual find; and (2) the angel who appeared to him is unnamed.

Having access now to Joseph Smith's earliest account, it can be demonstrated how Joseph refined his story, sometimes by eliminating certain details. The following is Joseph Smith's 1832 account.

> It came to pass when I was seventeen years of age I called again upon the Lord and he shewed unto me a

heavenly vision for behold an angel of the Lord came and stood before me and it was by night and he called me by name and he said the Lord had forgiven me my sins and he revealed unto me that in the Town of Manchester Ontario County N.Y. there was plates of gold upon which there was engravings which was engraven by Maroni [Moroni][1] & his fathers the servants of the living God in ancient days and deposited by the commandments of God and kept by the power thereof and that I should go and get them and he revealed unto me many things concerning the inhabitants of[2] the earth which since have been revealed in commandments & revelations and it was on the 22d day of Sept. AD 1822 [1823] and thus he appeared unto me three times in one night and once on the next day and then I immediately went to the place and found where the plates was deposited as the angel of the Lord had commanded me and straightway made three attempts to get them and then being excedingly frightened I supposed it had been a dreem of Vision but when I considred I knew that it was not therefore I cried unto the Lord in the agony of my soul why can I not obtain them behold the angel appeared unto me again and said unto me you have not kept the commandments of the Lord which I gave unto you therefore you cannot now obtain them for the time is not yet fulfilled therefore thou wast left unto temptation that thou mightest be made acquainted with the power of the advisary therefore repent and call on the Lord thou shalt be forgiven and in his own due time thou shalt obtain them for now I had been tempted of the advisary and saught the Plates to obtain riches and kept not the commandment that I should have an eye single to the glory of God.[3]

Joseph's 1832 account admits that the Devil tempted him and he sought the plates in order to get money, but the official account published in the *Times and Seasons* admits no such

---

[1]Notice that at this point in the 1832 account the unidentified "angel of the Lord" makes a third-person reference to Moroni.

[2]The manuscript repeats the word *of*.

[3]Jessee, *Papers of Joseph Smith*, 1:7-8. Cf. Faulring, *American Prophet's Record*, 6-7.

thoughts. However, the Prophet's mother and Oliver Cowdery both record that Joseph indulged in mercenary speculation when viewing the golden treasure. Lucy Mack Smith wrote about the second annual visit in September 1824:

> Therefore, having arrived at the place, and uncovering the plates, he put forth his hand and took them up, but, as he was taking them hence, the unhappy thought darted through his mind that probably there was something else in the box besides the plates, which would be of some pecuniary advantage to him. So, in the moment of excitement, he laid them down very carefully, for the purpose of covering the box, lest some one might happen to pass that way and get whatever there might be remaining in it. . . .[4]

Oliver Cowdery recorded in the church publication:

> No sooner did he behold this sacred treasure than his hopes were renewed, and he supposed his success certain; and without first attempting to take it from its long place of deposit, he thought, perhaps, there might be something more equally as valuable, and to take only the plates, might give others an opportunity of obtaining the remainder, which could he secure, would still add to his store of wealth. These, in short, were his reflections, without once thinking of the solemn instruction of the heavenly messenger, that all must be done with an express view of glorifying God. . . .[5]

David Whitmer reminisced in an 1881 interview:

> I had conversations with several young men who said that Joseph Smith had certainly golden plates, and that before he obtained them he had promised to share with them, but had not done so, and they were very much incensed with him. Said I, "How do you know that Joe Smith has the plates?" They replied, "we saw the plates

---

[4]L. M. Smith, *Biographical Sketches*, 85-86.
[5]*Latter Day Saints' Messenger and Advocate* 2 (October 1835): 197, with emphasis in original.

[place]⁶ in the hill that he took them out of just as he described it to us before he obtained them." These parties were so positive in their statements that I began to believe there must be some foundation for the stories then in circulation all over that part of the country.⁷

Likewise, Martin Harris reminisced in 1859:

The money-diggers claimed that they had as much right to the plates as Joseph had, as they were in company together. They claimed that Joseph had been traitor, and had appropriated to himself that which belonged to them. . . . The first time I heard of the matter, my brother Preserved Harris, who had been in the village of Palmyra, asked me if [I] had heard about Joseph Smith, jr., having a golden bible. My thoughts were that the money-diggers had probably dug up an old brass kettle, or something of the kind. I thought no more of it. This was about the first of October, 1827. . . . Joseph said the angel told him he must quit the company of the money-diggers. That there were wicked men among them. He must have no more to do with them.⁸

Brigham Young divulged information about the competition to obtain the plates:

It was priests who first persecuted Joseph Smith. I will here relate a few of the circumstances which I personally knew concerning the coming forth of the plates, from a part of which the Book of Mormon was translated. This fact may be new to several, but I had a personal knowledge with regard to many of those circumstances.
    I well knew a man who, to get the plates, rode over sixty miles three times the same season they were obtained by Joseph Smith. About the time of their being delivered to Joseph by the angel, the friends of this man sent for him, and informed him that they were

---

⁶David Whitmer wrote a letter to the editor of the *Chicago Times*, pointing out that the word *place* should have been printed here instead of *plates*. See Cook, *David Whitmer Interviews*, 71.

⁷*Kansas City Journal*, 5 June 1881, printed in Cook, *David Whitmer Interviews*, 60-61.

⁸*Tiffany's Monthly* 5, no. 4 (August 1859): 167, 169.

going to lose that treasure, though they did not know what it was. The man I refer to was a fortune-teller, a necromancer, an astrologer, a soothsayer, and possessed as much talent as any man that walked on the American soil, and was one of the wickedest men I ever saw. The last time he went to obtain the treasure he knew where it was, and told where it was, but did not know its value. Allow me to tell you that a Baptist deacon and others of Joseph's neighbors were the very men who sent for this necromancer the last time he went for the treasure. I never heard a man who could swear like that astrologer; he swore scientifically, by rule, by note. To those who love swearing, it was musical to hear him, but not so to me, for I would leave his presence. He would call Joseph everything that was bad, and say, "I believe he will get the treasure after all." He did get it, and the war commenced directly.[9]

Shortly before he joined the church, W. W. Phelps, who was to become the editor of the first church newspaper, *The Evening and the Morning Star*, stated in an 1831 letter that "the places where they dug for the plates, in Manchester, are to be seen."[10] Joseph evidently made more than his four annual visits to Cumorah if his mother's account is to be believed, for she recorded that shortly after his marriage in January 1827 he returned crestfallen from the hill:

Presently he smiled and said in a calm tone, "I have taken the severest chastisement that I have ever had in my life."

My husband, supposing that it was from some of the neighbors, was quite angry and observed, "I would like to know what business anybody has to find fault with you!"

"Stop, father, stop," said Joseph, "it was the angel of the Lord. As I passed by the hill of Cumorah, where the plates are, the angel met me and said that I had not been engaged enough in the work of the Lord; that the

---

[9]*Journal of Discourses* 2 (1855): 180-81.

[10]W. W. Phelps, Letter to E. D. Howe, 15 January 1831, printed in Howe, *Mormonism Unvailed*, 273.

time had come for the record to be brought forth; and
that I must be up and doing and set myself about the
things which God had commanded me to do. But,
father, give yourself no uneasiness concerning the
reprimand which I have received, for I now know the
course that I am to pursue, so all will be well."

It was also made known to him, at this interview
that he should make another effort to obtain the plates,
on the twenty-second of the following September, but
this he did not mention to us at that time.[11]

All writers seem to agree that Joseph suffered bodily
injury either at Cumorah or on the way home. He sustained
hurts on his breast, his head, his side, and his thumb before the
plates were safely deposited under his own hearthstone. Martin
Harris' account indicated that Joseph received an injury
when he got the plates:

While on his way home with the plates, he was met by
what appeared to be a man, who demanded the plates,
and struck him with a club on his side, which was all
black and blue. Joseph knocked the man down, and
then ran for home, and was much out of breath. When
he arrived at home, he handed the plates in at the
window, and they were received from him by his
mother. They were then hidden under the hearth in his
father's house.[12]

To keep the plates safe Joseph hid them in various places
—in a hollow log, under his hearth, in the Smith's cooper's
shop, and in a barrel of beans. They were moved from Cumorah
to his father's house in Manchester, thence to Pennsylvania,
and later back to New York. On at least three occasions during
the nearly two-year interval in which Joseph retained custody
of the plates the angel retrieved them for one reason or another.
Once as punishment for Joseph's dereliction in permitting
Martin Harris to borrow 116 pages of the translation. The

---

[11]Smith, *Biographical Sketches*, 99.
[12]*Tiffany's Monthly* 5, no. 4 (August 1859): 166-67.

Lord denied two requests but finally granted permission to show the work to a favored few after being importuned the third time. He became indignant when the pages were lost. At another time he transported them for Joseph from Harmony to Fayette. A third time the angel borrowed the plates to show to the three witnesses—Cowdery, Whitmer, and Harris—and then returned them so that Joseph could show them himself to eight additional witnesses. The proximity of the angel in moments of duress caused Whitmer to laconically remark, "When Joseph wanted to see the plates, this messenger was always at hand."[13]

---

[13]*Kansas City Journal*, 5 June 1881, printed in Cook, *David Whitmer Interviews*, 63. Lucy Mack Smith, in Vogel, *Early Mormon Documents*, 1:396, mentions one of the ancient Nephites carrying the plates to Manchester, where the eight witnesses saw them.

Figure 5

Oliver Cowdery

Reproduced from
the *Contributor* 5 (October 1883).

Figure 6

David Whitmer

Reproduced from
the *Contributor* 5 (October 1883).

Figure 7

Martin Harris

Reproduced from
the *Contributor* 5 (October 1883).

CHAPTER 5

The Witnesses

When or where has God suffered one of the witnesses
or first Elders of this Church to fall? Never, and
nowhere (Joseph Smith, *History of the Church*, 2:308).

Latter-day Saints accept the Book of Mormon on par with the
Bible as a legitimate record of God's dealings with men.
Hardly less important than the book itself in sustaining the
faith of the saints is the word of the men who believed in
Joseph and endorsed the work of his translation. The three
special witnesses were Oliver Cowdery, David Whitmer, and
Martin Harris. The eight witnesses were Christian Whitmer,
Jacob Whitmer, Peter Whitmer, Jr., John Whitmer, Hiram
Page, Joseph Smith, Sr., Hyrum Smith, and Samuel H. Smith.[1]
    The question as to the reality of the golden plates cannot
be lightly dismissed. It might even be suggested that if they
were only a figment of Joseph's imagination then all other
items relating to the supernatural in the birth and growth of the
church fall under suspicion. If on the other hand, an autoch-
thonous people actually kept a hieroglyphic record which God
made available to Joseph Smith through angelic interposition,
then the law of parsimony demands that serious consideration
be given Joseph's claims to divine seership. Now that the angel

---

[1]For information on the witnesses, see Richard L. Anderson, *Investigating the Book of Mormon Witnesses* (Salt Lake City: Deseret Book Co.,
1981).

has carried the plates to heaven, the strongest support for their physical reality is still the testimonies of the eleven men who affixed their signatures to their impressive testaments: "Be it known unto all nations, kindreds, tongues, and people, unto whom this work shall come: That we, through the grace of God the Father, and our Lord Jesus Christ have seen the plates. . ." (The Testimony of the Three Witnesses, in the Book of Mormon) and "Be it known unto all nations, kindreds, tongues, and people, unto whom this work shall come: That Joseph Smith, Jun., the translator of this work, has shown unto us the plates. . ." (The Testimony of Eight Witnesses, in the Book of Mormon).

There are problems to be solved in studying the testimonies of the three and the eight witnesses regarding the manner of their viewing the plates. Before the Book of Mormon was completed, the Lord said to Joseph:

> Oh ye unbelieving, ye stiffnecked generation, mine anger is kindled against you. . . . But this generation shall have my words, yea and the testimony of three of my servants shall go forth with my words unto this generation; . . . I will give them power, that they may behold and view these things as they are, and to none else will I grant this power, to receive this same testimony among this generation. . . . (Book of Commandments 4:3-4; cf. D&C 5:8, 10-11, 13-14).

Lest the reader interpret the "none else" as excluding the eight who were later chosen, authorities have been quick to explain that the view of the three was spiritual—achieved through condescension of an angel—whereas the experience of the eight was definitely physical; they "handled" and "hefted" the plates under the direction, not of an angel, but Joseph himself. If this appears specious, it at least supports a passage in the Book of Mormon: "And there is none other which shall view it, save it be a few according to the will of God" (2 Ne. 27:13).

A revealing insight into the nature of the experience of

the witnesses was written in 1838 by Stephen Burnett, who affirmed that he heard Harris declare in a public meeting "that he never saw the plates [of the Book of Mormon] with his natural eyes only in vision or imagination, neither Oliver [Cowdery] nor David [Whitmer]."[2] Another contemporary source confirms Harris' 1838 statement:

> Martin Harris, one of the subscribing witnesses, has come out at last, and says he never saw the plates, from which the book purports to have been translated, except in vision; and he further says that any man who says he has seen them in any other way is a liar, Joseph not excepted.[3]

Anthony Metcalf claims that about two years before Harris died at Clarkston, Utah, he told him, "I never saw the golden plates, only in a visionary or entranced state."[4] This seems to agree with a report made by Rev. John Alonzo Clark who also professed acquaintanceship with Harris:

> To know how much this testimony is worth I will state one fact. A gentleman in Palmyra, bred to the law, a professor of religion, and of undoubted veracity, told me that on one occasion, he appealed to Harris and asked him directly, "Did you see those plates?" Harris replied, he did. "Did you see the plates, and the engrav-

---

[2]Stephen Burnett, Letter to "Br. Johnson," April 1838, Joseph Smith's Letter Book, quoted in Marvin S. Hill, "Cultural Crisis in the Mormon Kingdom: A Reconsideration of the Causes of Kirtland Dissent," *Church History* 49 (September 1980): 295. Burnett also explained in this letter that when he heard Martin Harris' declaration, the "last pedestal gave way, in my view our foundations was sapped & the entire superstructure fell in a heap of ruins."

[3]Warren Parrish, Letter to E. Holmes, 11 August 1838, in the Carthage, Ohio, *Evangelist* 6 (1838): 226-27, quoted in Edward H. Ashment, "'A Record in the Language of My Father': Evidence of Ancient Egyptian and Hebrew in the Book of Mormon," in *New Approaches to the Book of Mormon: Explorations in Critical Methodology*, ed. Brent Lee Metcalfe (Salt Lake City: Signature Books, 1993), 332n10, 391.

[4]Anthony Metcalf, *Ten Years before the Mast* (Malad City, ID, 1888), 70.

ings on them with your bodily eyes?" Harris replied, "Yes, I saw them with my eyes—they were shown unto me by the power of God and not of man." "But did you see them with your natural—your bodily eyes, just as you see this pencil-case in my hand? Now say *no* or *yes* to this." Harris replied, "Why I did not see them as I do that pencil-case, yet I saw them with the eye of faith; I saw them just as distinctly as I see any thing around me—though at the time they were covered over with a cloth."[5]

The same Metcalf quoted above also claims he received the following letter from Whitmer dated in April 1887, answering a request for information concerning his testimony:

> In regards to my testimony to the visitation of the angel, who declared to us three witnesses that the Book of Mormon is true, I have this to say: Of course we were in the spirit when we had the view, for no man can behold the face of an angel, except in a spiritual view, but we were in body also, and everything was as natural to us, as it is at any time. Martin Harris, you say, called it "being in vision." We read in the Scriptures, Cornelius saw, in a vision, an angel of God, Daniel saw an angel in a vision, also in other places it states they saw an angel in the spirit. A bright light enveloped us where we were, that filled at noon day, and there in a *vision* or in the *spirit*, we saw and heard just as it is stated in my testimony in the Book of Mormon. . . .[6]

The saint who is inclined to accept the word of a Gentile with reservation may prefer Whitmer's remark to Pratt and Smith in their 1878 interview: "When we see things in the spirit and by the power of God they seem to be right here. . . ."[7] Royal Skousen, professor of English at Brigham Young University, opened up a real can of worms when he opened the

[5]John A. Clark, *Gleanings by the Way* (Philadelphia: W. J. and K. Simon, 1842), 256-57, with emphasis in original.

[6]Metcalf, *Ten Years*, 73-74, with emphasis in original.

[7]Orson Pratt/Joseph F. Smith, Interview with David Whitmer, 7-8 September 1878, printed in Cook, *David Whitmer Interviews*, 43.

possibility (in the face of many statements that Joseph Smith saw English words in the interpreters) that "it is possible that Joseph saw the text, so to speak, in his 'mind's eye.'" If it is considered possible that Joseph Smith may have seen the words of the Book of Mormon in his "mind's eye," can it not also be considered possible that the witnesses saw the plates in the same fashion?[8]

From March 1830 when the Book of Mormon came from the press up to the present time there have been many who have believed that the plates were imaginary or only visionary and that the witnesses were either deceived or deceiving. The condition of faith in viewing the plates is not contested by Latter-day Saints. Before permitting the angel to display them to the chosen three the Lord said:

> And it is by your faith that you shall obtain a view of them, even by that faith which was had by the prophets of old. And after that you have obtained faith, and have seen them with your eyes, you shall testify of them, by the power of God; And this you shall do that my servant Joseph Smith, Jun., may not be destroyed, that I may bring about my righteous purposes unto the children of men in this work. And ye shall testify that you have seen them, even as my servant Joseph Smith, Jun., has seen them; for it is by my power that he has seen them, and it is because he had faith (D&C 17:2-5).

The Lord also instructed Joseph in the words he wanted Harris to say regarding the spiritual view of the plates:

> Behold, I have seen the things which the Lord hath shown unto Joseph Smith Jun., and I know of a surety that they are true, for I have seen them, for they have been shown unto me by the power of God and not of man (D&C 5:25).

---

[8]Royal Skousen, "Translating the Book of Mormon: Evidence from the Original Manuscript," in *Book of Mormon Authorship Revisited: The Evidence for Ancient Origins*, ed. Noel B. Reynolds (Provo, UT: Foundation for Ancient Research and Mormon Studies, 1997), 64.

The threat to unworthy viewers of the plates was emphasized many times by the Lord, the angel, and Joseph—and then
repeated by both the devout and the cynical. Joseph declared
he must not show them to any undesignated persons for "if I
did I should be destroyed" (JS-H 1:42). The Rochester *Gem*,
15 May 1830 said: "At one time it was said that he was commanded of the Lord not to show the plates, on pain of instant
death."[9] Professor Charles Anthon of Columbia University
claimed Harris told him the "curse of God" would come on
those who dared to examine the plates.[10]

Joseph's father-in-law, Isaac Hale, contributed this perti-
nent information:

> I was shown a box in which it is said they [the plates]
> were contained, which had to all appearances, been used
> as a glass box of the common window glass. I was
> allowed to feel the weight of the box, and they gave me
> to understand, that the book of plates was then in a
> box—into which, however, I was not allowed to look.[11]

Even though Martin's wife, Lucy Harris, failed in a search
for the plates in the snow at Harmony, Pennsylvania, her curiosity had perhaps already been partially satisfied regarding the
appearance of the plates for Lucy had previously had a dream.
The Prophet's mother related the following:

> A personage appeared to her [Lucy Harris], who told
> her, that as she had disputed the servant of the Lord,
> and said his word was not to be believed, and had also
> asked him many improper questions, she had done that
> which was not right in the sight of God. After which he
> said to her, "Behold, here are the plates, look upon them,

---

[9]*The Gem* (Rochester, NY), 15 May 1830, printed in Kirkham, *New Witness for Christ*, 2:47.

[10]Charles Anthon, Letter to Eber D. Howe, printed in B. H. Roberts, *A Comprehensive History of The Church of Jesus Christ of Latter-day Saints, Century I* (Salt Lake City: The Church of Jesus Christ of Latter-day Saints, 1930), 1:104.

[11]Howe, *Mormonism Unvailed*, 264.

and believe."

After giving us an account of her dream, she described the Record very minutely, . . .[12]

In an 1859 sermon Brigham Young said some astounding things about those who had seen an angel of God:

> Some of the witnesses of the Book of Mormon, who handled the plates and conversed with the angels of God, were afterwards left to doubt and to disbelieve that they had ever seen an angel. One of the Quorum of the Twelve—a young man full of faith and good works, prayed, and the vision of his mind was opened, and the angel of God came and laid the plates before them [him], and he saw and handled them, and saw the angel, and conversed with him as he would with one of his friends; but after all this, he was left to doubt, and plunged into apostasy, and has continued to contend against the work.[13]

Lucy Mack Smith told the Reverend Caswell when he visited Nauvoo in 1842:

> I have myself seen and handled the golden plates: they are about eight inches long, and six wide; some of them are sealed together and are not to be opened, and some of them are loose. They are all connected by a ring which passes through a hole at the end of each plate, and are covered with letters beautifully engraved.[14]

Thirty-five years after the death of the Prophet, Emma Smith Bidamon, in response to a question from her son, Joseph Smith III, concerning the plates, answered:

> The plates often lay on the table without any attempt at concealment, wrapped in a small linen table cloth, which I had given him to fold them in. I once felt of the plates, as they thus lay on the table, tracing their outline and

---

[12]L. M. Smith, *Biographical Sketches*, 112.
[13]*Journal of Discourses* 7 (1860): 164.
[14]Caswall, *City of the Mormons*, 27.

shape. They seemed to be pliable like thick paper, and would rustle with a metallic sound when the edges were moved by the thumb, as one does sometimes thumb the edges of a book. . . .[15]

Failure of those outside the chosen circle to see the plates might account for Harris' remark in 1859: "The plates were kept from the sight of the world, and no one, save Oliver Cowdery, myself, Joseph Smith jr., and David Whitmer, ever saw them."[16] This seems to exclude the eight witnesses whose testimony, appearing in all editions of the Book of Mormon, is one of the strongest supports of the physical reality of the plates.

Another story touching on the contents of the box was recorded by the Prophet's mother in relating a court proceeding against Joseph at Lyons, New York, in 1829. Lucy Harris was the complainant and three unidentified witnesses testified that Joseph had told them that (1) the box contained nothing but sand, (2) it contained lead, and (3) there was nothing at all in the box; the plates story was a ruse to get Martin Harris' money away from him. Harris, defending the Prophet, testified:

> I can swear, that Joseph Smith never has got one dollar from me by persuasion, since God made me. I did once, of my own free will and accord, put fifty dollars into his hands, in the presence of many witnesses, for the purpose of doing the work of the Lord. . . And as to the plates which he professes to have, gentlemen, if you do not believe it, but continue to resist the truth, it will one day be the means of damning your souls.[17]

Beginning in October 1834 and continuing at intervals throughout the succeeding year Oliver Cowdery published eight letters concerning the origin and development of the

---

[15]J. Smith III, "Testimony of Sister Emma," 289-90.

[16]*Tiffany's Monthly* 5, no. 4 (August 1859): 166.

[17]L. M. Smith, *Biographical Sketches*, 134.

church in the *Messenger and Advocate*, the official church organ. The information was supplied by Joseph and the letters had his endorsement. In the eighth letter Oliver gave a description of the repository of the golden plates at Cumorah, which he said was a stone box "sufficiently large to admit a breast-plate" made of six separate stones (i.e.,top, bottom, and four sides). From the bottom of the box "arose three small [cement] pillars" on which the sacred record reposed.[18]

Joseph's own history which appeared a few years later stated that the plates rested on "two stones crossways of the box."[19] This is but a minor instance of an imposing list of discrepancies between the two histories which will be discussed elsewhere in this work.

In 1833 unbeliever Abigail Harris of Palmyra made what appears to be an enormously extravagant affidavit concerning the weight of the plates and other astonishing details alleged to have been gleaned from the Smiths a few years earlier, yet her story is only slightly more remarkable than details supplied by leading church officials at later dates. Abigail said:

> They [Joseph Smith Sen., and Lucy Mack Smith] said that the plates he then had in possession were but an introduction to the Gold Bible—that all of them upon which the bible was written, were so heavy that it would take four stout men to load them into a cart—that Joseph had also discovered by looking through his stone, the vessel in which the gold was melted from which the plates were made, and also the machine with which they were rolled; he also discovered in the bottom of the vessel three balls of gold, each as large as his fist. The old lady said also, that after the book was translated, the plates were to be publicly exhibited —admittance 25 cents. She calculated it would bring in annually an enormous sum of money—that money would then be very plenty, and the book would also sell

---

[18]*Latter Day Saints' Messenger and Advocate* 2 (October 1835): 196.
[19]*History of the Church*, 1:16.

for a great price, as it was something entirely new—that they had been commanded to obtain all the money they could borrow for present necessity, and to repay with gold.[20]

In a speech at Farmington, Utah, 17 June 1877, two months before his death, Brigham Young addressed the saints thus:

> I could relate many very singular circumstances. I lived right in the country where the plates were found from which the Book of Mormon was translated, and I know a great many things pertaining to that country. I believe I will take the liberty to tell you of another circumstance that will be as marvelous as anything can be. This is an incident in the life of Oliver Cowdery, but he did not take the liberty of telling such things in meeting as I take. I tell these things to you, and I have a motive for doing so. I want to carry them to the ears of my brethren and sisters, and to the children also, that they may grow to an understanding of some things that seem to be entirely hidden from the human family. Oliver Cowdery went with the Prophet Joseph when he deposited these plates. Joseph did not translate all of the plates; there was a portion of them sealed, which you can learn from the Book of Doctrine and Covenants. When Joseph got the plates, the angel instructed him to carry them back to the hill Cumorah, which he did. Oliver says that when Joseph and Oliver went there, the hill opened, and they walked into a cave, in which there was a large and spacious room. He says he did not think, at the time, whether they had the light of the sun or artificial light; but that it was just as light as day. They laid the plates on a table; it was a large table that stood in the room. Under this table there was a pile of plates as much as two feet high, and there were altogether in this room more plates than probably many wagon loads; they were piled up in the corners and along the walls. The first time they went there the sword of Laban hung upon the wall; but when they went again it had been taken down and laid upon the table across the gold

---

[20]Howe, *Mormonism Unvailed*, 253.

plates; it was unsheathed, and on it was written these words: "This sword will never be sheathed again until the kingdoms of this world become the kingdom of our God and his Christ." I tell you this as coming not only from Oliver Cowdery, but others who were familiar with it. . . .[21]

Abigail's cart load is humbled by Brigham's wagon load and her four stout men dwarfed by the ten referred to by his counselor, Heber C. Kimball:

How does it compare [crossing the plains with hand carts] with the vision that Joseph and others had, when they went into a cave in the hill Cumorah, and saw more records than ten men could carry? There were books piled up on tables, book upon book. Those records this people will yet have, if they accept of the Book of Mormon and observe its precepts, and keep the commandments.[22]

Edward Stevenson of the Council of Seventy corroborated the cave story, attributing the source to Cowdery through Whitmer:

It was likewise stated to me by David Whitmer in the year 1877 that Oliver Cowdery told him that the Prophet Joseph and himself had seen this room and that it was filled with treasure, and on a table therein were the breastplate and the sword of Laban, as well as the portion of gold plates not yet translated, and that these plates were bound by three small gold rings, and would also be translated, as was the first portion in the days of Joseph.[23]

There have been many estimates as to the number of plates of the Book of Mormon, ranging from a mere twenty-one to a magnificent two thousand. The first estimate is that

---

[21]*Journal of Discourses* 19 (1878): 38.
[22]*Journal of Discourses* 4 (1857): 105.
[23]Stevenson, *Reminiscences of Joseph*, 14.

of churchman Janne M. Sjodahl[24] and the second that of critic William Sheldon who reasoned: "Were the engraving coarse enough to be read, it would take about 2,000 such plates, or a stack of plates ten feet high to contain the Book."[25] Apostle John A. Widtsoe and Franklin S. Harris hypothesized that if the plates, described as being about six inches wide by eight inches long by six inches thick, were pure gold such a cube would weigh two hundred pounds. Knowing that Joseph carried the plates long distances, Widtsoe and Harris deduced that they must have been of an alloy and would, therefore, not have weighed over one hundred and seventeen pounds.[26] This conjecture clashed somewhat with the Book of Mormon statement that the twenty-four plates of Ether were "of pure gold" (Mosiah 8:9), making it reasonable to suppose that Mormon's plates were made of the same material. Either theory regarding the particular metal and its weight poses a problem in considering Joseph's run through the woods while repelling assailants, or Emma's moving the plates about in order to dust.

Oliver Cowdery

Cowdery, Whitmer, and Harris have been venerated by believers in the Book of Mormon; an imposing granite monument on the Salt Lake Temple grounds commemorates the miraculous experience of these three witnesses to the Book of Mormon. The story of their disaffection with the church and the subsequent return of Cowdery and Harris to the fold is well known among the saints but few are aware how harshly

---

[24]Janne M. Sjodahl, *An Introduction to the Study of the Book of Mormon* (Salt Lake City: Deseret News Press, 1927), 39.

[25]William Sheldon, *Mormonism Examined; or, Was Joseph Smith a Divinely Inspired Prophet?* (Broadhead, WI, [1876]), 132.

[26]John A. Widtsoe and Franklin S. Harris, Jr., *Seven Claims of the Book of Mormon: A Collection of Evidences* (Independence, MO: Zion's Printing Co., 1937), 37.

their character was assailed by Joseph and other church officials at Kirtland and in the church publications after 1838.

Nine charges against Cowdery were presented to the High Council of the church in April 1838, among which the following were sustained: urging vexatious lawsuits against the brethren, accusing the Prophet of adultery, not attending meetings, returning to the practice of law "for the sake of filthy lucre," "disgracing the church by being connected in the bogus business" (counterfeiting), and lastly, "retaining notes after they had been paid," and generally "forsaking the cause of God."[27] Whereupon he was expelled from the church.

After his excommunication Cowdery joined the Methodist Church at Tiffin, Ohio, and became a Sunday-school superintendent. This fact is not usually acknowledged by Mormon writers but verification comes from one of them:

> Others support the claim that he became a member of the Methodist Protestant Church while at Tiffin, Ohio. This last assumption is correct. Oliver did become a member of this Church, in fact, the minute books of said Church indicate that he was one of the Charter Members.[28]

While outside the church Oliver Cowdery wrote to his brother, Warren A. Cowdery, concerning that "dirty, nasty, filthy affair of his [Joseph Smith] and Fanny Alger's."[29]

This bit of doggerel proclaiming Cowdery's denial of the Book of Mormon appeared in the *Times and Seasons*:

> . . . Or prove that Christ was not the Lord
> Because that Peter cursed and swore?

---

[27]*History of the Church*, 3:16-17.

[28]Stanley Gunn, *Oliver Cowdery: Second Elder and Scribe* (Salt Lake City: Bookcraft, 1962), 179.

[29]Oliver Cowdery, Letter to Warren A. Cowdery, 21 January 1838, quoted in Todd Compton, *In Sacred Loneliness: The Plural Wives of Joseph Smith* (Salt Lake City: Signature Books, 1997), 28, 643.

Or Book of Mormon not his word
Because denied, by Oliver.[30]

Four years after Joseph Smith's death Cowdery returned to the church, was rebaptized, but according to his brother-in-law, David Whitmer, with whom he spent the year prior to his death in 1850, Oliver rejected the Doctrine and Covenants, the sacred book of God's revelations to Joseph.

David Whitmer

David Whitmer was the most-interviewed witness of the Book of Mormon. In an 1878 interview with Orson Pratt and Joseph F. Smith, Whitmer stated that he saw the angel and the plates, which were in a great light while seated on a log a few feet distant.[31]

After graduating from law school in 1885 James H. Moyle stopped in Richmond, Missouri, to talk to the aged David Whitmer. Moyle appealed to Whitmer to tell him the truth about his published testimony of the Book of Mormon, and Whitmer bore a strong testimony. However, Moyle wrote that Whitmer was "somewhat spiritual in his explanations. He was not as materialistic in his descriptions as I wished."[32] Moyle was clearly disappointed by the ethereal nature of Whit-

---

[30]Joel H. Johnson, poem, *Times and Seasons* 2 (15 July 1841): 482.

[31]Cook, *David Whitmer Interviews*, 25-26.

[32]James H. Moyle, Diary, 28 June 1885, located in the Archives, Historical Department, The Church of Jesus Christ of Latter-day Saints, Salt Lake City. At the end of his 1885 diary, Moyle adds a summary of the 2½-hour Whitmer interview, saying that "he [Whitmer] did see them [the plates] and the angel and heard him speak. But that it was indiscribable that it was through the power of God. . . . Because it is only seen in the Spirit. I was not fully satisfied with the explanation. It was more spiritual than I anticipated." R. L. Anderson, *Book of Mormon Witnesses*, 81, 91, quotes Moyle's diary concerning Whitmer's seeing but not handling the plates, but Anderson omits mentioning Moyle's dissatisfaction with the spiritual nature of Whitmer's testimony.

mer's description, expecting it to be more physical. After a lifetime of study of the Book of Mormon, Wesley P. Lloyd reported that B. H. Roberts in 1933 had come to a similar conclusion:

> Bro. Roberts made a special Book of Mormon study. Treated the problem systematically and historically and in a 400 type written page thesis set forth a revolutionary article on the origin of the Book of Mormon and sent it to Pres. Grant. It's an article far too strong for the average Church member but for the intellectual group he considers it a contribution to assist in explaining Mormonism. He swings to a psychological explanation of the Book of Mormon and shows that the plates were not objective but subjective with Joseph Smith, that his exceptional imagination qualified him psychologically for the experience which he had in presenting to the world the Book of Mormon and that the plates with the Urim and Thummim were not objective.[33]

In 1887 David Whitmer referred to his break with the church a half century earlier in these words:

> If you believe my testimony to the Book of Mormon; if you believe that God spake to us three witnesses by his own voice, then I tell you that in June, 1838, God spake to me again by his own voice from the heavens, and told me to "separate myself from among the Latter Day Saints, for as they sought to do unto me, so should it be done unto them."[34]

The psychologist might see Whitmer's visionary experiences conforming to a pattern and not be able to distinguish between the true and the false voices, but to the Latter-day Saint it is at once obvious that the angel-with-the-plates vision was authentic and the later manifestations spurious. While it

---

[33]B. H. Roberts, *Studies of the Book of Mormon*, ed. Brigham D. Madsen, 2d ed. (Salt Lake City: Signature Books, 1992), 23.

[34]David Whitmer, *An Address to All Believers in Christ* (Richmond, MO, 1887), 27.

is true Whitmer never denied his testimony of the former, it is equally true he did not repudiate Hiram Page, the Kirtland seeress, or God's voice in 1838.

It is not possible to deal here with the complicated pattern of events which led to widespread apostasy in the church in 1838; it is sufficient to note that deep scars were left and strongly worded accusations were hurled both by the apostates and by those remaining in authority. Joseph Smith in a December 1838 letter from Liberty Jail pronounced a severe fate for certain offenders:

> Such characters as ... D. Whitmer, O. Cowdery, and Martin Harris, are too mean to mention; and we had like to have forgotten them.... Therefore we say unto you, dear brethren, in the name of the Lord Jesus Christ, we deliver these characters unto the buffetings of Satan until the day of redemption, that they may be dealt with according to their works....[35]

In April 1838 David Whitmer was found guilty of unchristian-like conduct in not attending meetings, defaming the Prophet, neglecting his duties, and not observing the Word of Wisdom.[36]

Martin Harris

Of all the figures in early Mormonism none was more thoroughly discredited by friend and foe than Martin Harris. Even the Lord pronounced him a "wicked man" for losing the 116 pages of the translation (D&C 10:1, 7). In spite of the rebuke, or because of it, Martin mortgaged his farm to pay $3,000 for the printing of the Book of Mormon. Harris served on the committee to choose the Twelve Apostles and he was a High Councilman at Kirtland, but it was in the role of witness

---

[35]*History of the Church*, 3:32.
[36]*History of the Church*, 3:18-19.

that he found distinction. Martin was a joiner. During the 1840s he became a follower of Ann Lee and the Shakers, then switched allegiance to James Jesse Strang, claimant to Joseph's mantle, and served as a missionary in England for Strangite Mormonism. Altogether he joined eight different groups.

Even among his Mormon brethren Martin was often deflated. A twentieth-century church writer recorded:

> Martin Harris was an unaggressive, vacillating, easily influenced person who was no more pugnacious than a rabbit. . . . His conviction of one day might vanish and be replaced by doubt and fear before the setting of the sun. He was changeable, fickle, and puerile in his judgment and conduct.[37]

Rev. John A. Clark gave an account of one of Martin's prophecies, with the addition of the striking loss to be incurred by the prophet in the event of failure:

> I was informed by Judge S— of Palmyra, that he [Martin Harris] . . . uttered his prophecies so frequently that he at length told him, that he would not consent to his uttering his predictions any more orally, but that he must write them down and subscribe his name to them, or else seek some other place for the exercise of his prophetic gift. Harris instantly wrote down two predictions, attaching his signature to each.
>
> The one was a declaration that Palmyra would be destroyed, and left utterly without inhabitants, before the year 1836. The other prediction was that before 1838 the Mormon faith would so extensively prevail, that it would modify our national government, and there would at that period be no longer any occupant of the presidential chair of the United States. To these predictions he subjoined the declaration that if they were not literally fulfilled, any one might have full permission to cut off his head and roll it around the streets as a foot-ball.[38]

---

[37]McGavin, *Historical Background*, 23.
[38]J. A. Clark, *Gleanings by the Way*, 348.

Some forty years later in Clarkston, Utah, Martin was still willing to part with his head, but for a different reason. Comfort E. Godfrey Flinders, a faithful Relief Society sister who helped prepare Martin's body for burial, stated:

> I was living at my father's home in Clarkston, Utah, at the time of the death of Martin Harris, who lived there with his son a year or two before he died. Every one in the town knew Martin Harris and all were anxious to know about what he saw about the golden plates from which the Book of Mormon was translated. The following incident occurred at my father's home: Half a dozen boys were discussing the testimony of Martin Harris who was seen coming up the street towards them. Upon seeing him one of them said: "Here comes the old man now; let's ask him if he really saw the plates." Upon arriving at the point where the boys were they asked him the question: "Did you really see the plates?" He said: "Can you see that chopping block?" (upon which some of the boys were sitting). "Yes," replied the boys. "Well, just as plain as you see that chopping block, I saw the plates and sooner than I would deny it I would lay my head upon that chopping block and let you chop it off."[39]

The *Painesville Telegraph* of 15 March 1831 carried the news of Harris' visit to that northern Ohio town:

> He immediately planted himself in the bar-room of the hotel, where he soon commenced reading and explaining the Mormon hoax, and all the dark passages from Genesis to Revelations. He told all about the gold plates, Angels, Spirits, and Jo Smith. He had seen and handled them all, by the power of God! . . .[40]

In 1892 John H. Gilbert, the typesetter for the 1830 Book of Mormon, recalled the response of Martin Harris to his query

---

[39]Nels B. Lundwall, *Assorted Gems of Priceless Value* (Salt Lake City: 1944), 351.

[40]*Painesville Telegraph*, 15 March 1831, printed in Kirkham, *New Witness for Christ*, 2:97.

as to whether he had seen the golden plates with his naked eyes: "Martin looked down for an instant, raised his eyes up, and said 'No, I saw them with a spiritual eye.'"[41]

Many writers, professing to have known Martin, told of his encounters with celestial visitors. A miraculous visitation was recorded by a member of the LDS Church in her autobiography. Mary Elizabeth Rollins Lightner told that as a girl she attended a cottage meeting where the following transpired:

> After prayer and singing, Joseph began talking. Suddenly he stopped and seemed almost transfixed. He was looking ahead and his face outshone the candle which was on a shelf just behind him. I thought I could almost see the cheek bones. He looked as though a searchlight was inside his face [and shining through every pore. I could not take my eyes from his face]. After a short time he looked at us very solemnly and said, "Brothers and Sisters do you know who has been in your midst this night?" One of the Smith family said, "An angel of the Lord." Joseph did not answer.
>
> Martin Harris was sitting at the Prophet's feet on a box. He slid to his knees, clasped his arms around the Prophet's knees and said, "I know, it was our Lord and Savior, Jesus Christ." Joseph put his hand on Martin's head and answered, "Martin, God revealed that to you. Brothers and Sisters, the Savior has been in your midst. I want you to remember it. He cast a veil over your eyes for you could not endure to look upon Him. You must be fed with milk and not meat."[42]

---

[41]John H. Gilbert, Memorandum, 8 September 1892, printed in Wilford C. Wood, ed., *Joseph Smith Begins His Work* (Salt Lake City: Deseret News Press, 1958), 1:xxvii. Confirmation of Gilbert's statement is found in R. I. Anderson, *New York Reputation*, 172, where William H. Kelley's notes of his 1881 interview with Gilbert are transcribed as: "He [Martin Harris] saw the Book with his spiritual eyes." William H. Kelley, "The Hill Cumorah, and the Book of Mormon," *The Saints' Herald* 28 [1 June 1881]: 166, omitted this statement in the published report of his interview with Gilbert.

[42]Mary Elizabeth Rollins Lightner, Autobiography, typescript located in Manuscript 589, Manuscripts Division, J. Willard Marriott Library, University of Utah, Salt Lake City. The bracketed words, which appear to be authentic, are found in other typescript versions.

On a later occasion Martin was rebuked for his lack of judgment. It was recorded in Joseph Smith's account of the westward march of Zion's Camp from Ohio to Missouri in 1834 that:

> Martin Harris having boasted to the brethren that he could handle snakes with perfect safety, while fooling with a black snake with his bare feet, he received a bite on his left foot. The fact was communicated to me, and I took occasion to reprove him, and exhort the brethren never to trifle with the promises of God.[43]

Christopher G. Crary, a resident of Kirtland for whom Harris once worked, penned this sketch of his employee during the period of his ostracism from the church:

> Martin Harris remained in Kirtland twenty-five or thirty years after the Mormons left. His mind, always unbalanced on the subject of Mormonism, had become so demented that he thought himself a bigger man than Smith, or even Christ, and believed that most of the prophesies in the Old Testament referred directly to him. One day, when working for me, he handed me a leaflet that he got printed, taken from some of the prophets, telling of a wonderful person that should appear and draw all men after him. I looked it over and returned it to him. He said, "Who do you think it refers to?" I said, "Why, of course, it refers to you." He looked very much pleased, and said, "I see you understand the scriptures." . . .[44]

Upon hearing of Martin's pilgrimage to Salt Lake and his rebaptism, David Whitmer observed that "this singular action upon the part of Harris was wholly chargeable to the enfeebled conditions of his mind, which had begun to manifest certain positive symptoms of imbecility even before he entertained the

---

[43]*History of the Church*, 2:95, evidently written in an 1845 addendum.

[44]Christopher G. Crary, *Pioneer and Personal Reminiscences* (Marshalltown, IA: Marshall Printing Co., 1893), 44-45.

overtures from the Rocky Mountain saints."[45]

Martin at first protested rebaptism but when it was explained to him that all emigrating saints repeated the ritual upon arriving in Zion he consented. His sponsor, Edward Stevenson of the Council of Seventy, who had initiated arrangements for bringing the aged witness to Utah, wrote:

> That Martin Harris was very zealous, somewhat enthusiastic, and what some would term egotistical, is no doubt the case; but the Lord has shown this generation that He can carry on His work independently of all men, only as they live closely and humbly before Him. ... Having been absent so long from the body of the Church and considering his great age, much charity was necessary to be exercised in his behalf.[46]

The energizing force of Martin's testimony in sustaining the faith of other believers is shown by an 1870 letter, in which he said: "I will say concerning the plates, I do say that the angel did show to me the plates containing the Book of Mormon."[47] Also, William H. Homer, a Mormon missionary returning from England in 1869, stopped off at Kirtland and asked Harris the all-important question: "What about your testimony to the Book of Mormon? Do you still believe that the Book of Mormon is true and that Joseph Smith was a prophet?" He described the reaction of the venerable witness and his own feelings in these words:

> The effect was electric. A changed old man stood before me. It was no longer a man with an imagined

---

[45] *The Omaha Herald*, 17 October 1886, printed in Cook, *David Whitmer Interviews*, 195.

[46] Edward Stevenson, "The Three Witnesses to the Book of Mormon," *The Latter-day Saints' Millennial Star* 48 (21 June 1886): 390.

[47] *The True Latter Day Saints' Herald* 22 (1875): 630, quoted in Richard L. Anderson, "Personal Writings of the Book of Mormon Witnesses," in *Book of Mormon Authorship Revisited: The Evidence for Ancient Origins*, ed. Noel B. Reynolds (Provo, UT: Foundation for Ancient Research and Mormon Studies, 1997), 46.

grievance. It was a man with a message.

"Young man," answered Martin Harris with impressiveness, "Do I believe it? Do I see the sun shining? Just as surely as the sun is shining on us and gives us light, and the sun [moon] and stars give us light by night, just as surely as the breath of life sustains us, so surely do I know that Joseph Smith was a true prophet of God, chosen of God to open the last dispensation of the fulness of times; so surely do I know that the Book of Mormon was divinely translated. I saw the plates; I saw the Angel; I heard the voice of God. I know that the Book of Mormon is true and that Joseph Smith was a true prophet of God. I might as well doubt my own existence as to doubt the divine authenticity of the Book of Mormon or the divine calling of Joseph Smith." It was a sublime moment. It was a wonderful testimony. We were thrilled to the very roots of our hair. The shabby, emaciated little man before us was transformed as he stood with hand outstretched toward the sun of heaven. A halo seemed to encircle him. A divine fire glowed in his eyes. His voice throbbed with the sincerity and the conviction of his message. It was the real Martin Harris whose burning testimony no power on earth could quench. It was the most thrilling moment of my life.[48]

Examination of the statements of the three Book of Mormon witnesses shows that while they bore firm testimony both in and out of the church, sometimes the nature of that testimony has been misunderstood. The most drastic damage to the accepted image of the three witnesses is the very real possibility that their testimony may have been based on a visionary or mental experience, and not a physical one.

---

[48]William H. Homer, "The Passing of Martin Harris," *Improvement Era* 29 (March 1926): 469-70.

CHAPTER 6

The Translation Process

Take away the Book of Mormon and the revelations, and where is our religion? We have none ... (Joseph Smith, *History of the Church* 2:52).

The time line for the translation of the Book of Mormon is from April to June 1828 for the lost 116 pages and from April through June 1829 for the published text.[1] However real the golden plates were to Joseph Smith, there is no evidence from his scribes[2] or early associates that he actually used them in dictating the Book of Mormon. David Whitmer bluntly declared: "He did not use the plates in the translation, but would hold the interpreters to his eyes and cover his face with a hat."[3] Joseph Knight recorded an account of the translation process:

> Now the way he translated was he put the urim and thummim into his hat and Darkned his Eyes then he

[1]Royal Skousen, "Book of Mormon Manuscripts," in *Encyclopedia of Mormonism*, ed. Daniel H. Ludlow (New York: Macmillan Publishing Co., 1992), 1:185.

[2]Skousen, "Translating the Book of Mormon," 72-73, indicated that Joseph Smith himself was scribe for at least twenty-eight words in the Original Manuscript of the Book of Mormon.

[3]*Kansas City Journal*, 5 June 1881, printed in Cook, *David Whitmer Interviews*, 62.

would take a sentance and it would apper in Brite Roman Letters. Then he would tell the writer and he would write it. Then that would go away the next sentance would Come and so one. But if it was not Spelt rite it would not go away till it was rite, so we see it was marvelous. Thus was the hol [whole] translated.[4]

At another time David Whitmer described the process of translation:

I will now give you a description of the manner in which the Book of Mormon was translated. Joseph Smith would put the seer stone into a hat, and put his face in the hat, drawing it closely around his face to exclude the light; and in the darkness the spiritual light would shine. A piece of something resembling parchment would appear, and on that appeared the writing. One character at a time would appear, and under it was the interpretation in English. Brother Joseph would read off the English to Oliver Cowdery, who was his principal scribe, and when it was written down and repeated to Brother Joseph to see if it was correct, then it would disappear, and another character with the interpretation would appear. Thus the Book of Mormon was translated by the gift and power of God, and not by any power of man.[5]

The church has always been strongly committed to the belief that Joseph translated directly from the plates, but at least one modern LDS scholar, Nels L. Nelson, a professor at Brigham Young University, concluded otherwise: "Joseph Smith did not look directly at the plates while translating. In fact the plates, while they were in the possession of the Prophet, were probably not immediately at hand with him during most of the translation."[6]

Unbelievers of the 1830s frequently voiced a like opinion.

---

[4] Jessee, "Joseph Knight's Recollection," 35.

[5] Whitmer, *Address to All Believers*, 12.

[6] Nels L. Nelson, "Human Side of the Book of Mormon," *The Mormon Point-of-View: A Quarterly Magazine* 1 (1 April 1904): 125.

The *Evangelical Inquirer* of Dayton Ohio, 7 March 1831, observed: "However the angel (ghost!) that discovered the plates to him, likewise informed him that he would be inspired to translate the inscription without looking at the plates, while an amanuensis would record his infallible reading all of which was accordingly done."[7] The inspiration of the Holy Ghost was emphasized by a minister who lived near Fayette, New York, in 1830:

> The Angel indicated that the Lord destined him to translate these things into English from the ancient language, that under these plates were hidden spectacles, without which he could not translate these plates, that by using the spectacles, he (Smith) would be in a position to read these ancient languages, which he had never studied, and that the Holy Ghost would reveal to him the translation in the English language.[8]

The apostate Ezra Booth declared: "He does not pretend that he sees them with his natural, but with his spiritual eyes; and he says he can see them as well with his eyes shut, as with them open. So also in translating—the subject stands before his eyes in print, but it matters not whether his eyes are open or shut; he can see as well one way as the other."[9]

After a review of all the first- and second-hand evidence, two Mormon researchers concluded that "the Prophet, his face in a hat to exclude exterior light, would have been unable to view the plates directly even if they had been present during transcription" and that, therefore, the plates were not actually used during translation.[10]

Noting the agreement between three of the Prophet's

---

[7]David I. Burnett, "Something New—'The Golden Bible,'" *Evangelical Inquirer*, 7 March 1831, printed in Kirkham, *New Witness for Christ*, 2:112.

[8]Rev. Diedrich Willers, quoted in Quinn, "First Months of Mormonism," 326.

[9]Howe, *Mormonism Unvailed*, 186.

[10]Van Wagoner and Walker, "Gift of Seeing," 53.

closest associates—Whitmer, Harris, and wife Emma—each of whom at widely separated times and places spoke of the "face-in-the-hat" *modus operandi* of the translation, one literal-minded writer lamented:

> The only point of interest to me . . . is that the stone was placed in Joseph's hat. Just where the plates were I cannot tell, for if Joseph had the stone and his face buried in his hat, it is hardly probable that the plates could have been there too.[11]

Accepting, but not quite understanding, Joseph's fascinating procedure in translating, Nels L. Nelson of the Brigham Young University rationalized:

> Any object consecrated by God, and sufficiently believed in by man, would have had a like effect. Indeed, the crown of the hat, could faith have been made expectant enough by it, would have served the same purpose—provided it had also been accepted by God.[12]

Perhaps even the crown of the hat was superfluous to Joseph in formulating his ideas, for Mother Smith related that long before her son obtained the plates from Cumorah he would entertain the family in the evenings:

> Joseph would occasionally give us some of the most a-musing recitals that could be imagined. He would describe the ancient inhabitants of this continent, their dress, mode of traveling, and the animals upon which they rode; their cities, their buildings, with every particular; their mode of warfare; and also their religious worship. This he would do with as much ease, seemingly, as if he had spent his whole life among them.[13]

Mother Lucy's proud admission of Joseph's narrative skill provoked a wry comment from Richard C. Evans, for many

---

[11]Lamoni Call, *2000 Changes in the Book of Mormon* (Bountiful, UT, 1898), 23.

[12]Nelson, "Human Side," 142.

[13]L. M. Smith, *Biographical Sketches*, 85.

years a member of the First Presidency of the Reorganized Church of Jesus Christ of Latter Day Saints with Joseph Smith III:

> This is evidently why Smith did not require the *Plates* to be in his hat when he translated, but they could lie covered up on the table or even be in the woods when he did the job, as testified by his wife and her father, who tells of his talking through his hat.[14]

Speculation regarding the source of Joseph's ideas and his methods of translation became an indulgence of Mormon and non-Mormon writers alike. George Reynolds, secretary to President John Taylor and later a member of the Council of Seventy, explained:

> The translation was accomplished by no common method, by no ordinary means. It was done by divine aid. There were no delays over obscure passages, no difficulties over the choice of words, no stoppages from the ignorance of the translator; no time was wasted in investigation or argument over the value, intent, or meaning of certain characters, and there was no reference to authorities. These difficulties to human work were removed. All was as simple as when a clerk writes from dictation. The translation of the characters appeared on the Urim and Thummim, sentence by sentence, and as soon as one was correctly transcribed the next would appear.[15]

A certain professor at the University of Michigan at Ann Arbor when queried on the matter, reasoned: ". . . there seems to me but one logical conclusion, either the Lord intentionally made all the mistakes of the first edition and colored the writings with the provincialisms of New York state, or, that the Lord was unable to speak correctly or use other than the phrases and mannerisms of the locality in which Joseph Smith

---

[14]Richard C. Evans, *Forty Years in the Mormon Church: Why I Left It!* (Toronto, Canada, 1920), 153, with emphasis in original.

[15]Reynolds, *Myth of the "Manuscript Found,"* 71.

lived." To which Latter-day Saint Francis W. Kirkham rejoined: ". . . we realize that the Martin Harris theory of the interpretation is contrary to common sense and reason."[16]

While the church frowned on further exploration of the subject, Roberts continued to postulate:

> If the Book of Mormon is a real translation instead of a word-for-word bringing over from one language into another, and it is insisted that the divine instrument, Urim and Thummim, did all, and the prophet nothing—at least nothing more than to read off the translation made by Urim and Thummim—then the divine instrument is responsible for such errors in grammar and diction as did occur. But this is to assign responsibility for errors in language to a divine instrumentality, which amounts to assigning such errors to God. But that is unthinkable, not to say blasphemous.[17]

Another churchman, E. Cecil McGavin, reached the same conclusion:

> It is evident that the Prophet Joseph Smith did not see the English sentences appear upon the Urim and Thummim, neither did he hear a voice dictating the meaning of the original characters. He simply was inspired as to the meaning of the Nephite writings, but was left to himself to express those ideas in his own words. The language of the Book of Mormon is the language of Joseph Smith, not the language of Deity or of angelic messengers.[18]

Roberts was not in sympathy with the theory that the errors in the Book of Mormon might be charged to the typesetters. He reasoned:

> That errors of grammar and faults in diction do exist in the Book of Mormon (and more especially and abun-

---

[16]Roberts, *Defense of the Faith*, 1:307.

[17]Ibid., 1:278.

[18]E. Cecil McGavin, *An Apology for the Book of Mormon* (Salt Lake City: Deseret News Press, 1930), 16.

dantly in the first edition) must be conceded; and what is more, while some of the errors may be referred to inefficient proof-reading, such as is to be expected in a country printing establishment, yet such is the nature of the errors in question, and so interwoven are they throughout the diction of the book, that they may not be disposed of by saying they result from inefficient proof-reading, or referring them to the mischievous disposition of the "typos," or the unfriendliness of the publishing house. . . .

In the presence of these facts, only one solution to the difficulties presents itself, and that is . . . that the translator is responsible for the verbal and grammatical errors, in the translation.[19]

This solution, however plausible, may not satisfy the reader who interprets the Lord's word to Oliver Cowdery, through Joseph, as a guarantee of accuracy in the process of divine translation:

But, behold, I say unto you, that you must study it out in your mind; then you must ask me if it be right, and if it is right I will cause that your bosom shall burn within you; therefore, you shall feel that it is right. But if it be not right you shall have no such feelings, but you shall have a stupor of thought that shall cause you to forget the thing which is wrong; therefore, you cannot write that which is sacred save it be given you from me (D&C 9:8-9).

Substantial accuracy in the Book of Mormon seems implied in the Lord's assurance that "as your Lord and your God liveth it is true" (D&C 17:6), and in Joseph's positive pronouncement to the Nauvoo brethren that it was "the most correct of any book on earth."[20] Despite these confident assertions, the problems arising out of Joseph's alleged method of translation still remain. In a summation by Nels L. Nelson two dilemmas were revealed:

---

[19]Roberts, *Defense of the Faith*, 1:280-81.
[20]*History of the Church*, 4:461.

> On the one hand, it makes the Prophet a mere automa-
> ton, needing no other mental qualification than ability
> to read words on a signboard; and on the other it makes
> God responsible for all the errors—mistakes in spelling,
> grammar, punctuation, diction, sentential structure, and
> modern quotation—which are undoubtedly to be found
> in the translation. These are superficial errors, it is true,
> and therefore strong evidences of the genuineness of the
> book, if viewed as the personal equation of Joseph
> Smith; but inexplicable and therefore very damaging, if
> attributed to the Lord.[21]

It may be that the church will not soon re-open the doors
of inquiry into the processes of the translation of the Book of
Mormon, for the belief is strong that those doors were closed
by Joseph himself when he was importuned in 1831 by the
elders at Orange, Ohio, through his brother Hyrum, to
disclose the facts of the production of the Book of Mormon.
The Far West Record stated that "Br. Joseph Smith jr. said that
it was not intended to tell the world all the particulars of the
coming forth of the book of Mormon, & also said that it was
not expedient for him to relate these things."[22]

And so, in the meantime, the provocative question of B.
H. Roberts must go unanswered, remaining a constant challenge to the curiosity of the investigator:

> The translation of the Book of Mormon is English in
> idiom, and the idiom of the time and locality where it
> was produced, as all must know who read it, and espe-
> cially those who have read the first edition of it. . . . The
> question remains, Whose is it? The Urim and Thum-
> mim's, the Lord's, or is it Joseph Smith's? And who is
> responsible for its palpable errors? The Lord, or man?[23]

---

[21]Nelson, "Human Side," 138.

[22]Donald Q. Cannon and Lyndon W. Cook, ed., *Far West Record:
Minutes of The Church of Jesus Christ of Latter-day Saints, 1830-1844* (Salt
Lake City: Deseret Book Co., 1983), 23.

[23]Roberts, *Defense of the Faith*, 1:293.

CHAPTER 7

Responses to the Book of Mormon

The boldness of my plans and measures, can readily be tested by the touchstone of all schemes, systems, projects, and adventures—*truth*, for truth is a matter of fact; and the fact is, that by the power of God I translated the Book of Mormon from hieroglyphics; the knowledge of which was lost to the world: in which wonderful event I stood alone, an unlearned youth, to combat the worldly wisdom, and multiplied ignorance of eighteen centuries, with a new revelation (Joseph Smith, *Times and Seasons*, 4:372-73).

The critic who would evaluate the Book of Mormon is confronted by an impressive warning from Moroni: "He that condemneth let him be aware lest he shall be in danger of hell fire" (Morm. 8:17). Possibly this stopped some of the less intrepid for there are few appraisals that are both impartial and comprehensive. In contrast to the mass bibliography on biblical criticism, the Book of Mormon student must pick from a scant list of violently partisan commentaries. As though to avoid the fate of the complacent mentioned in the Revelation of St. John: "I know thy works, that thou art neither cold nor hot: . . . So then because thou art lukewarm, . . . I will spue thee out of my mouth" (Rev. 3:15-16), critics have aligned themselves like antipodes in all discussions of the subject.

That controversy would characterize Book of Mormon discussion seems inevitable, for few volumes have had the endorsement of Deity. Both in the narrative itself and in appendage thereto Christ gave tacit and expressed approval of its verity. Chapter twenty-three of Third Nephi records Jesus' reproof of Nephi's omission in the sacred record, thereby implying His acceptance of the remainder, and in modern revelation to Oliver Cowdery, the scribe, He declared that "the words or the work which thou hast been writing are true" (D&C 6:17). Again to the three witnesses, he said, "And he [Joseph Smith] has translated the book, even that part which I have commanded him, and as your Lord and your God liveth it is true" (D&C 17:6). Nevertheless, the title page of the book carries an apology and a plea by Moroni, which reads: "If there are faults they are the mistakes of men; wherefore, condemn not the things of God, that ye may be found spotless at the judgment-seat of Christ" (Book of Mormon, title page).

The Lord made frequent promises to the new saints that "a great and marvelous work is about to come forth unto the children of men" (cf. D&C 4:1; 6:1; 11:1; 12:1; 14:1) and in partial fulfilment of the prophecy five thousand copies of the Book of Mormon issued from the Palmyra press of Egbert B. Grandin in March 1830. It has been selected by the Grolier Club as one of one hundred books written before 1900 most to influence American life, thus taking its place alongside the writings of Benjamin Franklin, Thomas Paine, Mark Twain, and Mary Baker Eddy. In 1937 Henry A. Wallace, U.S. Secretary of Agriculture, made this statement:

> Of all the American religious books of the nineteenth century it seems probable that "The Book of Mormon" was the most powerful. It reached perhaps only one per cent of the people of the United States, but it affected this one per cent so powerfully and lastingly that all the people of the United States have been affected. . . .[1]

---

[1] "Wallace Extols Power of Great Books as National Fair Is Opened by Publishers," *The New York Times* 137 (5 November 1937): 3.

Every Mormon home has one or more copies of the sacred tome on its shelves; study groups throughout the church peruse its pages and memorize its text. Yet withal the book goes unread by a large segment of church population. Apostle Joseph Fielding Smith stated in the General Conference in October 1952: "It is my understanding, and I hope I am wrong, that a great multitude of our members have never read the Book of Mormon nor the Doctrine and Covenants." Reason for neglect might be found in a remark by Mark Twain: "The book [of Mormon] is a curiosity to me, it is such a pretentious affair, and yet so 'slow,' so sleepy; such an insipid mess of inspiration. It is chloroform in print."[2] Rudyard Kipling, the English writer, who toured America in the 1880s, commented: "Joseph Smith . . . produced a volume of six hundred closely printed pages, containing the books of Nephi, first and second, Jacob, Enos, Jarom, Omni, Mormon, Mosiah, the Record of Zeniff, the book of Alma, Helaman, the third of Nephi, the book of Ether (the whole thing is a powerful anæsthetic, by the way), and the final book of Mononi [sic]."[3]

A strong plea for objectivity in studying the Book of Mormon was made by Apostle Orson Pratt in 1850:

> The nature of the message in the Book of Mormon is such, that if true, no one can possibly be saved and reject it; if false, no one can possibly be saved and receive it. Therefore, every soul in all the world is equally interested in ascertaining its truth or falsity. In a matter of such infinite importance no person should rest satisfied with the conjectures or opinions of others: he should use every exertion himself to become acquainted with the nature of the message: he should carefully examine the evidences on which it is offered to the world: he should, with all patience and perseverance,

---

[2]Mark Twain, *Roughing It* (Hartford, CT: American Publishing Co., 1872), chap. xvi, 127.

[3]Rudyard Kipling, *From Sea to Sea: Letters of Travel* (New York: Doubleday and McClure Co., 1899), 2:114.

seek to acquire a certain knowledge whether it be of God or not. Without such an investigation in the most careful, candid, and impartial manner, he cannot safely judge without greatly hazarding his future and eternal welfare.

If, after a rigid examination, it be found an imposition, it should be extensively published to the world as such; the evidences and arguments on which the imposture was detected, should be clearly and logically stated, that those who have been sincerely yet unfortunately deceived, may perceive the nature of the deception, and be reclaimed, and that those who continue to publish the delusion, may be exposed and silenced, not by physical force, neither by persecutions, bare assertions, nor ridicule, but by strong and powerful arguments—by evidences adduced from scripture and reason.[4]

The following studies, chronologically listed, while not always reflecting Pratt's call for sober judgment, are nonetheless among the most critical reviews that have been written on the subject:

1. Alexander Campbell, *Delusions: An Analysis of the Book of Mormon* (1831).
2. Eber D. Howe, *Mormonism Unvailed* (1834).
3. Clark Braden and E. L. Kelly, *Public Discussion of the Issues between the Reorganized Church of Jesus Christ of Latter Day Saints and the Church of Christ (Disciples), held in Kirtland, Ohio* (1884).
4. M. T. Lamb, *The Golden Bible* (1887).
5. Charles Shook, *The True Origin of the Book of Mormon* (1914).
6. Fawn M. Brodie, *No Man Knows My History: The Life of Joseph Smith, The Mormon Prophet* (1945, 2d ed. 1995).
7. Jerald and Sandra Tanner, *Mormonism: Shadow or Reality* (1964, 5th ed. 1987).

---

[4]Orson Pratt, *Divine Authenticity of the Book of Mormon* (Liverpool, England: R. James, 1850), 1.

8. B. H. Roberts, *Studies of the Book of Mormon* (1985, 2d ed. 1992).
9. Brent Lee Metcalfe, ed., *New Approaches to the Book of Mormon: Explorations in Critical Methodology* (1993).
10. Stan Larson, *Quest for the Gold Plates: Thomas Stuart Ferguson's Archaeological Search for the Book of Mormon* (1996).

Three of the above reviewers were ministers—Campbell, Braden, and Lamb—who to various degrees sought to impose their own particular credos while deflating Mormonism. Two others—Howe and Brodie—were concerned not so much with appraisal of the new scripture as with the panorama of Mormonism and the character of its founder. Shook was more interested in establishing the charge of plagiarism and in debunking the so-called "external evidences in support of the Book of Mormon" than in analyzing the text. The Tanners' book, which is the most popular of the scores of titles they have published on various aspects of Mormonism, contains a profusion of quotations, mostly from Mormon sources. The Metcalfe volume is an up-to-date compilation, bringing together ten studies that question the historicity of the Book of Mormon. Larson's study focuses on one person's odyssey in the field of Book of Mormon archaeology—beginning with his intense enthusiasm and ending with his critical disillusionment. The controversial study penned by Roberts on the Book of Mormon was published over fifty years after his death from manuscripts written from 1921 to 1927. Roberts' volume is far and above the most dangerous to the faithful because it was penned not only by the foremost intellectual in Mormonism but by one who served the church as a general authority.

Some of the most significant defenses of the Book of Mormon by LDS Church writers are as follows:

1. Charles Thompson, *Evidences in Proof of the Book of Mormon* (1841).

2. Orson Pratt, *Divine Authenticity of the Book of Mormon* (1850).
3. B. H. Roberts, *Defense of the Faith and the Saints*, 2 vols. (1907-1912).
4. Janne M. Sjodahl, *An Introduction to the Study of the Book of Mormon* (1927).
5. John A. Widtsoe and Franklin S. Harris, Jr., *Seven Claims of the Book of Mormon* (1937).
6. Sidney B. Sperry, *Problems of the Book of Mormon* (1964).[5]
7. Hugh Nibley, *Since Cumorah: The Book of Mormon in the Modern World*, 2d ed. (1988).
8. Diane E. Wirth, *The Challenge to the Critics: Scholarly Evidences of the Book of Mormon* (1988).
9. Michael T. Griffith, *Refuting the Critics: Evidences of the Book of Mormon's Authenticity* (1993).
10. Noel Reynolds, ed., *Book of Mormon Authorship Revisited* (1997)

Thompson and Pratt generally ignored the objections of the critics in favor of assertions and proofs of the book's divine origin. Sjodahl was the first serious attempt to utilize archaeological evidence. Widtsoe and Harris presented a compilation of evidence from a number of sources. Sperry frankly discussed a number of problematic passages in the Book of Mormon. Nibley has written many volumes in defense of the Book of Mormon, and *Since Cumorah* is a good representation of Nibley's scholarship. Wirth and Griffith summarize the external evidence for the Book of Mormon. The Reynolds compilation provides the insights of fourteen modern writers in favor of the authenticity of the Book of Mormon.

B. H. Roberts forthrightly defended the book against

---

[5]One of the apostles told Sperry that there are no *Problems of the Book of Mormon*, so when the second edition of his book came out three years later, he had to rename it *Answers to Book of Mormon Questions.*

assailants and seldom quailed in face of arguments considered irrefutable by the opposition. Notice that Roberts has the unusual distinction of being in both lists—his earliest studies ardently in support of the Book of Mormon and his latest studies cautiously in opposition to it.

Changes in the Book of Mormon

B. H. Roberts asks an important question regarding responsibility for the "palpable errors" in the Book of Mormon and answers that "the translator is responsible for the verbal and grammatical errors in the translation."[6] This statement may not reflect the official views of the church, but if the charge of Joseph's authorship can be sustained, it helps to explain the unabashed revisions of the text in later editions. Estimates of word changes in the Book of Mormon range from two thousand by Lamoni Call to four thousand by Jerald and Sandra Tanner to five thousand by Clark Braden—the difference in definition of exactly what is a "change" varying from author to author.[7] These alterations in the sacred text prompted an irate query from an outspoken Mormon iconoclast, Heber Bennion:

> If we are at liberty to change the grammar and rhetoric of the Book on account of the illiteracy of the translator, where will it end? If the grammar is defective for lack of inspiration, why is not the rhetoric, and the logic, and the facts, and figures subject to the same imputation? In fact the whole book?

---

[6]Roberts, *Defense of the Faith*, 1:281, 293.

[7]See Call, *2000 Changes*; Jerald Tanner and Sandra Tanner, *3913 Changes in the Book of Mormon* (Salt Lake City: Modern Microfilm Co., n.d.); and Clark Braden and E. L. Kelly, *Public Discussion of the Issues between the Reorganized Church of Jesus Christ of Latter Day Saints and the Church of Christ (Disciples), held in Kirtland, Ohio* (St. Louis, MO: Christian Publishing Co, 1884; reprint, Rosemead, CA: Old Paths Book Club, 1955), 184.

There are no published statements from the church in answer to Mr. Bennion's query, but George Reynolds, secretary to President John Taylor, once admitted in an official church organ that there were as many as thirty corrections or changes in the text. Reynolds listed a few such corrections but ignored the important differences.[8] The Reorganized Church at Independence, more forthright in the matter than the larger Utah Church, once published six columns of corrections.[9]

The reaction of the Gentiles to the redaction of the Book of Mormon is typified in this cynical report from the Utah Gospel Mission of Cleveland, Ohio:

> This first edition of the Book of Mormon is valuable in part from the fact that by comparing it with the present edition we learn that over two thousand changes have been made in the book since this copy was printed—two thousand changes in what claims to be a Book of God! . . . These two thousand changes have been necessary to make the language even half-way passable, and still the book has many errors which even a good schoolboy might correct![10]

The case against the book's divinity because of alterations may not be quite as damaging as here implied. The most significant changes are those which have to do with such meaningful and non-mechanical subjects as the authorship of the volume, the identity of God, the identity and roles of certain characters in the story, the translating media used by the prophets, land locations, the wording of certain portions of the Isaiah text, and the exact words of Jesus to the Nephites. However, the greater portion of the Book of Mormon is unchanged, except

---

[8]George Reynolds, "History of the Book of Mormon," *The Contributor* 5 (August 1884): 408.

[9]"Book of Mormon Committee Report," *The Saints' Herald* 31 (23 August 1884): 545-48.

[10]John D. Nutting, *Mormonism Proclaiming Itself a Fraud* (Cleveland, OH: Utah Gospel Mission, 1901), 8.

for grammatical corrections. If the unbeliever found inconsistencies in the first edition he will find them in the last, for little attempt has been made to improve the story or make it more palatable for popular consumption.

The second edition of the Book of Mormon was printed at Kirtland, Ohio, in 1837. The publishers, Parley P. Pratt and John Goodson, stated in the preface that because of "numerous typographical errors which always occur in manuscript editions . . . the whole has been carefully re-examined and compared with the original manuscripts, by elder Joseph Smith, Jr., the translator of the book of Mormon, assisted by the present printer, brother O. Cowdery. . . ." The third edition stated: "carefully revised by the translator." This would seem to indicate a thorough examination of the text but such was not the case, for hundreds of changes were made after the death of Joseph Smith—some in 1879, some in 1920, and most recently in 1981. In 1898 Lamoni Call complained:

> They are correcting the commonest kinds of grammatical errors. The number of both nouns and verbs is changed. Adjectives are changed for adverbs. The tense of verbs is changed. Superfluous words and clauses are eliminated. Words and clauses are added to complete or amend the sentence. Pronouns are changed. The ancient form is changed to the modern in hundreds of places, . . .[11]

While the church in Utah remained silent under these barbs, a member of the Reorganized Church has openly called for even further revision: "We need a corrected edition of the Book of Mormon, *not changed in the sense of the text*—there would be great objection to this—but corrected in spelling, diction, grammar, and punctuation."[12]

---

[11]Call, *2,000 Changes*, 53.

[12]James D. Wardle, "Shall We Improve the Book of Mormon?" *The Saints' Herald* 102 (21 March 1955): 10, with emphasis in original.

Views Expressed by Critics

The first published condemnation of the Book of Mormon came 2 April 1830, only a week after the book was offered for sale at Palmyra, New York. The *Rochester Daily Advertiser* in near-by Rochester printed the following:

BLASPHEMY
Book of Mormon—Alias the "Golden Bible"

The Book of Mormon has been placed in our hands. A viler imposition was never practiced. It is an evidence of fraud, blasphemy, and credulity, shocking both to Christians and moralists. The author and proprietor is Joseph Smith, Jr., a fellow who by some hocus pocus acquired such influence over a wealthy farmer of Wayne County that the latter mortgaged his farm for $3,000 which he paid for printing and binding five-thousand copies of the blasphemous work.[13]

Other unfavorable reviews followed. In Ohio the *Painesville Telegraph* reported in late 1830:

If the book of *Mormon*, as it is called, with the pretensions of its apostles, is a fabrication, it is one of the most infamous and blasphemous character; and we must confess, after having an opportunity to canvass some of its claims to a true revelation from God, we have not been able to discover testimony which ought to elicit faith in any prudent or intelligent mind.[14]

In 1831 Alexander Campbell, the founder of the Disciples of Christ, blasted the Book of Mormon for providing answers to current theological controversies:

This prophet Joseph, through his stone spectacles, wrote on the plates of Nephi, in his book of Mormon, every error and almost every truth discussed in N. York

---

[13] *Rochester Daily Advertiser*, 2 April 1830, printed in Kirkham, *New Witness for Christ*, 2:40.

[14] *Painesville Telegraph*, 30 November 1830, with emphasis in original, printed in Kirkham, *New Witness for Christ*, 2:43.

for the last ten years. He decides all the great controversies—infant baptism, ordination, the trinity, regener-
ation, repentance, justification, the fall of man, the
atonement, transubstantiation, fasting penance, church
government, religious experience, the call to the ministry, the general resurrection, eternal punishment, who
may baptize, and even the question of freemasonry,
republican government, and the rights of man.[15]

Josiah Priest, a writer on American antiquities, stated:

This work is ridiculous enough, it is true; as the whole
book of Mormon, bears the stamp of folly, and is a poor
attempt at an imitation of the Old Testament Scriptures, and is without connection, object, or aim; shew-
ing every where language and phrases of too late a
construction, to accord with the Asiatic manner of
composition, which highly characterized the style of the
Bible.[16]

Origen Bacheler, the Brooklyn minister, wrote this summation of his review in 1838:

Many things I have omitted to notice for want of room.
But enough has been brought into view to show, that it
is perhaps the most gross, the most ridiculous, the most
imbecile, the most contemptible concern, that was ever
attempted to be pawned off upon society as a revelation.
... It has no merit even as a forgery.... My conclusion
therefore is that he [the author] was either a quiz, or a
blockhead; for no *ingenious* imposter would ever have
written *such* a work, intending it for general belief....[17]

Professor Jonathan B. Turner of Illinois College commented curtly in 1842:

---

[15]Alexander Campbell, *Delusions: An Analysis of the Book of Mormon*
(Boston: B. H. Green, 1831), 13.

[16]Josiah Priest, *American Antiquities and Discoveries in the West*
(Albany, NY: Hoffman and White, 1833), 73.

[17]Origen Bacheler, *Mormonism Exposed, Internally and Externally*
(New York, 1838), 36, with emphasis in original.

Did not this book claim divine authority, it would perhaps be about as harmless as the same amount of nonsense could well be, and might be read with no direct evil, excepting loss of time.[18]

In 1844 Rev. James H. Hunt concluded:

It bears the stamp of imposition upon every page. If the God of all creation should condescend to give us a written declaration of his will, it would not be filled with such idle vagaries as would disgrace a common scribbler; the fact is, this Book of Mormon is the most contemptible piece of presumption that has ever come under our own observation, and as an admixture of blackguardism and nonsense we will poise it against the world.[19]

The erudite Frenchman, Jules Remy, visited Utah in 1855 and denounced the Book of Mormon as "a jumble of bad imitations of Scripture, anachronisms, contradictions, and bad grammar."[20] To Artemus Ward, humorist, the book was "ponderous, but gloomy and at times incoherent."[21] Pomeroy Tucker, who as editor of the *Wayne County Sentinel* was very close to the scene when the Book was printed, waited thirty-seven years before making this indictment:

The Book of Mormon, viewed in any sense as a literary production, is scarcely worthy of criticism or remark; but when considered "as the accepted groundwork of the religious faith of a people whose growth has been most extraordinary, and whose fanaticism is an astonishing phenomenon in psychology, the book has more

---

[18]Turner, *Mormonism in All Ages*, 19.

[19]James H. Hunt, *Mormonism, Embracing the Origin, Rise, and Progress of the Sect, with an Examination of the Book of Mormon, also Their Troubles in Missouri, and Final Expulsion from the State* (St. Louis: Ustick and Davies, 1844), 15.

[20]Jules Remy, *A Journey to Great Salt Lake City* (London: W. Jeffs, 1855), 1:265.

[21]Artemus Ward, *Artemus Ward: His Travels* (New York: Carleton, 1865), 215.

than an ephemeral interest" for the student of human philosophy. As a curiosity merely, not as a readable romance, it commands a place in respectable libraries.[22]

William Sheldon, a critic in 1876, thought that the book betrayed its weakness in imitating the style of Bible phraseology.

> Had the Bible never been translated into the English language until the present day, our ordinary language would have been used, instead of phraseology out of date; and as its present phraseology is not the style required by the original, Joseph's imitation of this outdated phraseology in his pretended translation of a new work, or an old work newly found, is a strong proof against its divine origin; for Inspiration would not speak in an obsolete language, for the sake of making it sound like the Bible.[23]

The psychoanalyst, I. Woodbridge Riley, after dubbing it a "monument of misplaced energy," further declared:

> As literature it is not worth reading—the educated Mormons fight shy of it; as history it merely casts a side light on a frontier settlement in the twenties; but as biography it has value, it gives, as it were, a cross section of the author's brain.[24]

Samuel W. Traum gave it the scientific brush-off in 1910:

> Since the book is wrong in its alleged geographical, topographical, ethnological, philological, domestic, social, and religious facts, it fails to meet the test to which an accredited history would yield, and failing in that, it is manifestly not a real history of a real people, and if not a history it is spurious, and being spurious it is fraudulent, and being fraudulent it can not be consistently claimed that God had anything to do with it. . . .

---

[22]Tucker, *Origin, Rise, and Progress*, 111.

[23]Sheldon, *Mormonism Examined*, 82-83.

[24]I. Woodbridge Riley, *The Founder of Mormonism: A Psychological Study of Joseph Smith, Jr.* (New York: Dodd, Mead and Co., 1902), 163.

The book is of modern origin, and the claim that it is anything else must fail for lack of support to accredited testimony.[25]

The Rt. Rev. Franklin S. Spalding, one-time Episcopal Bishop in Utah, stressed the need for sober appraisal in 1912:

If the Book of Mormon is true, it is, next to the Bible, the most important book in the world. . . . If this book is what it claims to be, it throws light upon matters of the first importance.[26]

The English investigator, Stuart Martin, thought it "a conglomeration of vain imaginings, intermingled with definite instances of plagiarism from the Bible."[27]

One of the most penetrating, though brief, criticisms of the Book of Mormon was made by Fawn M. Brodie. Acknowledging Joseph Smith as the author, she wrote:

His talent, it is true, was not exceptional, for his book lacked subtlety, wit, and style. He was chiefly a tale-teller and preacher. His characters were pale, humorless stereotypes; the prophets were always holy, and in three thousand years of history not a single harlot was made to speak. But he began the book with a first-class murder, added assassinations, and piled up battles by the score. There was plenty of bloodshed and slaughter to make up for the lack of gaiety and the stuff of humanity.[28]

To many of the above criticisms concerning the Book of

---

[25]Samuel W. Traum, *Mormonism against Itself* (Cincinnati, OH: Standard Publishing Co., 1910.), 151-52.

[26]Franklin S. Spalding, *Joseph Smith, Jr., as a Translator* (Salt Lake City: The Arrow Press, 1912), 3.

[27]Stuart Martin, *The Mystery of Mormonism* (New York: E. P. Dutton and Co., 1920), 16.

[28]Brodie, *No Man Knows My History*, 62.

Mormon the LDS Church accorded an official silence,[29] pre-ferring to let time, faith, and even science vindicate the great latter-day scripture which was dedicated to "convincing of the Jew and Gentile that JESUS is the CHRIST, the ETERNAL GOD, manifesting himself unto all nations." Replies were sometimes made, many *ex officio*, but were not always specific answers to specific objections. The delayed-action formula paid off in the instance of the charge that Joseph had used Solomon Spaulding's "Manuscript Story" as the plot basis for the Book of Mormon. Until 1884 when the document was found in Honolulu (of all places), the scornful Gentile world had rested its case largely on the charge of plagiarism. Brief rebuttals were made by certain church officials but they lacked the note of triumph that came after the discovery of the actual manuscript.[30]

B. H. Roberts, LDS general authority and church writer, wrote the following in 1922 but it was first published in 1985:

> Anti-Christs among the Nephites . . . are all of one breed and brand; so nearly alike that one mind is the author of them, and that a young and undeveloped, but piously inclined mind. The evidence I sorrowfully submit, points to Joseph Smith as their creator. It is difficult to believe that they are the product of history, that they come upon the scene separated by long periods of time, and among a race which was the ances-tral race of the red man of America. . . .
>
> And now, I doubt not, at the conclusion of this review of the Nephite and Jaredite wars of extinction, some will be led to exclaim—and I will set it down for them—"Is all this sober history inspired written and

---

[29]An exception was made in the case of Mrs. Brodie's book. LDS Church officials Albert E. Bowen, John A. Widtsoe, and Milton R. Hunter each wrote unfavorable reviews, as did also Francis W. Kirkham and Hugh Nibley.

[30]For a review of the Spaulding theory for the origin of the Book of Mormon, see Lester E. Bush, Jr., "The Spaulding Theory Then and Now," *Dialogue: A Journal of Mormon Thought* 10 (Autumn 1977): 40-69.

true, representing things that actually happened? Or is it a wonder-tale of an immature mind, unconscious of what a test he is laying on human credulity when asking men to accept his narrative as solemn history?"[31]

Harold Bloom, professor of humanities at Yale University, expressed his view in 1992:

The Book of Mormon was not only his [Joseph Smith's] first work; it is the portrait of a self-educated, powerful mind at the untried age of twenty-four. It has bravura, but beyond question it is wholly tendentious and frequently tedious.[32]

Anthony A. Hutchinson, a critic in 1993, clearly stated his conclusion:

My thesis is simple. I will state it as directly as possible for the sake of understanding and discussion. Members of the Church of Jesus Christ of Latter-day Saints should confess in faith that the Book of Mormon is the word of God but also abandon claims that it is a historical record of the ancient peoples of the Americas. We should accept that it is a work of scripture inspired by God in the same way that the Bible is inspired, but one that has as its human author Joseph Smith, Jr.[33]

---

[31]Roberts, *Studies of the Book of Mormon*, 271, 283. Because of the controversial nature of his three manuscripts, Robert did not want them published and read by members of the church. However, now that the book is available, it behooves anyone interested in the origin of the Book of Mormon to read this book. On the important question of whether B. H. Roberts believed in the *historicity* of the Book of Mormon during the last decade of his life, see Daniel C. Peterson, "Is the Book of Mormon True? Notes on the Debate," in *Book of Mormon Authorship Revisited: The Evidence for Ancient Origins*, ed. Noel B. Reynolds (Provo, UT: Foundation for Ancient Research and Mormon Studies, 1997), 163-64, 176n76.

[32]Harold Bloom, *The American Religion: The Emergence of the Post-Christian Nation* (New York: Simon and Schuster, 1992), 85.

[33]Anthony A. Hutchinson, "The Word of God is Enough: The Book of Mormon as Nineteenth-Century Scripture," in *New Approaches to the Book of Mormon: Explorations in Critical Methodology*, ed. Brent Lee Metcalfe (Salt Lake City: Signature Books, 1993), 1.

After an internal examination of population patterns in the Book of Mormon, John C. Kunich stated:

> Given the evidence presented in this essay, it is reasonable to conclude that some of the details of events in the Book of Mormon are not literally historical. Whether this is due to modern scribal error, misinterpretation, the nature of revelation, the mode of transmission of the Book of Mormon text, or the nature of the text itself is left to individual interpretation.[34]

In 1993 David P. Wright expressed the following judgment about viewing the Book of Mormon as a nineteenth-century production:

> Some might think that acceptance of the conclusion that Joseph is author of the Book of Mormon requires rejecting the work as religiously relevant and significant. I append this afterword to make it clear that such a rejection does not follow from this critical judgment. . . . Adopting the critical conclusion about authorship made in this paper might lead one to appreciate the Book of Mormon as a window to Joseph Smith's life, revealing the sharpness of his intellect and portraying his religious growth. It records many of his questions and answers. It reflects his internal struggles and spiritual challenges in the context of his social and religious environment.[35]

---

[34]John C. Kunich, "Multiply Exceedingly: Book of Mormon Population Sizes," in *New Approaches to the Book of Mormon: Explorations in Critical Methodology*, ed. Brent Lee Metcalfe (Salt Lake City: Signature Books, 1993), 265. Cf. James E. Smith, "How Many Nephites? The Book of Mormon at the Bar of Demography," in *Book of Mormon Authorship Revisited: The Evidence for Ancient Origins*, ed. Noel B. Reynolds (Provo, UT: Foundation for Ancient Research and Mormon Studies, 1997), 255-93.

[35]David P. Wright, "'In Plain Terms That We May Understand': Joseph Smith's Transformation of Hebrews in Alma 12-13," in *New Approaches to the Book of Mormon: Explorations in Critical Methodology*, ed. Brent Lee Metcalfe (Salt Lake City: Signature Books, 1993), 211, 213.

Views Expressed by Supporters

In the fourteen years that Joseph Smith expounded the principles of the gospel to his people, he did not often seek support from the Book of Mormon, which had "sprung from the earth" in fulfilment of prophecy. Joseph Smith summarized the Book of Mormon for John Wentworth of the *Chicago Democrat* in 1842:

> In this important and interesting book, the history of ancient America is unfolded, from its first settlement by a colony that came from the tower of Babel, at the confusion of languages to the beginning of the fifth century of the Christian era. We are informed by these records that America in ancient times has been inhabited by two distinct races of people. The first were called Jardites and came directly from the tower of Babel. The second race came directly from the city of Jerusalem, about six hundred years before Christ. They were principally Israelites, of the descendants of Joseph. The Jaredites were destroyed about the time that the Israelites came from Jerusalem, who succeeded them in the inheritance of the country. The principal nation of the second race fell in battle towards the close of the fourth century. The remanant are the Indians that now inhabit this country. . . .[36]

On another occasion Joseph told the Twelve Apostles that the "Book of Mormon was the most correct of any book on earth, and the keystone of our religion, and a man would get nearer to God by abiding by its precepts, than by any other book,"[37] while Brigham Young asserted: "We believe it [the Book of Mormon] contains the history of the aborigines of our continent, just as the Old Testament contains the history of the Jewish nation."[38]

---

[36]"Church History," *Times and Seasons* 3 (1 March 1842): 707-708.

[37]*History of the Church*, 4:461.

[38]John A. Widtsoe, ed., *Discourses of Brigham Young* (Salt Lake City: Deseret Book Co., 1973), 109.

In a missionary pamphlet William A. Morton averred:

Now, when someone succeeds in making me believe that twenty-four blackbirds were caught, killed, plucked, baked in a pie, and that when the pie was opened the birds came out and began to sing, then perhaps I may be led to believe that Joseph Smith manufactured, out of whole cloth, his wonderful story of the origin of the Book of Mormon. But not until then.[39]

Josiah Hickman saw the book as being on trial before the courts of modern science and academic research:

It has given to the world a new history and has asked all nations to read and believe. Its contents are strange; its advent, having come through the intervention of an angel, is supernatural. As a result only a comparative few read and believe—though the reading public is increasing yearly. The public in general ask for reasons why they should believe this marvelous story. If it is true, there must be abundant evidence somewhere, for truth becomes illumined through time and experience. Her evidence is accumulative, her assertions impregnable; in the courts of evidence she is amply vindicated. On the other hand, deception crumbles and fades; its tenets are shaken to dust before the searchlight of evidence. The Latter-day Saints keenly realize the situation and urge the earnest inquiries of the thinking public. If the claims of the Book be false, what an unparalleled deception![40]

Heber J. Grant, president of the LDS Church from 1918 to 1945, maintained that "a man ought to have his head tapped for the simples who would undertake to say that any would be idiotic enough to write a book like the Book of Mormon as a

---

[39]William A. Morton, *Why I Believe the Book of Mormon to Be the Word of God* (Salt Lake City: Deseret News Press, 1966), 5-6.

[40]Josiah E. Hickman, *The Romance of the Book of Mormon* (Salt Lake City: Deseret News Press, 1937), 39-40.

novel, hoping to sell it to the people,"[41] and on another occasion insisted that "there is not one single expression in the Book of Mormon that would wound in the slightest degree the sensitiveness of any individual. There is not a thing in it but what is for the benefit and uplift of mankind."[42] E. Cecil McGavin believed that "the scholars of the world will yet agree that the Book of Mormon could not have been written by an unlearned young man in a frontier village. The evidence is overwhelming that this book is a companion volume of the Bible, another chapter of the word of God, a divine and worthy witness to the Bible."[43]

After a lifetime of careful study on the subject, Francis W. Kirkham decided that the evidence pointed to but one conclusion:

> Joseph Smith told the truth. He was not deceived. The Book of Mormon cannot be explained in terms of the mind content of Joseph Smith. The record of the book gives more than one thousand years of the history of a great people. It contains glorious spiritual teachings far beyond the ability of Joseph Smith. It seems incredible to believe that one person could dictate, from day to day for about three months, such a book, which has been proved to be consistent with its claims if he was in a constant, peculiar mental state. Moreover, such mental conditions would be easily discovered by the persons assisting him. . . .[44]

Churchman, teacher, and mission president Bryant S. Hinckley wrote:

> The Book of Mormon is, however, in all respects a marvelous work and a wonder. There is no other book like it in the world. It is marvelous in the manner in

---

[41] *Conference Reports*, 5 April 1908, 57.

[42] *Conference Reports*, 7 April 1929, 128-29.

[43] E. Cecil McGavin, *Cumorah's "Gold Bible,"* 2d ed. (Salt Lake City: Bookcraft, 1948), 274.

[44] Kirkham, *New Witness for Christ*, 1:394.

which it came forth, in the way in which it was translated, in the story which it tells, in the teachings which
it gives, and in the prophecies which it contains. This
book is marvelous in the effects which it has produced.
It is marvelous because of the faith it has built in the
souls of those who have read it with prayerful hearts.
Owing to its influence, thousands upon thousands of
God's children have been saved from spiritual and
temporal poverty, degradation, and sin and lifted to the
highest level.[45]

Verla L. Birrell, a faculty member at the University of
Utah, compiled a 583-page geographical guide to the Book of
Mormon and wrote the following assessment of depth of its
message:

The Book of Mormon is an amazing book. Every verse
is charged with valuable information. The total scope of
the Book cannot be judged by one reading, but is
gradually unfolded by continuous study. The surprising
observation of those who have given the Book of
Mormon serious consideration is that a large amount of
new material may be discovered with each additional
reading.[46]

J. Reuben Clark, Jr., United States Ambassador to Mexico under Herbert Hoover and member of the First Presidency
of the LDS Church for more than a score of years, asked
scoffers to consider the following:

. . . the Book of Mormon alone has a vocabulary of
5,500 different words (Joseph was an unschooled, un-
lettered young man of twenty-four when this book was
finished); that this scripture contains many passages of
the very highest literacy excellence; that there is not one
salacious story of erotic incident in all the scripture he
produced—more than can be said of the Bible; that the

---

[45]Bryant S. Hinckley, *Doctrine and Covenants Studies* (Salt Lake City:
Deseret Sunday School Union Board, 1948), 9.
[46]Verla L. Birrell, *Book of Mormon Guide Book* (Salt Lake City, 1948),
xxvii.

Book of Mormon is almost four times as large as the Books of Moses; . . .[47]

Modern apostle, Jeffrey R. Holland, recently affirmed:

No other origin for the Book of Mormon has ever come to light because no other account than the one Joseph Smith and these witnesses [Oliver Cowdery, David Whitmer, and Martin Harris] gave can truthfully be given. There is no other clandestine "author," no elusive ghostwriter still waiting in the wings after a century and a half for the chance to stride forward and startle the religious world. Indeed, that any writer—Joseph Smith or anyone else—could create the Book of Mormon out of whole cloth would be an infinitely greater miracle than that young Joseph translated it from an ancient record by "the gift and power of God."[48]

Recently President Gordon B. Hinckley declared:

Think of [this] tremendous book of 522 [531] pages, which is being read across the world. More than three million copies of this marvelous record were distributed last year alone. No one, I am satisfied, can prayerfully read the Book of Mormon without coming to a knowledge that it is what it purports to be, and that is another witness of the Lord Jesus Christ speaking out of the dust to those of this generation concerning the Redeemer of the world.[49]

My Concluding Position

And so the Book of Mormon has received its fair measure of maledictions and encomiums. Always the storm center in the controversy that has raged over the divinity of the LDS

---

[47]J. Reuben Clark, Jr., *On the Way to Immortality and Eternal Life* (Salt Lake City: Deseret Book Co., 1949), 220-21.

[48]Jeffrey R. Holland, *Christ and the New Covenant: The Messianic Message of the Book of Mormon* (Salt Lake City: Deseret Book Co., 1997), 349.

[49]Gordon B. Hinckley, *Teachings of Gordon B. Hinckley* (Salt Lake City: Deseret Book Co., 1997), 44.

Church itself, it has inspired among connoisseurs of the Mormon drama a unity of opposites. That it is the crux of every matter pertaining to Mormonism is acknowledged by Apostle Joseph F. Merrill: "The divinity of the establishment of this Church stands or falls with the validity of that book. I say this, of course, in perfect confidence that no matter what discoveries may be made, the validity of that book will never be impeached."[50]

This black-or-white, either-or position is questioned by some students of Mormon history. Marvin S. Hill, professor of history at Brigham Young University, cautioned that "some in the Church have expressed doubts as to its [the Book of Mormon's] historicity but still accept it as a divine revelation and scripture."[51] While previously such a controversial position was not even mentioned, an LDS writer in the new *Encyclopedia of Mormonism* acknowledges that some Mormon researchers question the historicity of the Book of Mormon.[52]

Likewise, Brigham D. Madsen, who edited the controversial *Studies of the Book of Mormon* written by B. H. Roberts in the 1920s, declared:

> B. H. Roberts had the instinct for what is significant in Mormonism—not such issues as those listed above, important as they are, but the true origins of the LDS faith—the Book of Mormon as history or as a figment of Joseph Smith's imagination and creativity. . . .
> While LDS leaders in Salt Lake City continue their aggressive preaching of the Book of Mormon, despite the overwhelming scientific proofs of its fictional char-

---

[50]Joseph F. Merrill, "The Place the Book of Mormon along with Cardinal Teachings Holds in the Lives of Latter-day Saints," *Deseret News*, 19 January 1929, Church Department, sect. 3, p. 6.

[51]Marvin S. Hill, "Afterword," *Brigham Young University Studies* 30 (Fall 1990): 121.

[52]Stephen D. Ricks, "Book of Mormon Studies," in *Encyclopedia of Mormonism*, ed. Daniel H. Ludlow (New York: Macmillan Publishing Co., 1992), 1:209.

acter, the Reorganized Church of Jesus Christ of Latter Day Saints has . . . "soft-pedalled the Book of Mormon. . . ."

It is possible, as did B. H. Roberts during the last decade of his life, to emphasize the religious and spiritual values in the Book of Mormon and to use these moral lessons as a driving force for missionary work. . . .

Most of the thousands of Mormon disbelievers in the Book of Mormon want to retain their activity and membership in their church because of the values they perceive in it. They cherish the Word of Wisdom and its rules of health; they applaud the church's stand for strong family values in a time of moral decay; they sustain the old puritan virtues espoused by their church leaders; they rejoice in their proud traditions of sacrifice; they thrill to the strains of the old hymn, "Come, Come Ye Saints." . . .[53]

The immediate theme of the Book of Mormon, and in fact Mormonism in general, is the constant contest between good and evil. Nephites are seen as white and delightsome, Lamanites as dark and loathsome, inhabitants as righteous or unrighteous with little visible degree of variation. One's status is usually described as either/or. Percentages of good or evil are not determinable.

Missionaries are now instructed to avoid pejorative statements against other churches, such as "mother of abominations," "whore of all the earth," "mother of harlots," and other offensive designations. But such unfortunate words cannot be erased from the LDS scriptures. Also, in Third Nephi it is related that Jesus is the architect and executioner of thousands of his people (designated as "unrighteous") by drowning, burning, and smothering them in sixteen major cities. To survivors who were "more righteous than they" he then promises in redundant phrases to gather and protect them "as a hen gathereth

---

[53]Brigham D. Madsen, "Reflections on LDS Disbelief in the Book of Mormon as History," *Dialogue: A Journal of Mormon Thought* 30 (Fall 1997): 95-97.

her chickens" (3 Ne. 9:1-22; 10:1-6).

As past hostilities recede, there becomes renewed hope for brotherly love, for giving the lie to the cynic who says, "He that lives on hope will die fasting." While religion can promote love, power, beauty, and graceful genuflection, it can also promote hatred, division, war, and decimation. Are there pathways to ecumenism, tolerance, and amelioration? Can virtue be triumphant, peace attainable? Mormons think so. Their tenth Article of Faith states "that Christ will reign personally upon the earth; and, that the earth will be renewed and receive its paradisiacal glory" (A of F 10).

A possible scenario for the future of the Book of Mormon is that the prophets, seers, and revelators of the Church of Jesus Christ of Latter-day Saints, plus 60,000 missionaries, will continue to promote the book as holy scripture, a guide for the world's missions in order that they may attain a place in the heavenly Kingdom of God.

Nevertheless, the debate concerning the Book of Mormon will long continue for it is unlikely that critics will suddenly heed the Bible dictum: "Refrain from these men, and let them alone: for if this counsel or this work be of men, it will come to nought: But if it be of God, ye cannot overthrow it; lest haply ye be found even to fight against God" (Acts 5:38-39).

THE

BOOK OF MORMON:

AN ACCOUNT WRITTEN BY THE HAND OF MOR-
MON, UPON PLATES TAKEN FROM
THE PLATES OF NEPHI.

Wherefore it is an abridgment of the Record of the People of Nephi; and also of the Lamanites; written to the Lamanites, which are a remnant of the House of Israel; and also to Jew and Gentile; written by way of commandment, and also by the spirit of Prophesy and of Revelation. Written, and sealed up, and hid up unto the LORD, that they might not be destroyed; to come forth by the gift and power of GOD unto the interpretation thereof; sealed by the hand of Moroni, and hid up unto the LORD, to come forth in due time by the way of Gentile; the interpretation thereof by the gift of GOD; an abridgment taken from the Book of Ether.

Also, which is a Record of the People of Jared, which were scattered at the time the LORD confounded the language of the people when they were building a tower to get to Heaven: which is to shew unto the remnant of the House of Israel how great things the LORD hath done for their fathers; and that they may know the covenants of the LORD, that they are not cast off forever; and also to the convincing of the Jew and Gentile that JESUS is the CHRIST, the ETERNAL GOD, manifesting Himself unto all nations. And now if there be fault, it be the mistake of men; wherefore condemn not the things of GOD, that ye may be found spotless at the judgment seat of CHRIST.

BY JOSEPH SMITH, JUNIOR,
AUTHOR AND PROPRIETOR.

PALMYRA:

PRINTED BY E. B. GRANDIN, FOR THE AUTHOR.

1830.

Figure 8

1830 Edition of the Book of Mormon

Appendices

Martin Harris
on Mormonism

INTERVIEW BY JOEL TIFFANY[1]

The following narration we took down from the lips of Martin Harris, and read the same to him after it was written, that we might be certain of giving his statement to the world. We made a journey to Ohio for the purpose of obtaining it, in the latter part of January, 1859. We did this that the world might have a connected account of the origin of Mormonism from the lips of one of the original witnesses, upon whose testimony it was first received. For it will be remembered that Martin Harris is one of the three witnesses selected to certify to the facts connected with the origin of that revelation.

---

[1]Joel Tiffany interviewed Martin Harris at his home in Kirtland, Ohio, in January 1859, and this interview was (after being approved by Harris) published in "Mormonism—No. II," *Tiffany's Monthly* 5, no. 4 (August 1859): 163-70. In a previous issue of his magazine Joel Tiffany, "Mormonism," *Tiffany's Monthly* 5, no. 1 (May 1859): 50, says the following about Martin Harris: "We were personally acquainted with Martin Harris, the real father of earthly Mormonism. He was the first associated with the Prophet Joseph Smith, and the one most intimate with him at the time the revelation commenced. Mr Harris had conversed with us many times upon the subject, giving us the history of its earthly development, and desiring us to write it from his lips. It is but simple justice to Mr. Harris, that we should state that he is still an earnest and sincere advocate of the spiritual and divine authority of the Book of Mormon."

Mr. Harris says: "Joseph Smith, jr., found at Palmyra, N.Y., on the 22d day of September, 1827, the plates of gold upon which was recorded in Arabic, Chaldaic, Syriac, and Egyptian, the Book of Life, or the Book of Mormon. I was not with him at the time, but I had a revelation the summer before, that God had a work for me to do. These plates were found at the north point of a hill two miles north of Manchester village. Joseph had a stone which was dug from the well of Mason Chase, twenty-four feet from the surface. In this stone he could see many things to my certain knowledge. It was by means of this stone he first discovered these plates.

"In the first place, he told me of this stone, and proposed to bind it on his eyes, and run a race with me in the woods. A few days after this, I was at the house of his father in Manchester, two miles south of Palmyra village, and was picking my teeth with a pin while sitting on the bars. The pin caught in my teeth, and dropped from my fingers into shavings and straw. I jumped from the bars and looked for it. Joseph and Northrop Sweet, also did the same. We could not find it. I then took Joseph on surprise, and said to him—I said, 'Take your stone.' I had never seen it, and did not know that he had it with him. He had it in his pocket. He took it and placed it in his hat—the old white hat—and placed his face in his hat. I watched him closely to see that he did no look one side; he reached out his hand beyond me on the right, and moved a little stick, and there I saw the pin, which he picked up and gave to me. I know he did not look out of the hat until after he had picked up the pin.

"Joseph had had this stone for some time. There was a company there in that neighborhood, who were digging for money supposed to have been hidden by the ancients. Of this company were old Mr. Stowell—I think his name was Josiah— also old Mr. [Alva] Beman, also Samuel Lawrence, George Proper, Joseph Smith, jr., and his father, and his brother Hiram Smith. They dug for money in Palmyra, Manchester, also in

Pennsylvania, and other places. When Joseph found this stone, there was a company digging in Harmony, Pa., and they took Joseph to look in the stone for them, and he did so for a while, and then he told them the enchantment was so strong that he could not see, and they gave it up. There he became acquainted with his future wife, the daughter of old Mr. Isaac Hale, where he boarded. He afterwards returned to Pennsylvania again, and married his wife, taking her off to old Mr. Stowell's, because her people would not consent to the marriage. She was of age, Joseph was not.

"After this, on the 22d of September, 1827, before day, Joseph took the horse and wagon of old Mr. Stowell, and taking his wife, he went to the place where the plates were concealed, and while he was obtaining them, she kneeled down and prayed. He then took the plates and hid them in an old black oak tree top which was hollow. Mr. Stowell was at this time at old Mr. Smith's, digging for money. It was reported by these money-diggers, that they had found boxes, but before they could secure them, they would sink into the earth. A candid old Presbyterian told me, that on the Susquehannah flats he dug down to an iron chest, that he scraped the dirt off with his shovel, but had nothing with him to open the chest; that he went away to get help, and when they came to it, it moved away two or three rods into the earth, and they could not get it. There were a great many strange sights. One time the old log school-house south of Palmyra, was suddenly lighted up, and frightened them away. Samuel Lawrence told me that while they were digging, a large man who appeared to be eight or nine feet high, came and sat on the ridge of the barn, and motioned to them that they must leave. They motioned back that they would not; but that they afterwards became frightened and did leave. At another time while they were digging, a company of horsemen came and frightened them away. These things were real to them, I believe, because they were told to me in confidence, and told by different ones, and their stories agreed, and they seemed to be in earnest—I knew they were in earnest.

"Joseph did not dig for these plates. They were placed in this way: four stones were set up and covered with a flat stone, oval on the upper side and flat on the bottom. Beneath this was a little platform upon which the plates were laid; and the two stones set in a bow of silver by means of which the plates were translated, were found underneath the plates.

"These plates were seven inches wide by eight inches in length, and were of the thickness of plates of tin; and when piled one above the other, they were altogether about four inches thick; and they were put together on the back by three silver rings, so that they would open like a book.

"The two stones set in a bow of silver were about two inches in diameter, perfectly round, and about five-eighths of an inch thick at the centre; but not so thick at the edges where they came into the bow. They were joined by a round bar of silver, about three-eighths of an inch in diameter, and about four inches long, which, with the two stones, would make eight inches.

"The stones were white, like polished marble, with a few gray streaks. I never dared to look into them by placing them in the hat, because Moses said that 'no man could see God and live,' and we could see anything we wished by looking into them; and I could not keep the desire to see God out of my mind. And beside, we had a command to let no man look into them, except by the command of God, lest he should 'look aught and perish.'

"These plates were usually kept in a cherry box made for that purpose, in the possession of Joseph and myself. The plates were kept from the sight of the world, and no one, save Oliver Cowdery, myself, Joseph Smith, jr., and David Whitmer, ever saw them. Before the Lord showed the plates to me, Joseph wished me to see them. But I refused, unless the Lord should do it. At one time, before the Lord showed them to me, Joseph said I should see them. I asked him, why he would break the commands of the Lord? He said, you have done so much I am afraid you will not believe unless you see them. I replied, 'Joseph, I know all about it. The Lord has showed to me ten times more about it than you know.'" Here we inquired of Mr. Harris—How did the Lord show you these things? He replied, "I am forbidden to say anything how the Lord showed them to me, except that by the power of God I have seen them."[2]

Mr. Harris continues: "I hefted the plates many times, and should think they weighed forty or fifty pounds.

"When Joseph had obtained the plates, he communicated the fact to his father and mother. The plates remained concealed in the tree top until he got the chest made. He then went after them and brought them home. While on his way home with the plates, he was met by what appeared to be a man, who demanded the plates, and struck him with a club on his side, which was all black and blue. Joseph knocked the man down, and then ran for home, and was much out of breath. When he arrived at home, he handed the plates in at the window, and the were received from him by his mother. They were then hidden under the hearth in his father's house. But the wall being partly down, it was feared that certain ones, who were trying to get possession of the plates, would get under the house and dig them out. Joseph then took them out, and hid them under the old cooper's shop, by taking up a board and digging in the ground and burying them. When they were

---

[2]On this point Joel Tiffany, "Mormonism," *Tiffany's Monthly* 5, no. 1 (May 1859): 50-51, explained concerning the use by Martin Harris of this phrase: "His common expression when conversing upon the subject is, 'the Lord showed me this,' and 'the Lord told me that.' Observing that he frequently used such expressions, we inquired of him, How we were to understand the Lord showed to him certain things, and in what manner He spake with him. He informed us that these revelations came by way of impression. That he was 'impressed by the Lord.'"

taken from there, they were put into an old Ontario glass-box. Old Mr. Beman sawed off the ends, making the box the right length to put them in, and when they went in he said he heard them jink, but he was not permitted to see them. He told me so.

"The money-diggers claimed that they had as much right to the plates as Joseph had, as they were in company together. They claimed that Joseph had been traitor, and had appropriated to himself that which belonged to them. For this reason Joseph was afraid of them, and continued concealing the plates. After they had been concealed under the floor of the cooper's shop for a short time, Joseph was warned to remove them. He said he was warned by an angel. He took them out and hid them up in the chamber of the cooper's shop among the flags. That night some one came, took up the floor, and dug up the earth, and would have found the plates had they not been removed.

"These things had all occurred before I talked with Joseph respecting the plates. But I had the account of it from Joseph, his wife, brothers, sisters, his father and mother. I talked with them separately, that I might get the truth of the matter. The first time I heard the of the matter, my brother Preserved Harris, who had been in the village of Palmyra, asked me if had heard about Joseph Smith, jr., having a golden bible. My thoughts were that the money-diggers had probably dug up an old brass kettle, or something of the kind. I thought no more of it. This was about the first of October, 1827. The next day after the talk with my brother, I went to the village, and there I was asked what I thought of the Gold Bible? I replied, The Scripture says, He that answereth a matter before he heareth it, it is foolishness unto him. I do not wish to make myself a fool. I don't know anything about it. Then said I, what is it about Joe's Gold Bible? They then went on to say, that they put whiskey into the old man's cider and got him half drunk, and he told them all about it. They then repeated his account, which I found afterwards to agree substantially with the account given by Joseph. Then said I to them, how do you know that he has not got such gold plates? They replied, 'Damn him! angels appear to men in this enlightened age! Damn him, he ought to be tarred and feathered for telling such a damned lie!' Then I said, suppose he has told a lie, as old Tom Jefferson said, it did matter to him whether a man believed in one god or twenty. It did not rob his pocket, nor break his shins. What is it to us if he has told a lie? He has it to answer for if he has lied. If you should tar and feather all the liars, you would soon be out of funds to purchase the material.

"I then thought of the words of Christ, The kingdom divided against itself cannot stand. I knew they were of the devil's kingdom, and if that is of the devil, his kingdom is divided against itself. I said in my heart, this is something besides smoke. There is some fire at the bottom of it. I then determined to go and see Joseph as soon as I could find time.

"A day or so before I was ready to visit Joseph, his mother came over to our house and wished to talk with me. I told her I had no time to spare, she might talk with my wife, and, in the evening when I had finished my work I would talk with her. When she commenced talking with me, she told me respecting his bringing home the plates, and many other things, and said that Joseph had sent her over and wished me to come and see him. I told her that I had a time appointed when I would go, and that when the time came I should then go, but I did not tell her when it was. I sent my boy to harness my horse and take her home. She wished my wife and daughter to go with her; and they went and spent most of the day. When they came home, I questioned them about them. My daughter said, they were about as much as she could lift. They were now in the glass-box, and my wife said they were very heavy. They both lifted them. I waited a day or two, when I got up in the morning, took my breakfast, and told my folks I was going to the village, but went directly to old Mr. Smith's. I found that

Joseph had gone away to work for Peter Ingersol[l] to get some flour. I was glad he was absent, for that gave me an opportunity of talking with his wife and the family about the plates. I talked with them separately, to see if their stories agreed, and I found they did agree. When Joseph came home I did not wish him to know that I had been talking with them, so I took him by the arm and led him away from the rest, and requested him to tell me the story, which he did as follows. He said: 'An angel had appeared to him, and told him it was God's work.'" Here Mr. Harris seemed to wander from the subject, when we requested him to continue and tell what Joseph then said. He replied, "Joseph had before this described the manner of his finding the plates. He found them by looking in the stone found in the well of Mason Chase. The family had likewise told me the same thing.

"Joseph said the angel told him he must quit the company of the money-diggers. That there were wicked men among them. He must have no more to do with them. He must not lie, nor swear, nor steal. He told him to go and look in the spectacles, and he would show him the man that would assist him. That he did so, and he saw myself, Martin Harris, standing before him. That struck me with surprise. I told him I wished him to be very careful about these things. 'Well,' said he, 'I saw you standing before me as plainly as I do now.' I said, if it is the devil's work I will have nothing to do with it; but if it is the Lord's, you can have all the money necessary to bring it before the world. He said the angel told him, that the plates must be translated, printed and sent before the world. I said, Joseph, you know my doctrine, that cursed is every one that putteth his trust in man, and maketh flesh his arm; and we know that the devil is to have great power in the latter days to deceive if possible the very elect; and I don't know that you are one of the elect. Now you must not blame me for not taking your word. If the Lord will show me that it is his work, you can have all the money you want.

"While at Mr. Smith's I hefted the plates, and I knew from the heft that they were lead or gold, and I knew that Joseph had not credit enough to buy so much lead. I left Mr. Smith's about eleven o'clock and went home. I retired to my bedroom and prayed God to show me concerning these things, and I covenanted that if it was his work and he would show me so, I would put forth my best ability to bring it before the world. He then showed me that it was his work, and that it was designed to bring in the fullness of the gospel to the gentiles to fulfill his word, that the first shall be last and the last first. He showed this to me by the still small voice spoken in the soul. Then I was satisfied that it was the Lord's work, and I was under a covenant to bring it forth.

"The excitement in the village upon the subject had become such that some had threatened to mob Joseph, and also to tar and feather him. They said he should never leave until he had shown the plates. It was unsafe for him to remain, so I determined that he must go to his father-in-law's in Pennsylvania. He wrote to his brother-in-law Alvah Hale, requesting him to come for him. I advised Joseph that he must pay all his debts before starting. I paid them for him, and furnished him money for his journey. I advised him to take time enough to get ready, so that he might start a day or two in advance: for he would be mobbed if it was known when he started. We put the box of plates into a barrel about one-third full of beans and headed it up. I informed Mr. Hale of the matter, and advised them to cut each a good cudgel and put into the wagon with them, which they did. It was understood that they were to start on Monday; but they started on Saturday night and got through safe. This was the last of October, 1827. It might have been the first of November."

Problems in Early Mormon Texts[1]

We discussed in the first chapter the evolution of the story of Joseph Smith's First Vision. In this appendix we will examine other texts in early LDS history that have been quietly altered. Consider the development of the concept of priesthood authority. In 1838 Joseph dictated the official narrative of the restoration of the Holy Priesthood, which had been lost to the earth since shortly after the advent of the Savior. The restoration was a double event: the first half being an ordination of Joseph Smith and Oliver Cowdery by the resurrected John the Baptist with the bestowal of the Aaronic, or lesser, Priesthood on 15 May 1829,[2] and the second being the conferring of the Melchizedek Priesthood with the gift of the Holy Ghost by Peter, James, and John sometime later. Historical research in early Mormon documents shows that the term "priesthood" was not used until 1831.[3]

The "full history of the rise of the church of the Latter

---

[1] An earlier version of this appendix was separately published as LaMar Petersen, *Problems in Mormon Text* (Salt Lake City, 1957).

[2] D. Michael Quinn, "150 Years of Truth and Consequences about Mormon History," *Sunstone* 16 (February 1992): 13, states that "in November 1910, Church President Joseph F. Smith told the Salt Lake Temple fast meeting that Elder Roberts doubted that Joseph Smith had actually received a priesthood restoration from John the Baptist."

[3] Prince, *Power from on High*, 11-12.

Day Saints,"[4] which was written by Oliver Cowdery in 1834, should surely contain the details of these miraculous events, but though there is indeed an ecstatic account of the ordination by an angel, other particulars are notably lacking. The angel is unidentified (if Joseph and Oliver then knew him to be John the Baptist they did not reveal it),[5] there is no mention of two Priesthoods, Aaronic or Melchizedek, lesser or higher, no promise of the Holy Ghost, no visit of Peter, James, and John (which in 1834 should have been a matter of historical record for five years),[6] no mention of the baptism and ordination of each other, and finally, a different wording of the angelic conferment. Oliver Cowdery's 1834 account was "the first time Mormons learned that a heavenly conferral of authority occurred before the church's organization."[7]

According to Oliver Cowdery's account in 1834, the angel said: "Upon you my fellow servants, in the name of Messiah I confer this priesthood and this authority, which shall remain upon earth, that the sons of Levi may yet offer an offering unto the Lord in righteousness!" (JS-H 1:71*n*). In Joseph Smith's dictation in 1838, the angel said: "Upon you my fellow servants, in the name of Messiah, I confer the Priesthood of Aaron, which holds the keys of the ministering of angels, and of the gospel of repentance, and of baptism by immersion for the remission of sins, and this shall never be

---

[4]*Latter Day Saints' Messenger and Advocate* 1 (October 1834): 13.

[5]Cook, *David Whitmer Interviews*, 155, quoted David Whitmer's statement in 1885: "I never heard that an Angel had ordained Joseph and Oliver to the Aaronic priesthood until the year 1834 5. or 6—in Ohio. . . . I do not believe that John the Baptist ever ordained Joseph and Oliver as stated and believed by some, . . ."

[6]The period of five years assumes the traditional date of May or June 1829 date for the visitation of Peter, James, and John. However, Bushman, *Joseph Smith*, 163, 240-41*n*55 suggests the summer of 1830, after the organization of the church.

[7]D. Michael Quinn, *The Mormon Hierarchy: Origins of Power* (Salt Lake City: Signature Books, 1994), 15.

taken again from the earth, until the sons of Levi do offer again an offering unto the Lord in righteousness" (D&C 13). It will be noted that in the first there is no mention of Aaron, the keys, or baptism by immersion, and an entirely different meaning is conveyed in "*that* the sons of Levi may yet offer and offering" than in "*until* the sons of Levi do offer again an offering."[8]

It has been officially declared that the angel, in conferring the priesthood, set a perfect pattern for the elders of the church to follow, yet several problems here present themselves:

(1) John, who baptized Christ, and whose name bespeaks his mission, did not baptize either Joseph or Oliver. Although this fact is made quite clear in the 1842 account, Joseph added somewhat ambiguously: ". . . we were baptized and ordained under the hand of the messenger."[9] This was slightly altered in modern editions to read: ". . . we were ordained under the hand of this messenger, and baptized" (JS-H 1:72).

(2) John conferred the priesthood on unbaptized men and, according to a third account, ordained them to the office of Priest which ordination they repeated upon each other. At no time since has it been the custom to ordain before baptizing, or to repeat the ordination.

(3) Joseph, unbaptized, baptized Oliver. This is a pattern not since observed.

(4) John, filled with the Holy Ghost from his mother's womb (D&C 84:27), could not impart the gift of the Holy Ghost to the two initiates; nevertheless, they too were filled with the Holy Ghost. A distinction is made between merely

---

[8]The 1834 wording agrees more nearly with the Malachi quote in 3 Ne. 24:3 than does the 1838 wording. D&C 13 first appeared as LDS scripture in the 1876 edition of the Doctrine and Covenants. See Lyndon W. Cook, *The Revelations of the Prophet Joseph Smith: A Historical and Biographical Commentary of the Doctrine and Covenants* (Salt Lake City: Deseret Book, 1985), 22-23.

[9]"History of Joseph Smith," *Times and Seasons* 3 (1 August 1842): 666.

having the Holy Ghost and having the gift of the Holy Ghost.

(5) It has often been asserted by church officials that at the time of John the Baptist's visit to restore the priesthood there was no one living on the earth with priesthood authority, yet in Mormon scripture the Lord promised John the Apostle who had asked to have power over death, "thou shalt tarry until I come in my glory" (D&C 7:3). He had likewise promised the three Nephite disciples "ye shall never taste of death; but ye shall live to behold all the doings of the Father unto the children of men, even until all things shall be fulfilled according to the will of the Father, when I shall come in my glory with the powers of heaven" (3 Ne. 28:7). The whereabouts of these four ordained mortals in 1829 has never been explained.

Three months before Joseph was murdered at Carthage, he gave other particulars of his first ordination:

> I went into the woods to inquire of the Lord, by prayer, His will concerning me, and I saw an angel, and he laid his hands upon my head, and ordained me to [be] a Priest after the order of Aaron, and to hold the keys of the Priesthood, which office was to preach repentance and baptism for the remission of sins, and also to baptize. But I was informed that this office did not extend to the laying on of hands for the giving of the Holy Ghost.[10]

Two points here are of interest: (1) Oliver seems to be excluded from the experience, and (2) the angel bypassed the offices of Deacon and Teacher in ordaining Joseph a Priest. There is evidently some confusion here in semantics. Despite the two references to "office," historian Joseph Fielding Smith affirms, "Joseph Smith and Oliver Cowdery, as the record shows, were not ordained to any office, but the Priesthood was

---

[10]*History of the Church*, 6:249-50.

conferred upon them."[11]

The important details that are missing from the "full history" of 1834 are likewise missing from the Book of Commandments in 1833. The student would expect to find all the particulars of the restoration in this first treasured set of revelations, the chronological order of which encompassed the bestowals of the two Priesthoods, but they are conspicuously absent. There is only one reference to an angelic visitation: "But after truly repenting, God ministered unto him by an holy angel... that he should translate a book" (Book of Commandments 24:7). The notable revelations on priesthood in the Doctrine and Covenants before referred to—Sections 2 and 13—are missing, and Chapter 28 gives no hint of the restoration which, if actual, had been known for four years. More than four hundred words were added to this revelation of September 1830 in Section 27 of the Doctrine and Covenants, the additions made to include the names of heavenly visitors and two separate ordinations. The Book of Commandments gives the duties of Elders, Priests, Teachers, and Deacons and refers to Joseph's apostolic calling, but there is no mention of Melchizedek Priesthood, High Priesthood, High Priests, nor High Councilors. These words were later inserted into the revelation on church organization and government given in 1830, making it appear that they were known at that date, but they do not appear in the original, Chapter 24 of the 1833 Book of Commandments. Similar interpolations were made in the revelations now known as Sections 42 and 68.

There seems to be no support for the historicity of the restoration of the priesthood in journals, diaries, letters, nor printed matter prior to October 1834. David Whitmer declared that the offices of Elder, Priest, and Teacher—parts of a single

---

[11]Joseph Fielding Smith, *Church History and Modern Revelation* (Salt Lake City: The Council of the Twelve Apostles of the Church of Jesus Christ of Latter-day Saints, 1953), 1:61.

priesthood—were in evidence long before the formal organization of the church on 6 April 1830. This conflicts with Joseph's statement that he and Oliver ordained each other Elders on that historic day and that these ordinations were the first to be made to a definite office since the conferment by the angel. Whitmer contends that the only ordination Joseph received was that of Prophet, Seer, and Revelator and that the idea of dual priesthoods conferred by heavenly beings was not known in the early years of the church.[12] This helps to explain the mystery in Joseph's annotation of the fourth conference of the church at Kirtland, 3 June 1831: "The authority of the Melchizedek Priesthood was manifested and conferred for the first time upon several of the Elders."[13] Joseph's comment is in conflict with the later statement: "The office of an elder comes under the priesthood of Melchizedek" (D&C 107:7). It has been suggested that this refers to the ordination of the first High Priests and does not mean what it says, but another instance of the bestowal of Melchizedek Priesthood upon Elders is found in William Smith's account of the conference which followed at Orange, Ohio, 25 October 1831 "where Elders, Priests, Teachers, and Deacons received some general instructions from the leaders of the church concerning the priesthood of Melchisedec, to which they had not as yet been ordained."[14] As these statements were written in retrospect they may not conclusively establish that the term "Melchizedek Priesthood" was in use at the specified dates. However, the apostate Ezra Booth referred to the order of Melchizedek in 1831.

Some have believed that the revelation to Cowdery and Whitmer in June 1829 when they were called "with that same calling with which he [Paul] was called" (D&C 18:9) is

---

[12]See Whitmer, *Address to All Believers*, 32-35, 64.

[13]*History of the Church*, 1:175-76.

[14]W. Smith, *William Smith on Mormonism*, 19-20.

evidence that they held the Melchizedek Priesthood at that time. If so, Whitmer's reply to a question from Joseph F. Smith and Orson Pratt in 1878 gives no clue. He was asked: "Can you tell the date of the restoration of the Apostleship by Peter, James, and John?" He replied: "I do not know, Joseph never told me. I can only tell you what I know: I will not testify to anything I do not know."[15]

A rude paragraph awaits the faithful who read the history of the church as viewed by Joseph Smith III, son of the Prophet. Referring to the visit of the three angels he wrote: "There is no historical evidence of such an event. Nor is there any evidence that Peter, James, and John were present, either when the instruction was given to ordain or when the ordination actually took place.... It is not safe then to write historically that Joseph Smith and Oliver Cowdery were ever ordained literally under the hands of Peter, James, and John."[16] In a footnote to the story of the restoration of the High Priesthood B. H. Roberts wrote similarly: "There is no definite account of the event in the history of the Prophet Joseph, or, for matter of that, in any of our annals. . . ."[17] This lack of historical proof will not alter belief in the divine commission. These matters are to be accepted by faith, not proven by chapter and verse. In Mormon belief authority to act in God's name comes not from an inner conviction of one's sonship with God but by the backward tracing of authority from one priest to another through the imposition of hands. It is a transfer of privilege, not an inalienable right.

A study of changes made in the revelations indicates that many things came by evolution rather than endowment. In the

---

[15]Cook, *David Whitmer Interviews*, 25.

[16]Joseph Smith III and Heman C. Smith, *History of the Church of Jesus Christ of Latter Day Saints* (Lamoni, IA: Board of Publication of the Reorganized Church of Jesus Christ of Latter Day Saints, 1897), 1:64-65.

[17]*History of the Church*, 1:40. Paragraphs believed to substantiate the priesthood restoration in D&C 18:9; 20:2,3; 27:12; 128:20 are cited.

1833 Book of Commandments the Lord said: "[Joseph] has a gift to translate the book, and I have commanded him that he shall pretend to no other gift, for I will grant him no other gift" (Book of Commandments 4:2). But a more expansive program is outlined for Joseph in the same revelation as it appeared two years later: "And you have a gift to translate the plates; and this is the first gift that I bestowed upon you; and I have commanded that you should pretend to no other gift until my purpose is fulfilled in this; for I will grant unto you no other gift until it is finished" (D&C 5:4). [18] Even as Cowdery's "full history" omitted the story of the baptism so does the revelation of March 1829 in the Book of Commandments fail to indicate the importance of the rites of ordination soon to be initiated: "Whosoever believeth in my word, them will I visit with the manifestation of my Spirit, and they shall be born of me. . . ." (Book of Commandments 4:4). These words were affixed in the 1835 Doctrine and Covenants: ". . . even of water and of the Spirit. And you must wait yet a little while, for ye are not yet ordained" (D&C 5:16-17).

Many improvements were made in the Lord's word. "The gift of working with the rod" (Book of Commandments 7:3) became "the gift of Aaron" (D&C 8:6). "Power to translate" (Book of Commandments 9:1) became "power given unto you to translate by the means of the Urim and Thummim" (D&C 10:1). "The Lord your God suffered death in the flesh" (Book of Commandments 15:13) became "the Lord your Redeemer suffered death in the flesh" (D&C 18:11). "Administer the flesh and blood of Christ" (Book of Commandments 24:32) became "administer bread and wine—the emblems of the flesh and blood of Christ" (D&C 20:40). "Neither the teachers nor deacons have authority to baptize nor administer the sacra-

---

[18]Karl F. Best, "Changes in the Revelations, 1833-1835," *Dialogue: A Journal of Mormon Thought* 25 (Spring 1992): 98, frankly stated that this change can either be considered "a clarification or a fraud."

ment" (Book of Commandments 24:41) became "neither teachers nor deacons have authority to baptize, administer the sacrament, or lay on hands" (D&C 20:58). The words of encouragement to Emma, "And thou needest not fear, for thy husband shall support thee *from* the church" (Book of Commandments 26:8) became "And thou needest not fear, for thy husband shall support thee *in* the church" (D&C 25:9). "Behold, thou shalt consecrate *all* thy properties, that which thou hast unto me" (Book of Commandments 44:26) became "behold, thou wilt remember the poor, and consecrate of thy properties for their support" (D&C 42:30). "I will consecrate the riches of the Gentiles unto my people" (Book of Commandments 44:32) became "I will consecrate of the riches of those who embrace my gospel among the Gentiles unto the poor of my people" (D&C 42:39). "The calling of twelve disciples in these last days" (Book of Commandments 15 superscription) became "the calling of Twelve Apostles in these last days" (D&C 18 superscription).

In the transfer of the revelations from the Book of Commandments to the Doctrine and Covenants the alterations were matched by as many deletions, one of the least explicable being the removal of Christ's prophetic words of March 1829: "I will establish my church, like unto the church which was taught by my disciples in the days of old" (Book of Commandments 4:5; cf. D&C 5).

The Book of Commandments was given the divine seal of approval in the first chapter:

> Search these commandments, for they are true and faithful, and the prophesies and promises which are in them shall all be fulfilled. What I the Lord have spoken, I have spoken, and I excuse not myself, and though the heavens and the earth pass away, my word shall not pass away, but shall all be fulfilled, whether by mine own voice, or by the voice of my servants, it is the same: For behold, and lo, the Lord is God, and the Spirit beareth record, and the record is true, and the truth abideth forever and ever: Amen (Book of Commandments 1:7).

That the book was vouchsafed as the word of God is implicit in the statement of the First Presidency of the church, viz., Joseph Smith, Sidney Rigdon, and Frederick G. Williams, on 25 June 1833 as they noted four typographical errors:

> We have found the following errors in the Commandments, as printed: fortieth chapter, tenth verse, third line, instead of "corruptable," put *corrupted*. Fourteenth verse of the same chapter, fifth line, instead of "respecter to persons," put *respecter of persons*. Twenty-first verse, second line of the same chapter, instead of "respecter to" put *respecter of*. Forty-fourth chapter, twelfth verse, last line, instead of "hands," put *heads*.[19]

For connoisseurs of Mormonism the chore of locating extant copies of this rare little volume offers one of the more intriguing facets of Latter-day Saint history. Its worth as a collector's item, many thousands of dollars per copy, is enhanced by the controversy surrounding its genesis.

Shortly before he died at age eighty-three, David Whitmer wrote sadly:

> Early in the spring of 1833, at Independence, Mo., the revelations were printed in the Book of Commandments. Many of the books were finished and distributed among the members of the church, and through some of the unwise brethren, the world got hold of some of them. From that time the ill-felling toward us began to increase; and in the summer of 1833 the mob came upon us, tore down the printing press, and drove the church out of Jackson county. . . . And when the Book of Commandments was printed, Joseph and the church received it as being printed correctly. This I know. In the winter of 1834 they saw that some of the revelations in the Book of Commandments *had to be changed*, because the heads of the church had gone too far, and had done things in which they had already gone ahead of some of the former revelations. So the book of

---

[19]*History of the Church*, 1:364, with italics added to show the corrections.

"Doctrine and Covenants" was printed in 1835, and some of the revelations changed and added to. By the providence of God I have one of the old Book of Commandments published in 1833. I will prove by a revelation in it, which is changed in the Doctrine and Covenants, a revelation that was given through the "stone" and is true—I will prove that God called Brother Joseph to translate the Book of Mormon only, and that he was not called to organize and establish the church any more than the rest of us Elders. That God commanded him that he should pretend to no other gift but to translate the Book of Mormon, that God would grant him no other gift.[20]

It is debatable whether the hundreds of changes which have been made in official church literature such as the Book of Mormon, *The Evening and the Morning Star*, the Book of Commandments, the Doctrine and Covenants, and the "History of Joseph Smith" help to clarify or confuse the study of Mormon history and dogma.

For example, the prime purpose of the Book of Mormon, according to its title page, is "to the convincing of the Jew and Gentile that Jesus is the Christ, the Eternal God," yet additions to the original text of First Nephi declared Christ to be "the *son* of" the Eternal God (1 Ne. 11:18, 21, 32; 13:40). The obvious error on page 236 that Jesus is "the Son of the only begotten of the Father" was corrected to "the Son, the Only Begotten of the Father"(Alma 5:48), yet Christ's strange references to "mine Only Begotten Son" (D&C 29:42,46) are permitted to remain. Two independent alterations of the text from the name Benjamin to Mosiah (Mosiah 21:28; Ether 4:1) were made to eliminate an internal anachronism. The omission of phrases such as "and the land which was between the land of Zarahemla"(3 Ne. 3:23) and "according to the crime which he hath committed"(Mosiah 29:15) were probably accidental and have now been rectified. The term "directors" was changed to

---

[20]Whitmer, *Address to All Believers*, 55-57, with emphasis in original.

"interpreters"(Alma 37:21,24) in an effort to clarify the reference to the translating stones. Other alterations from the first edition such as part of the Isaiah text in 2 Ne. 12:9 or the wording of the Lord's prayer in 3 Ne. 13:9-13 do little to enlighten, the original being more in accord with the Bible than the altered text.

Hundreds of grammatical errors, tautological expressions, and provincialisms have been eliminated. It is difficult to understand why such phrases as "state of awful woundedness" (1 Ne. 13:32), "diseases which was subsequent to man" (Alma 46:40), and "the numerority of their forces having slain a vast number" (Alma 56:10) were re-written but other phrases such as "I am consigned that these are my days" (Hel. 7:9), "he being stabbed by his brother by a garb of secrecy" (Hel. 9:6), and "they knew not whither they should steer the ship, insomuch that there arose a great storm" (1 Ne. 18:13) were left untouched. Improvements were made in "he that eatheth this bread, eatheth of my body to their soul" (3 Ne. 20:8), "they did not fight against God no more" (Alma 23:7), "the Devil is the preparator of it" (1 Ne. 15:35), and "that all might see the writing which he had wrote upon the rent" (Alma 46:19), but not in "they should observe to do all these things for to keep these commandments" (Mosiah 13:25), "retaining a remission of their sins" (Alma 4:14), "until we repair unto them the many murders" (Alma 27:8), "to bring about the bowels of mercy" (Alma 34:15), nor in "there can be no labor performed" (Alma 34:33). Repetitions and ambiguities were deleted from 1 Ne. 8:7; Alma 17:3; 29:4; 3 Ne. 10:4; and Morm. 9:34, but not from 1 Ne. 4:9; 1 Ne. 17:5,6; 2 Ne. 3:4-21; Jacob 5:65; Alma 5:6; 3 Ne. 10:4-6; nor Ether 2:17.

The rephrasing of the text of the revelations as originally printed in *The Evening and the Morning Star* and the Book of Commandments, plus the inclusion of material foreign to the original meaning, make it difficult for all but the persistent to understand the chronology of events. Except for the withdrawal of the controversial Lectures on Faith in 1921, the Doctrine and Covenants has undergone little revision since 1876, although a comparison of that edition with earlier ones reveals unique changes in the concepts of marriage and an increased need for priestly authority. One interesting addition, made sometime after the Manifesto of 1890, is the superscription of Section 132 in which plurality of wives is made an appendage to the new and everlasting covenant of marriage, rather than the covenant itself.

The reasons for certain changes in the "History of Joseph Smith" are understandable. Joseph was sometimes more forthright than his redactors would permit. It was more sophisticated for Martin Harris to "urge" or "importune" Joseph to seek information from the Lord than to "tease."[21] It was more accurate to prophesy: "Orson Hyde... *may* stand on earth and bring souls till Christ comes" than to insist: "Orson Hyde . . . *shall* stand on earth and bring souls till Christ comes."[22] It was kinder to read that "prophesyings" were pronounced upon the enemies of Christ at the Kirtland Temple than "cursings."[23] It would not do for a Prophet to cheer some tired brethren with "a couple of dollars with directions to replenish the bottle [of whisky] to stimulate them in the fatigues of their sleepless journey"; the offending clause had to be removed.[24] Joseph's assertion that "Water, Fire, Truth, and God are all the same" emerged "water, fire, truth, and God are all realities."[25] The elimination of the last clause of Joseph's dire prophecy concerning the fate of the government rendered it less fearsome: "While discussing the petition to Congress, I prophesied, by virtue of the holy Priesthood vested in me, and

---

[21]*History of the Church*, 1:21.
[22]*History of the Church*, 2:189, with italics added to show word change.
[23]*History of the Church*, 2:431.
[24]*History of the Church*, 5:450.
[25]*History of the Church*, 3:297.

in the name of the Lord Jesus Christ, that, if Congress will not hear out our petition and grant us protection, they shall be broken up as a government *and God shall damn them, and there shall be nothing left of them—not even a grease spot!*"[26]

Many of Joseph's entries that were eligible for emendation were left intact: imprecations, boasts, extravagant prophecies, personal piques, astrological and phrenological interpretations, and trivia. Despite these cankers Joseph emerges as a man of abundant energy and imagination, a man interested in people, in giving final answers to all perplexing theological questions, and in building the perfect society. Whether one accepts his visions as objective realities, subjective illusions, or only as fabrications, one cannot deny him his place as a vigorous and unique American: founder of a church, editor of a paper, reviser of the Bible, temple builder, banker, collector of Egyptian documents, proponent of adult education and westward expansion, city planner and councilman, merchant, land agent, mayor, lieutenant-general of the Nauvoo Legion, polygamist, Mason, and candidate for president of the United States. In Mormon belief these roles were all eclipsed by one far greater: vicegerent of God and intercessor with Christ and holy angels. The injunction reads: "For his word ye shall receive, as if from mine own mouth, in all patience and faith" (D&C 21:5) and so Joseph's pronouncements could never be companion to the adage: "Truth is forever on the scaffold; wrong forever on the throne." His definitions of God and eschatology (i.e., the doctrines of death, judgment, heaven, and hell) were absolute and there could be no retraction or modification. His task of re-instituting Zion was formidable. This was to be the third and final attempt at establishing Christ's church upon the earth. If it were to stand forever and break all other kingdoms in pieces according to Daniel's prophecy, the historical record must be free of contradictions and obscuri-

---

[26]*History of the Church*, 6:116 with italics added to show deleted words.

ties—free of all but the lucid, the forthright, and the explicit. A scribe at his elbow and the church press at his side, these aids would help insure accuracy in the preservation of God's word.

One of the distinguishing features of Mormonism is its concept of an anthropomorphic God, a sentient being of body, parts, and passions. Having conversed with God in 1820, Joseph should have known him to be a physical entity distinct from the other two members of the Trinity, but the Book of Mormon ten years later described the triune God of the Christian world: the three-in-one personage sometimes known as the great Incomprehensible. Mormon wrote, "unto the Father, and unto the Son, and unto the Holy Ghost, which is one God" (Morm. 7:7).[27] Abinadi said:

> I would that ye should understand that God himself shall come down among the children of men, and shall redeem his people. And because he dwelleth in flesh he shall be called the Son of God, and having subjected the flesh to the will of the Father, being the Father and the Son—The Father, because he was conceived by the power of God; and the Son, because of the flesh; thus becoming the Father and Son—And they are one God, yea, the very Eternal Father of heaven and of earth (Mosiah 15:1-4).

Zeezrom said:

> Thou sayest there is a true and living God? And Amulek said: Yea, there is a true and living God. Now Zeezrom said: Is there more than one God? and he answered, No.... Now Zeezrom saith again unto him: Is the Son of God the very Eternal Father? And Amulek said unto him: Yea, he is the very Eternal Father of heaven and of earth, and all things which in them are; he is the beginning and the end, the first and the last (Alma 11:26-29, 38, 39).

---

[27]In promotion of either better grammar or plurality this was changed in the second edition to read, "which *are* one God."

To the brother of Jared Christ said: "I am the Father and the Son . . . and man have I created after the body of my spirit" (Ether 3:14,16). In contrast to the oneness in these expressions there are several instances in the Book of Mormon where Jesus prays to his Father. The unity, yet separateness, expressed in "that I may be in them as thou, Father, art in me, that we may be one," used by Mormon theologians as proof of the individuality of the Father and Son, is perplexing in relation to the verse which follows: "And when Jesus had spoken these words he came again unto his disciples; and behold they did pray steadfastly, without ceasing, unto him: and he did smile upon them again" (3 Ne. 19:30). The injunction to pray only to God in the name of Christ is disobeyed frequently throughout the Book of Mormon as Christ permits the Nephites to pray directly to him.

The three witnesses to the reality of the Golden Plates —Cowdery, Whitmer, and Harris—subjoined their testimony with, "And the honor be to the Father, and to the Son, and to the Holy Ghost, which is one God." This is interpreted today to mean "one in purpose" and not one in person, but this explanation is not harmonious with Cowdery's reference to the Trinity or Godhead as an "exalted personage" in the *Messenger and Advocate*.[28] The first definitions of the Father and Son as separate personages appeared in Kirtland in the "Lectures on Faith," a set of seven theological essays comprising the first seventy-five pages of the Doctrine and Covenants. God was identified as a personage of spirit and Christ as a personage of tabernacle, the two possessing the same mind. This common mind was the Holy Spirit, not yet an individual personage. Question No. 3 of the catechism asked: "How many personages are there in the Godhead?" and the answer was "Two."

The incorporeal God of Kirtland became corporeal at

---

[28]Oliver Cowdery, Letter to William Frye, *Messenger and Advocate* 2 (December 1835): 236.

Nauvoo: "The Father has a body of flesh and bones as tangible as man's" (blood not included) and the Holy Ghost was advanced to the status of a personage (D&C 130:22).

Controversies inevitably ensued as to the character and identity of God. A half century later Wilford Woodruff, fourth president of the LDS Church, was to plead:

> Cease troubling yourselves about who God is; who Adam is, who Christ is, who Jehovah is. For heaven's sake, let these things alone. . . . God is God. Christ is Christ. The Holy Ghost is the Holy Ghost. That should be enough for you and me to know. If we want to know any more, wait till we get where God is in person. I say this because we are troubled every little while with inquiries from Elders anxious to know who God is, who Christ is, and who Adam is. I say to the Elders of Israel, stop this."[29]

The numerous assertions throughout Mormon scripture that Christ is the Father, the creator of our spirits (2 Ne. 11:7; Mosiah 5:15; Alma 22:10; Ether 3:15,16; D&C 29:34) led to an exposition by Apostle James E. Talmage, which was no doubt intended to be the definitive answer to the question of God's identity:

> We claim scriptural authority for the assertion that Jesus Christ was and is God the Creator, the God who revealed Himself to Adam, Enoch, and all the antediluvial patriarchs and prophets down to Noah; the God of Abraham, Isaac, and Jacob; the God of Israel as a united people, and the God of Ephraim and Judah after the disruption of the Hebrew nation; the God who made Himself known to the prophets from Moses to Malachi; the God of the Old Testament record; and the God of the Nephites. We affirm that Jesus Christ was and is Jehovah, the Eternal One.[30]

----

[29]*Latter-day Saints' Millennial Star* 57 (6 June 1895): 355-56.

[30]James E. Talmage, *Jesus the Christ: A Study of the Messiah and His Mission according to Holy Scriptures both Ancient and Modern* (Salt Lake City: The Deseret News, 1915), 32.

Despite the tone of finality, and possibly in response to continued speculation, the First Presidency of the church, together with the Quorum of the Twelve Apostles, issued a doctrinal essay on 30 June 1916 in which they stressed that "Jesus Christ is not the Father of the spirits who have taken or yet shall take bodies upon this earth, for He is one of them."[31] The dissertation might well have been extended to include a discussion of such antithetical passages as these:

> Never have I showed myself unto man whom I have created [The Lord showing himself to the brother of Jared] (Ether 3:15).
>
> And the Lord appeared unto them [Adam, Seth, Methuselah, et al.] (D&C 107:54).
>
> And I [Enoch] saw the Lord and he stood before my face (Moses 7:4).
>
> Thus I, Abraham, talked with the Lord, face to face, as one man talketh with another; and he told me of the works which his hands had made (Abr. 3:11).
>
> No man hath seen God at any time (John 1:18).
>
> And without the ordinances thereof, and the authority of the priesthood, the power of godliness is not manifest unto men in the flesh; For without this no man can see the face of God, even the Father, and live (D&C 84:21,22).
>
> It was on the morning of a beautiful, clear day, early in the spring of 1820. . . . I saw two Personages, whose brightness and glory defy all description, standing above me in the air. One of them spake unto me, calling me by name, and said, pointing to the other—*This is My Beloved Son. Hear Him!* [Joseph, without the ordinances or the priesthood in 1820, lived to tell that he had seen God] (JS-H 1:14,17).

---

[31]"The Father and the Son," *Improvement Era* 19 (August 1916): 942.

Other deific problems in Mormonism such as God's continual growth vs. his immutability, his oneness vs. his plurality, his geographical confinement near Kolob vs. his omnipresence, have enlivened many discussions in Mormon circles. Orson Pratt, who often discoursed on God's physical characteristics, once gave a definition which offered surprisingly little comfort to materialists:

> When we speak of only one God, and state that He is eternal, without beginning or end, and that He is in all worlds at the same instant, let it be distinctly remembered, that we have no reference to any particular person or substance, but to *truth* dwelling in a vast variety of substances. Wherever you find a fulness of wisdom, knowledge, truth, goodness, love, and such like qualities, there you find God in all His glory, power, and majesty, therefore, if you worship these adorable perfections, you worship God.[32]

After reflecting at some length on the character of God one Mormon educator, something of an iconoclast, wrote: "It follows, therefore, from the very nature of things, that the honest man's conception of God is a progressively growing ideal. . . . Let no council of ecclesiastics presume to lay an embargo on his soul, by pronouncing once for all what God is or is not."[33]

The Book of Mormon, cornerstone of the faith, "the most correct book on earth," reveals God in varying attitudes toward his children. He encircles them about "eternally in the arms of his love"(2 Ne. 1:15). He commands the murder of the prostrate Laban(1 Ne. 4:18). He sends the Spirit of the Lord to Nephi to interpret his father's dream, part of which concerns the fountain of living water, a representation of the love

---

[32]Orson Pratt, "The Pre-existence of Man," *The Seer* 1 (February 1853): 24.

[33]Nels L. Nelson, *Scientific Aspects of Mormonism; or, Religion in Terms of Life* (New York: G. P. Putnam's Sons, 1904), 20.

of God which is a representation of awful hell prepared for the wicked(1 Ne. 8:13-32; 11:25; 12:16; 15:26-29). He forbids Adam and Eve to eat the fruit, but hopes they will: the entire plan of peopling the earth and redeeming man from the fall will be "frustrated" unless they disobey(2 Ne. 2:22, 23; Alma 12:26). He curses the hard of heart and their posterity with dark skins and blesses with whiteness those who unite with the righteous (2 Ne. 5:20-25; 3 Ne. 2:14-16). He directs the building of barges with holes in the top and holes in the bottom, guiding the barges, filled with people, animals, and supplies for 344 days as the waves toss them towards the promised land (Ether 2:16-25; 6:2-12). He takes vengeance upon the wicked by burning, drowning, and smothering the inhabitants of sixteen cities, calling to the survivors: "O ye that are spared because ye were more righteous than they, will ye not now return unto me, and repent of your sins, and be converted, that I may heal you?" (3 Ne. 9:1-13). He says much about whoredoms, fornications, adulteries, abominations, se-cret combinations, secret oaths, concubines, and plural wives—all of which he is against.

God speaks frequently of love, his bowels of mercy, and the resurrection, but not of the home, the family, children, laughter, music, nor kindness to animals. He speaks of repentance and baptism, but not of baptism for the dead, salvation by proxy, marriage for time and eternity, sealing ordinances to insure the celestial continuation of families, nor the Three Degrees of Glory. He watches in sorrow as the Jaredites, lacking the priesthood, flourish in an area adjacent to a narrow neck of land (defined as Central America by Joseph Smith and Mormon geographers), and annihilate themselves several centuries before Christ at the hill Ramah (located in what is now New York State). He bestows the priesthood upon a second group, the Nephites, and again watches in sorrow as history repeats itself: they flourish in Central America and annihilate themselves (nearly) at the same hill in

New York (now known as Cumorah) a thousand years later.

God tolerates his foe, the Devil, who at times is an unwitting ally, as in the tempting of Eve: the Devil enacted the role requisite to the plan of life and salvation, thus preventing the scuttling of the divine program. Rejected from heaven because of his plan of redemption by coercion, Satan is the only one of the great interstellar authorities, save the Holy Ghost, who is bodiless. He has his own priesthood, and duties that often overlap those of God, the term "Destroyer" being applicable to either. In the early days of the church the ubiquitous man of sin was seen at conference, in the missions, and at the temple. He visited church leaders, once pulling Sidney Rigdon from his bed by the heels three times in one night.[34] President John Taylor wrote: "But again, who is Satan? He is a being of God's own make, under his control, subject to his will, cast out of Heaven for rebellion";[35] and at another time asked the moot question: "Why is it, in fact, that we should have a devil? Why did not the Lord kill him long ago? Because he could not do without him."[36] Jedediah M. Grant, counselor to Brigham Young, asserted: "The Lord our God absolutely gave Lucifer a mission to this earth,"[37] and President Young announced: "You cannot get your endowment without the devil's being present."[38] The Devil seems less active in the church today and it may be that Nephi's prophecy 2,500 years ago is being fulfilled: "The time speedily cometh that Satan shall have no more power over the hearts of the children of men" (1 Ne. 22:15). But even with waning power his existence

---

[34]Rigdon's interesting encounter with the Devil was recorded in L. M. Smith, *Biographical Sketches*, 196, but has been deleted from modern editions of the book.

[35]John Taylor, *The Government of God* (Liverpool, England: S. W. Richards, 1852), 81.

[36]*Journal of Discourses* 23 (1883):336.

[37]*Journal of Discourses* 2 (1855): 11.

[38]*Journal of Discourses* 3 (1856): 50

must be acknowledged, the *Deseret News* concluding:

> The point is, he is real. Lucifer is as much a person as Christ himself. . . . We in this Church must believe as definitely that there is a Devil as that we believe there is a God.[39]

The controversial aspects of early Mormonism are many —and so are its achievements. The desert has blossomed, an empire of homes has arisen, a culture has been implanted. Benevolent, wealthy, and influential, the LDS Church is expanding constantly in membership and material assets. It has produced its quota of leaders in the arts and sciences, in education and in government. The notable work of the auxiliary organizations, the Primary, the Mutual Improvement Association, and the Relief Society, has won wide acclaim. As an ethical society it provides opportunity for social work, participation in music, sports, public speaking, dancing, and dramatics. Its study classes include civics, homemaking, and English literature. As in other faiths the church is the instrument for many to express the best in their lives. The church maintains a missionary force of thousands of workers and disseminates the gospel message in many varieties of the printed page. The investigator will find thousands of items open for his inspection at the LDS Church Archives in the Historical Department, 50 East North Temple, Salt Lake City, Utah. Perhaps one day *all* documents, including those now restricted, will be available to him, if not the original, then by means of microfilm or photocopy. That the broadest possible understanding be promoted, and history served, the contents of all church records should be open for evaluation.

A wellspring of Mormon belief is that the earth will one day be renewed and receive its paradisiacal glory: the glory of peace under Christ, and the glory of universal brotherly love.

---

[39]Editorial, *Deseret News*, Church News, 15 January 1955, 12.

In this quest for ultimate justice it is hoped that the church will not overlook two immediacies: a more active participation in those organizations dedicated to the achievement of world peace, and the recognition of the equality of all peoples before God.

Serious consideration should be given Nephi's declaration that "all men are privileged the one like unto the other, and none are forbidden. . . and he denieth none that come unto him, black and white, bond and free, male and female; and he remembereth the heathen; and all are alike unto God, both Jew and Gentile" (2 Ne. 26:28,33). The symbol of special privilege, which was exemplified by the only two black men who received the priesthood during Joseph Smith's lifetime (Elijah Abel and Walker Lewis),[40] was finally demolished by Spencer W. Kimball's bold revelation in June 1978.[41] However, it must be stated that there is still much to do in order to make the brotherhood of man not merely a hopeful phrase but in truth a demonstrable fact.

Mormonism embraces much that is wholesome and ennobling. Its thirteenth Article of Faith approaches in idealism the tenets of Robert G. Ingersoll, the Gentile philosopher, who said:

> I belong to the Great Church that holds the world within its starlit aisles; that claims the great and good of

---

[40]Jessie L. Embry, *Black Saints in a White Church: Contemporary African American Mormons* (Salt Lake City: Signature Books, 1994), 23.

[41]It was accepted by the membership of the LDS Church as a revelation at the September 1978 general conference. Actually, the First Presidency and Quorum of the Twelve Apostles voted to give the priesthood to blacks in December 1969, with Kimball being one of those in the majority in favor of this action. However, Harold B. Lee was absent when the vote was taken, and when he returned a couple of days later, there was a new vote, rescinding the earlier decision. See Edwin B. Firmage, ed., *An Abundant Life: The Memoirs of Hugh B. Brown* (Salt Lake City: Signature Books, 1988), 142, and D. Michael Quinn, *The Mormon Hierarchy: Extensions of Power* (Salt Lake City: Signature Books, 1997), 14.

every race and clime; that finds with joy the grain of gold in every creed, and floods with light and love the germs of good in every soul.[42]

The doctrine of that church professing Jesus Christ as founder must be broad enough to include the religion of reason, the creed of science:

To love justice, to long for the right, to love mercy, to pity the suffering, to assist the weak, to forget wrongs and remember benefits—to love the truth, to be sincere, to utter honest words, to love liberty, to wage relentless war against slavery in all its forms, to love wife and child and friend, to make a happy home, to love the beautiful in art, in nature, to cultivate the mind, to be familiar with the mighty thoughts that genius has expressed, the noble deeds of all the world, to cultivate courage and cheerfulness, to make others happy, to fill life with the splendor of generous acts, the warmth of loving words, to discard error, to destroy prejudice, to receive new truths with gladness, to cultivate hope, to see the calm beyond the storm, the dawn beyond the night, to do the best that can be done and then to be resigned—this is the religion of reason, the creed of science. This satisfies the brain and heart.[43]

[42]Tryon Edwards, comp., *The New Dictionary of Thoughts: A Cyclopedia of Quotations* (New York: Standard Book Co., 1952), 82.

[43]*The Works of Robert G. Ingersoll* (New York: The Dresden Publishing Co., 1901), 4:290-91.

A Discussion with James E. Talmage

M y first major encounter with a general authority, where a religious question was being discussed, was early in 1933.[1] My friend, Omer Stewart, who later became the head of the Department of Anthropology at Boulder, Colorado, had returned from a mission in France and was now engaged in the study of anthropology under Julian Steward at the University of Utah.

Omer had written a paper on the Book of Mormon[2] which he brought to me and which, I confess, startled me at the time because he raised questions that I was totally unprepared to deal with. It had to do with the physical side of the Book of Mormon: with the flora and fauna and the grains, the terrain, the geography, the mountains, the rivers—anything physical; not doctrinaire at all, but merely the conditions that were supposed to have prevailed while the Nephites were flourishing

---

[1] The LaMar Petersen Oral Interview, which was conducted by Kent Walgren on 21 March 1978, is located in the LaMar Petersen Collection, Manuscript 524, Box 2, Manuscripts Division, J. Willard Marriott Library, University of Utah, Salt Lake City.

[2] The May 1932 paper, entitled "Book of Mormon and Modern Science," is located in the Omer C. Stewart Collection, Manuscript 612, Box 4, Fd 14, Manuscripts Division, J. Willard Marriott Library, University of Utah. For an up-to-date comparison of the requirements of the Book of Mormon contrasted with the currently known evidence in Mesoamerican archaeology, see Appendix D.

in Central America. Because evidently the conclusions that he made were not harmonious with the belief in the Book of Mormon as a divine record, I felt that someone should at least answer this or deal with it so that we could understand the questions that he had raised. Omer urged me to make contact with Dr. James E. Talmage, which I did. I talked to his secretary and she finally granted us, I think on a Friday afternoon, a fifteen-minute appointment where Dr. Talmage would have time to look at the paper and perhaps advise us regarding it.

Well, we met there, and the interview came about very promptly. Dr. Talmage was very courteous and expressed great interest when he saw the nature of the paper and he was kind. He began reading it but as he read on, he became exercised and somewhat distraught. And he turned to Omer and he said, "Young man, what have you done since you returned from your mission?" and Omer said, "Well, I've gone to the University and I've gotten married." And Dr. Talmage said, "Young man, it's quite possible that you have sinned because evidently you have lost the testimony you had as a missionary. This is not a faith-promoting work. You are questioning the validity of the Book of Mormon." And as he read on, he became more excited about this. Strangely enough, he became most interested, and I thought not to the point at all, in criticizing the grammar, the construction, the punctuation, which we were not interested in really—I did not care whether there was a comma there or a period or a new paragraph, but he seemed to think that Omer had goofed in a number of places where the structure, the mechanics of the presentation were not what he wanted, and of course he was a man of some precision and perhaps what he was saying was a valid criticism, but we wanted him to deal not with that aspect of the paper, but with the content. He really did not get into this very much, except to shake his head and say, "I've thought of that too. This bothered me when I was a young man, but I overcame that." And he then had a Book of Mormon on the desk and it was very impressive. He put his hand on the Book and he said, "This book cannot be put aside by any such kind of study as you have made, Brother Stewart. I have a firm testimony of the divinity of this book and nothing can shake it." But, he had already confessed that in his youth he had been shaken, too, by some of the same questions that Omer had raised and rather than deal with them and give us some kind of explanation, he just avoided them and turned a finger of accusation, which of course is not helpful in any way.

Finally, the interview we could see, was going on toward three hours—our fifteen minutes had long since passed and I guess the secretary was chafing at the bit, but in any case, we did stay three hours and when we left, he gave us some friendly admonitions, but we went down the church steps and Omer said, "Well, do you feel that he answered or helped us in any way regarding the problems I've raised?" And I said, "No, I can't think of a single thing in which he dealt honestly or helpfully."

Book of Mormon Archaeological Tests

BY STAN LARSON[1]

Thomas Stuart Ferguson was a popular LDS lecturer and writer on Book of Mormon archaeology during the early 1940s through the late 1960s.[2] Late in 1974 he received an unusual request, which led him—after a lifetime of studying the Book of Mormon—to write a twenty-nine-page analysis of what he felt were the most important archaeological problems relating to its historicity.

Ferguson's paper was part of a "Written Symposium on the Book of Mormon." David A. Palmer, a chemical engineer with an interest in the Book of Mormon, felt that the time was

---

[1]This appendix is an updated version of chapter 5 in Stan Larson, *Quest for the Gold Plates: Thomas Stuart Ferguson's Archaeological Search for the Book of Mormon* (Salt Lake City: Freethinker Press in association with Smith Research Associates, 1996), 175-234.

[2]Thomas Stuart Ferguson wrote the following books: *Cumorah—Where?*, *Great Message of Peace and Happiness*, *One Fold and One Shepherd*, *Ancient America and the Book of Mormon* (coauthored with Milton R. Hunter), as well as articles in *The Improvement Era*, *University Archaeological Society Newsletter*, *Bulletin of the University Archaeological Society*, *The Messenger of Northern California*, *The Millennial Star*, *Christianity Today*, and *Newsletter and Proceedings of the Society for Early Historical Archaeology*. After the 1967 discovery and translation of original Egyptian papyri used by Joseph Smith, Ferguson lost faith in the authenticity of the Book Abraham and then rejected the historicity of the Book of Mormon.

right for LDS students of the Book of Mormon to try to reach a general agreement concerning the main aspects of its geography. In 1974 Palmer proposed a two-stage written symposium to tackle this problem. In the first stage V. Garth Norman[3] and John L. Sorenson[4] were to make fresh revisions of their varying geographical theories. In the second stage selected LDS scholars were to offer constructive criticism of these two geographies in a "Book of Mormon Non Conference Symposium" and mail their response to the other participants.[5] Palmer enlisted the following individuals to join him in this unique symposium: B. Keith Christensen, a commercial illustrator; Thomas Stuart Ferguson, founder of the New World Archaeological Foundation; Fred W. Nelson, Jr., a chemist and archaeologist; V. Garth Norman, a New World Archaeological Foundation archaeologist; John L. Sorenson, a BYU professor of anthropology; Calvin D. Tolman, an offset pressman at the Deseret News; Bruce W. Warren, a doctoral student in anthropology; and J. Nile Washburn, a writer on Book of Mormon geography. Palmer required each participant to "make a *substantive* evaluation" of both geographical theories.[6]

In his contribution to this symposium Ferguson focused more attention on the position paper of John L. Sorenson:

---

[3]V. Garth Norman, "Book of Mormon Geography Study on the Narrow Neck of Land Region," Book of Mormon Geography Working Paper, no. 1, typescript, 1966, rev. 1972, and "Reconstruction and Correlation of the Geography of the Land Southward, Border Regions of the Book of Mormon," Book of Mormon Geography Working Paper, no. 2, typescript, 1975; both of which are located in the Calvin D. Tolman Collection, Accession 1445, Manuscripts Division, J. Willard Marriott Library, University of Utah, Salt Lake City; hereafter abbreviated to Tolman Collection.

[4]John L. Sorenson, "Where in the World? Views on Book of Mormon Geography," Book of Mormon Working Paper, no. 8, typescript, 1974, in Tolman Collection.

[5]David A. Palmer, form letter, 8 September 1974, in Tolman Collection.

[6]David A. Palmer, letter to Geography Symposium Participants, 20 December 1974, with emphasis in original, in Tolman Collection.

Sorenson lays down some factual requirements that the correlation of Jaredite-Nephite places must meet to be valid and acceptable: (1) configuration, (2) dimensions, (3) directions, (4) topography, (5) plant life, (6) animal life, (7) climate. . . . These are objective tests. To Sorenson's list of requirements—his "test" list—I think there should be added two additional items, (1) metals and (2) scripts, bringing the list of requirements to nine. He gives but one paragraph to his first test, "configuration." . . . He gives seven full pages to item two, "dimensions." . . . Four and a half pages are devoted to his test three, "directions." Sorenson's discussion of test four, "topography," encompasses seven pages. He quits after covering his first four items.

In my opinion, the most demanding and exacting tests (and therefore the most substantial) are "plant life," "animal life," "metals," and "scripts." Neither Norman nor Sorenson applies any of these more significant and truth-testing factors to their hypotheses. This is my main criticism of each of the papers.[7]

While Ferguson's initial assignment was to respond to the Norman and Sorenson geographical theories, his paper addressed more broadly what he saw as the critical difficulties in Book of Mormon archaeology. He divided these problems into four areas: the Plant-Life Test, the Animal-Life Test, the Metallurgy Test, and the Script Test. This insightful document reveals Ferguson's perception of what he termed "the big weak spots" involved in attempting to authenticate the Book of

---

[7]Thomas Stuart Ferguson, "Written Symposium on Book of Mormon Geography: Response of Thomas S. Ferguson to the Norman and Sorenson Papers," typescript, 12 March 1975, 1-2, in the Thomas Stuart Ferguson Collection, Accession 1350, Manuscripts Division, J. Willard Marriott Library, University of Utah, Salt Lake City; hereafter abbreviated to Ferguson Collection, UU. The text of Ferguson's study is reproduced in "Thomas Stuart Ferguson on Book of Mormon Archaeology" of the author's *Quest for the Gold Plates*, 235-68. It was first published in Jerald Tanner and Sandra Tanner, eds., *Ferguson's Manuscript Unveiled* (Salt Lake City: Utah Lighthouse Ministry, 1988).

Mormon through archaeology.[8] Ferguson also described his paper for the symposium as being a study "pointing up Book of Mormon problems raised by archaeology."[9]

Ferguson became aware of the earlier investigation into similar problems of the Book of Mormon made by B. H. Roberts, a member of the LDS First Council of Seventy, when Jerald and Sandra Tanner published the text in 1980. In 1921 William E. Riter of Salina, Utah, wrote to Apostle James E. Talmage for an answer to five questions which a friend of his in Washington, D.C., had asked about the Book of Mormon. The questions concerned the development of native American languages, the presence of the horse in the New World, knowledge of steel and metallurgy, use of metal swords and cimiters, and possession of silk. Talmage passed this letter on to Roberts for his answer. Roberts wrote a 141-page study entitled "Book of Mormon Difficulties: A Study," which discussed these five problems in three chapters.[10] In January 1922 Roberts presented this paper to the First Presidency and the Twelve Apostles, but their only response was silence. The following month Roberts condensed these problems into a short, positive letter in reply to Riter, not discussing any of the difficulties he had found in the Book of Mormon.

Roberts felt very unsatisfied, and during the first three

---

[8]Ferguson, letter to Mr. and Mrs. Harold W. Lawrence, 9 February 1976, in Ferguson Collection, UU.

[9]Ferguson, handwritten response on letter of J. Don Cerchione to Ferguson, 21 July 1976, in Ferguson Collection, UU.

[10]B. H. Roberts, "Book of Mormon Difficulties: A Study," typescript, 1921, in the B. H. Roberts Collection, Manuscript 106, Box 9, Book 1, Manuscripts Division, J. Willard Marriott Library, University of Utah, Salt Lake City; hereafter abbreviated to Roberts Collection. The incomplete manuscript (missing part II of "Difficulties") was reproduced in Jerald Tanner and Sandra Tanner, eds., *Roberts' Manuscripts Revealed: A Photographic Reproduction of Mormon Historian B. H. Roberts' Secret Studies on the Book of Mormon* (Salt Lake City: Modern Microfilm Co., 1980) and the complete manuscript was published in Roberts, *Studies of the Book of Mormon*, 61-148.

months of 1922 he delved further and wrote "A Book of Mormon Study," which discussed the controversial idea that Joseph Smith might have produced the Book of Mormon himself, using his own creative imagination and possibly Ethan Smith's *View of the Hebrews*.[11] This was followed in October 1927 by "A Parallel," which condensed "A Book of Mormon Study" into eighteen comparisons between the *View of the Hebrews* and the Book of Mormon.[12] Many LDS students consider these controversial analyses by Roberts concerning problems in the Book of Mormon to still be thought-provoking, even though Roberts wrote the two studies over seventy-six years ago. Because Ferguson did not become aware of Roberts's study until at least five years after his own, it provides a comparative analysis.

The written criticisms by Ferguson and the others participating in the 1975 symposium were taken into account by both Norman and Sorenson. Norman chose not to publish his geographical position. However, after careful revision Sorenson published his viewpoint a decade later as *An Ancient American Setting for the Book of Mormon*.[13] Deanne G. Matheny, who for-

---

[11]B. H. Roberts, "A Book of Mormon Study," typescript, 1922, in Box 9, Books 2-3, Roberts Collection; Roberts, *Studies of the Book of Mormon*,149-319.

[12]B. H. Roberts, "A Parallel," typescript, 1927, in Box 16, Fd 3, Roberts Collection; Roberts, *Studies*, 321-44. John W. Welch, *Finding Answers to B. H. Roberts' Questions and "An Unparallel"* (Provo, UT: Foundation for Ancient Research and Mormon Studies, 1985), responded to the problems proposed in Roberts' studies.

[13]John L. Sorenson, *An Ancient American Setting for the Book of Mormon* (Salt Lake City: Deseret Book Co., 1985; Provo, UT: Foundation for Ancient Research and Mormon Studies, 1985). Citing BYU Religious Instruction Administrative Council Minutes for 31 May 1978, Gary James Bergera and Ronald Priddis, *Brigham Young University: A House of Faith* (Salt Lake City: Signature Books, 1985), 86, 408n73, indicated that Sorenson's manuscript "was rejected for publication by BYU's Religious Studies Center because Elder Mark E. Petersen found the topic to be ' too touchy,'" and only after Petersen died did the Deseret Book Company and F.A.R.M.S. jointly publish the book. Also see John L. Sorenson, "The

merly taught anthropology at BYU, reviewed Sorenson's book in 1993.[14] Sorenson himself (then a BYU emeritus professor) responded to Matheny the following year.[15] Ferguson's study is now twenty-three years old, but using all these sources and the most current archaeological and historical evidence provides an opportunity to place the problems he raised into better perspective and to update the discussion to the present.

Before discussing the four types of tests, Ferguson made a plea to consult the Book of Mormon text in order to find out precisely what it contains:

> What are the demands of the text of the Book of Mormon for the dirt, soil, earth, and ground of the Book of Mormon places? Let's turn to the text of the Book of Mormon for some of the specific things that must be found in the ground occupied 2,500 years by the people from Iraq and for 1,000 years by the people from Israel.[16]

The Book of Mormon account of the Jaredites, Nephites, Lamanites, and other groups reveals a diverse record of their material cultures. Though such details are not the purpose of the Book of Mormon, there is enough incidental information provided to enable these important tests of its authenticity. Ferguson's goal was to produce a dispassionate analysis of the perceived problems of the Book of Mormon, approached from four different angles.

Book of Mormon as a Mesoamerican Record," in *Book of Mormon Authorship Revisited: The Evidence for Ancient Origins*, ed. Noel B. Reynolds (Provo, UT: Foundation for Ancient Research and Mormon Studies, 1997), 391-521.

[14]Deanne G. Matheny, "Does the Shoe Fit? A Critique of the Limited Tehuántepec Geography," in *New Approaches to the Book of Mormon: Explorations in Critical Methodology*, ed. Brent Lee Metcalfe (Salt Lake City: Signature Books, 1993), 269-328.

[15]John L. Sorenson, "Viva Zapato! Hurray for the Shoe!" review of "Does the Shoe Fit?" by Deanne G. Matheny, in *Review of Books on the Book of Mormon* 6, no. 1 (1994): 297-361.

[16]Ferguson, "Written Symposium," 4-5, Ferguson Collection, UU.

No.1—The Plant-Life Test of the Book of Mormon

In what Ferguson called the "Plant-Life Test," he presented quotations from the Book of Mormon that mention wheat, barley, figs, and grapes, then repeated the same list and attached the word "none" to each in order to indicate that no known evidence supports the existence of these plants in Mesoamerica. Ferguson then continued:

> This negative score on the plant-life test should not be treated too lightly. An abundance of evidence supporting the existence of these plants has been found in other parts of the world of antiquity. The existence of numerous non-Book-of-Mormon plants (maize,[17] lima beans, tomatoes, squash, etc.) has been supported by abundant archaeological findings. . . . Art portrayals in ceramics, murals, and sculptured works—of ancient plant life—are fairly commonplace. Thousands of archaeological holes in the area proposed have given us not a fragment of evidence of the presence of the plants mentioned in the Book of Mormon—the holes include the great one dug by Edwin Shook at Tehuacán, Puebla, Mexico. He excavated a cave—going down and back to 5,000 B.C., finding most of the major plants of the area. But no wheat, barley, figs, or grapes.[18]

To his credit Ferguson showed awareness—both here and in his discussion of the animal-life and the metallurgy tests—of the difference between the direct evidence of archaeological discoveries and the indirect evidence from sculptural and pictorial representations.

However, Ferguson did not explain that all of the occurrences of "grapes" and "figs" in the Book of Mormon are con-

---

[17]Ferguson's statement that "maize" is a non-Book-of-Mormon plant is incorrect, for the three instances of "corn" at Mosiah 7:22; 9:9,14, correspond with the known staple food. Jeremy A. Sabloff, *The New Archaeology and the Ancient Maya* (New York: Scientific American Library, 1990), 114, stated that Mesoamerican people of the Preclassic period "grew maize as their principal subsistence crop."

[18]Ferguson, "Written Symposium," 6-7, in Ferguson Collection, UU.

tained in biblical quotations. It could conceivably be argued that such quotations refer only to the Old World plants. The four instances of the term "grapes" in 2 Ne. 15:2-4 are imbedded within a thirteen-chapter-long quotation from Isaiah. Also, in the Book of Mormon the resurrected Jesus asked the people at Bountiful: "Do men gather grapes of thorns, or figs of thistles?" (3 Ne. 14:16), using the same wording as found in Matthew 7:16. Native grapes were used in northern Mexico.[19] In the sixteenth century Diego de Landa mentioned the existence of wild vines with edible grapes, though Mayan wine or *balche* was made by fermenting tree bark, honey, and water.[20] Evidence of a wild fig has been discovered at Don Martín in Chiapas.[21] Accordingly, Ferguson was mistaken both when he assumed that grapes and figs were Book of Mormon plants and when he asserted that no varieties of grapes or figs were known in Mesoamerica.

For archaeological confirmation of the Book of Mormon to be significant, it must come from both the right time period and the right place. The site at Don Martín, near Santa Rosa (which Sorenson identified as Zarahemla) has produced plant remains dating to the Late Preclassic time (200 B.C. to A.D. 200). Deanne G. Matheny, wife of and fellow archaeologist with Raymond T. Matheny, said the following concerning the discovered plants at this site:

> The seeds of more than fifty species of plants and other plant parts were among the remains recovered from the

---

[19]Weston La Barre, "Native American Beers," *American Anthropologist* 40 (April-June 1938): 232, quoted in Sorenson, "Viva Zapato!" 336.

[20]Diego de Landa, *Landa's Relación de las cosas de Yucatán,* ed. and trans. by Alfred M. Tozzer (Cambridge, MA: Peabody Museum, Harvard University, 1941), 92, 198.

[21]Alejandro Claudio Martínez Muriel, "Don Martín, Chiapas: Inferencias Economico-sociales de una Communidad Arqueologica" (M.A. thesis, Escuela Nacional de Antropología e Historia, Mexico City, 1978), 104, quoted in D. G. Matheny, "Does the Shoe Fit?" 302.

pits [at Don Martín]. . . . Several of those identified were domesticates, including the jack bean (*Canavalia*), manioc (*Manihot*), two species of maize (*Zea mays*), and two species of common bean (*Phaseolus*). Other species that may have been cultivated include amaranth (*Amaranthus*), chili pepper (*Capsicum*), goose foot (*Chenopodium*), sunflower (*Helianthus*), tobacco (*Nicotiana*), and *Crescentia, Acromia mexicana,* and *Sideroxylon tempisque*. Five wild plants were gathered: fig, palm, *portulaca, vitis,*[22] and *annonaceae*.

At other archaeological sites in Mesoamerica dating to pre-Columbian times, pollen studies and studies of seeds and other plants have revealed similar plant assemblages. But thus far no Old World plants have been identified by the presence of their pollens or other remains.[23]

Mesoamerican plant remains have thus been discovered in the archaeological record during the stated times of the Book of Mormon, showing the domestication of maize, beans, squash, avocado, chili peppers, and the bottle gourd.[24] John A. Price, professor of anthropology at York University, summarized the evidence for New World plants:

No Native Americans made grape wine or wheat bread. Instead, native plants . . . were domesticated: corn, beans, squashes, potatoes, tomatoes, manioc, . . . The Jaredites and Nephites are portrayed as having had plow agriculture of wheat and barley . . . , but nothing remotely resembling this kind of culture has ever been found, either archaeologically or ethnographically, in the aboriginal New World. . . . This was not plow agriculture; the animal drawn plow was absent in the pre-

---

[22]Sorenson, "Viva Zapato!" 339, pointed out that "when Matheny wrote out the names of some of Martínez's plants, she put down '*vitis,*' apparently unable to bring herself to say 'grape'!"

[23]D. G. Matheny, "Does the Shoe Fit?" 301-302.

[24]Richard E. Blanton et alia, *Ancient Mesoamerica: A Comparison of Change in Three Regions*, 2d ed. (Cambridge, England: Cambridge University Press, 1993), 40, explained that the bottle gourd was never eaten, but was used "as a container for carrying water."

Columbian world. It was hand agriculture of corn or manioc or potatoes, not wheat or barley.[25]

Wheat is mentioned in Mosiah 9:9 in a list of other seeds, and occurs metaphorically in the words of the resurrected Jesus to a multitude, warning them to avoid temptation since Satan wanted to "sift you as wheat" (3 Ne. 18:18). Since there are several other cultural adaptations–such as the replacement of "farthing" by "senine" (3 Ne. 12:26; cf. Matt. 5:26)—it should be assumed that, if the Nephites in the first century A.D. did not have wheat, Jesus would have substituted it with a more appropriate plant name. Barley occurs four times—at Mosiah 7:22; 9:9; and Alma 11:7,15.

Ferguson pointed out the lack of verification for the existence of wheat and barley during Book of Mormon times in Mesoamerica. B. H. Roberts also listed these two plants.[26] John L. Sorenson, professor of anthropology at BYU, reported that in 1982 some domesticated barley was discovered in Arizona.[27] Raymond T. Matheny, another professor of anthropology at BYU, countered that this was an indigenous American species in the Hohokam culture (dated about A.D. 900), and "has nothing to do with the Old World horticum [*Hordeum*] barley."[28] However, the Book of Mormon does not specify whether the barley referred to was an Old World transplant they brought in the form of seeds to the New World or a native vari-

---

[25]John A. Price, "The Book of Mormon vs. Anthropological Prehistory," *The Indian Historian* 7 (Summer 1974): 38. Though Price was LDS, he had been away from Mormon culture for years and his article exhibits several errors characteristic of non-Mormon treatments.

[26]Roberts' "Difficulties," chap. ii, 1, in Roberts Collection; Roberts, *Studies of the Book of Mormon*, 95.

[27]Sorenson, *Ancient American Setting*, 184.

[28]Raymond T. Matheny, "Book of Mormon Archaeology: Sunstone Symposium #6, Salt Lake Sheraton Hotel, August 25, 1984," typescript, 1984, in the David J. Buerger Collection, Manuscript 622, Box 33, Fd 17, Manuscripts Division, J. Willard Marriott Library, University of Utah, Salt Lake City. Matheny's remarks were transcribed without permission.

ety they found at or soon after their arrival here. More recently Sorenson reported the discovery of this North American barley in Illinois and Oklahoma.[29] The lack of evidence for the existence of wheat in the New World remains a major difficulty in verifying the antiquity of the Book of Mormon.[30]

No. 2—*The Animal-Life Test of the Book of Mormon*

In the "Animal-Life Test" Ferguson presented Book of Mormon quotations for the ass, bull, calf, cattle, cow, goat, horse, ox, sheep, sow (swine), and elephant. After citing the relevant passages for each of these items, Ferguson repeated the same list of names, emphatically adding the word "none" with each. Ferguson then commented:

> Evidence of the foregoing animals has not appeared in any form—ceramic representations, bones or skeletal

---

[29]Sorenson, "Viva Zapato!" 341.

[30]Because no pre-Columbian wheat has been found anywhere in the Americas, Sorenson tried to get out of the difficulty by suggesting that perhaps Joseph Smith may have dictated the mistranslation "wheat" for the native plant "amaranth." Then Sorenson, *Ancient American Setting*, 185-86, quoted with approval the identification of the Book of Mormon plant *sheum* with the Akkadian *s(h)e'um* "barley." However, since both *barley* and *sheum* are mentioned in the same verse (Mosiah 9:9), Sorenson admitted that reference is made to two different grains. Then, curiously, he suggested that amaranth might be the Book of Mormon *sheum*. But amaranth can not be used to identify *sheum* and to solve the problem of the absence of wheat. Clearly, there is a problem here that no amount of linguistic gymnastics in lexicons can solve. William J. Hamblin, "Basic Methodological Problems with the Anti-Mormon Approach to the geography and Archaeology of the Book of Mormon," *Journal of Book of Mormon Studies* 2 (Spring 1993): 191-93, handled the absence of wheat in another way. After quoting Luke P. Wilson's criticism that the lack of wheat, barley, linen (presumably from flax), grapes, and olives is a problem for the Book of Mormon, Hamblin then examined possibilities concerning each of these items—except wheat. That topic is completely avoided, both in Hamblin's text and footnotes. Cf. Luke P. Wilson, "The Scientific Search for Nephite Remains," *Heart and Mind: The Newsletter of Gospel Truths Ministries* (Fall 1992): 2-3, 5.

remains, mural art, sculptured art, or any other form. However, in the regions proposed by Norman and Sorenson, evidence has been found in several forms of the presence in Book of Mormon times of other animals —deer, jaguars, dogs, turkeys, etc. The zero score presents a problem that will not go away with the ignoring of it. Non-LDS scholars of first magnitude, some who want to be our friends, think we have real trouble here. That evidence of the ancient existence of these animals is not elusive is found in the fact that proof of their existence in the ancient Old World is abundant. The absence of such evidence in the area proposed for our consideration in this symposium is distressing and significant, in my view.[31]

Pre-Columbian Mayan hieroglyphs and ceramic art depict various mammals, such as jaguars, tapirs, deer, monkeys,[32] dogs, peccaries, coatimundis, armadillos, rabbits, gophers, and leaf-nosed bats.[33] The largest mammals alive in Mesoamerica when the Europeans arrived were jaguars, pumas, tapirs, and deer. After quoting numerous passages listing various Book of Mormon animals, B. H. Roberts of the LDS First Council of Seventy stated that this "unequivocally commits the Book of Mormon to the existence and use of the horse and the other Old World domestic animals mentioned above—horses, asses, oxen, cows, sheep, goats, swine (the last, however, only among

---

[31]Ferguson, "Written Symposium," 12-13, in Ferguson Collection, UU.

[32]Mary Baker, "Capuchin Monkeys (*Cebus capucinus*) and the Ancient Maya," *Ancient Mesoamerica* 3 (Fall 1992): 219-28, suggested that the hieroglyphic depictions represent capuchin monkeys rather than howler monkeys or spider monkeys.

[33]J. Eric S. Thompson, *A Catalog of Maya Hieroglyphs* (Norman, OK: University of Oklahoma Press, 1962), 336, 340-41, 343, 366, 375, 379-81; Robert J. Sharer, *The Ancient Maya*, 5th ed. (Stanford, CA: Stanford University Press, 1994), 623, 628; and Jeanette Favrot Peterson, *Precolumbian Flora and Fauna: Continuity of Plant and Animal Themes in Mesoamerican Art* (San Diego: Mingei International Museum of World Folk Art, 1990), passim.

the Jaredites)."³⁴

In the second century B.C. the Lamanites mistreated the people of Limhi, with the Book of Mormon stating that they "began to put heavy burdens upon their backs, and drive them as they would a dumb ass" (Mosiah 21:3). However, Roberts quoted an early twentieth-century authority to the effect that "before the time of Columbus, *no tribe had an animal able to carry a man.*"³⁵ No assses or other domesticated animals could be used to transport either humans or heavy loads, because "no animals large enough to carry cargo lived in Mesoamerica before the coming of the Spanish."³⁶

Enos, a nephew of the Nephi who was one of the original colonists, provided an early description of the domesticated animals among the Nephites:

> And it came to pass that the people of Nephi did till the land, and raise all manner of grain, and of fruit, and flocks of herds,³⁷ and flocks of all manner of cattle of every kind, and goats, and wild goats, and also many horses (Enos 1:21).

Many times in the Book of Mormon "flocks" and "herds" are mentioned. However, unless there is some specification as to what animal is actually being referred to in that particular flock or herd, it is useless to speculate as to the intended animal. For example, John L. Sorenson proposed that the Book of Mormon "flocks" and "herds" might have consisted of any one of

---

³⁴Roberts, "Difficulties," chap. ii, 6, in Roberts Collection; Roberts, *Studies of the Book of Mormon*, 98.

³⁵Roberts, "Difficulties," chap. ii, 8, in Roberts Collection; Roberts, *Studies of the Book of Mormon*, 99. B. H. Roberts is here quoting Clark Wissler, *The American Indian: An Introduction to the Anthropology of the New World* (New York: Douglas C. McMurtrie, 1917), 37, with Roberts adding the emphasis to Wissler's wording.

³⁶Linda Schele and David Freidel, *A Forest of Kings: The Untold Story of the Ancient Maya* (New York: William Morrow, 1990), 60.

³⁷This enigmatic Book of Mormon phrase occurs only here.

the following twenty animals: deer, peccaries, turkeys, Muscovy ducks, Tinamou ducks,[38] quail, pheasants, partridges, doves, *curassow*, *cotinga*, roseate spoonbills, macaws, *chachalaca*, parrots, hares, rabbits, *paca*, *agouti*, and fattened dogs.[39] In this menagerie of possible animals to be considered as part of a flock, the only animal actually mentioned in the Book of Mormon is the dog. The domestic dog certainly may have been a source of food,[40] but in the Book of Mormon the dog serves as an example in metaphors: people should not throw holy things to dogs (3 Ne.14:6), nor should they depart from righteousness and turn to iniquity like a dog which eats his own vomit (3 Ne. 7:8).

The Book of Mormon mentions sheep a total of twenty-six times. There are also twenty-two instances of shepherd and one reference to wool in 2 Ne. 8:8, which is a quotation from Isa. 51:8. Sheep, however, are not native American animals.[41] All the various animals mentioned in the Book of Mormon must be compared with the evidence available concerning animals in the Americas. Careful examination of many thousands of New World images on pottery and stone reveals no artistic renditions of Old World domestic animals. In the 1960s Sidney B. Sperry, professor of religion at BYU, admitted that "the problem of demonstrating the use of domestic animals among

---

[38]D. G. Matheny, "Does the Shoe Fit?" 303*n*20, pointed out that the Tinamou is not a duck, but "belongs to the family Tinamidae."

[39]Sorenson, *Ancient American Setting*, 292-93.

[40]Richard E. W. Adams, *Prehistoric Mesoamerica*, rev. ed. (Norman, OK: University of Oklahoma Press, 1991), 37, explained that domesticated dogs were eaten, but were "no substitute for cattle, sheep, goats, or pigs, all of which were important in the Old World Neolithic but lacking in the New World."

[41]Sorenson, *Ancient American Setting*, 296-97, asserted that "real sheep's wool was found in a burial site at Cholula," but examining Sorenson's source one finds that Sigvald Linné, *Mexican Highland Cultures: Archaeological Researches at Teoithuacán, Calpulalpan, and Chalchicomula in 1934-35* (Stockholm: Ethnographical Museum of Sweden, 1942), 156, indicated that "the grave is not with certainty stated to be pre-Spanish."

ancient American peoples is the most difficult scientific problem faced by Book of Mormon scholars at the present time."[42] Because considerable study has been done on the elephant and the horse, these two animals are examined in some detail.

Elephants among the Jaredites

In Ferguson's list of the various animals in the "Animal-Life Test" he qualified the negative verdict on elephants by explaining that there are "none contemporary with [the] Book of Mormon."[43] It seems justifiable for Ferguson to understand the meaning of the word "elephant" to include the extinct mammoth and mastodon of North America. The Book of Mormon contains the following reference to elephants: "and they also had horses, and asses, and there were elephants and cureloms and cumons; all of which were useful unto man, and more especially the elephants and cureloms and cumoms" (Ether 9:19). This indicates that the Jaredites found the elephants to be particularly helpful. However, it should be kept in mind that this solitary verse with its two occurrences of elephants is comparatively early in their history, since Emer is estimated to have lived about 2,500 B.C.[44]

Jean Frédéric Waldeck, who lived for a year in the Mesoamerican jungles during the early 1830s, published drawings of various Mayan hieroglyphic inscriptions. Waldeck's conviction that the Mayan culture was derived from the Old World "distorted his perceptions and drove him to see nonexistent"

---

[42]Sidney B. Sperry, *Answers to Book of Mormon Questions (formerly Problems of the Book of Mormon)* (Salt Lake City: Bookcraft, 1967), 164.

[43]Ferguson, "Written Symposium," 13, in Ferguson Collection, UU.

[44]Sorenson, *Ancient American Setting,*119, 298.

influences in the hieroglyphs.[45] Waldeck drew two elephant heads in his creative rendition of the middle panel of glyphs in the Temple of the Inscriptions at Palenque.[46] This should be compared with Annie Hunter's more accurate drawings of the same set of glyphs.[47] John L. Sorenson cited Albert S. Gatschet's 1887 article on "Elephants in America," in which Gatschet quoted Davyd Ingram's sixteenth-century fanciful description of elephants supposedly seen roaming in the eastern part of North America.[48] Ingram showed his lack of dependability as an eyewitness in his description of a grotesque headless animal purportedly sighted on this same journey:

> He [Ingram] did alsoe see one other Straunge Beaste bigger than a Beare, yt had nether heade nor necke, his eyes and mouthe weare in his breast; this beaste is verye ouglie to beholde and Cowardlie of kynde, yt beareth a very fyne skynne like a Ratte, full of sylver heare.[49]

Sorenson commented that Ingram's account "at least, shows some of the difficulty eye-witnesses and non-eye-witnesses have with perception and labeling."[50] It seems rather that this account illustrates how an unreliable observer with a vivid imagination can embellish a genuine travel narrative. Informed

---

[45]The editors of Time-Life Books, *The Magnificent Maya,* Lost Civilizations (Alexandria, VA: Time-Life Books, 1993), 21.

[46]Claude François Baudez, *Jean-Frédéric Waldeck, peintre: le premier explorateur des ruines mayas* ([Paris]: Fernand Hazan Editions, 1993), 127, fig 23.

[47]Alfred P. Maudsley, *Archaeology,* in *Biologia Centrali-Americana; or, Contributions to the Knowledge of the Fauna and Flora of Mexico and Central America,* ed. F. Duncane Godman and Osbert Salvin (London: R. H. Porter, and Dulau and Co., 1889-1902), vol. 4, pl. 61.

[48]John L. Sorenson, *Animals in the Book of Mormon: An Annotated Bibliography* (Provo, UT: Foundation for Ancient Research and Mormon Studies, 1992), 12.

[49]Albert S. Gatschet, "Elephants in America," *The American Antiquarian and Oriental Journal* 9 (1887): 202-203.

[50]Sorenson, *Animals,* 12.

writers realized that the mammoth had been extinct for a long time. A New York writer in the 1823 *Palmyra Herald* showed such awareness: "What wonderful catastrophe destroyed at once the first inhabitants, with the species of mammoth, is beyond the researches of the best scholar and greatest antiquarian."[51]

Numerous reasons have been proposed to explain the extinction of the large mammals during the late Pleistocene era.[52] The two major theories to account for this extinction are climatic changes and human hunting.[53] In North America prehistoric remains of the Columbian mammoth (*Mammuthus columbi*) and the American mastodon (*Mammut americanum*) have been found.[54] Gary Haynes, professor of anthropology at the University of Nevada, Reno, pointed out that mammoths and mastodons disappeared during the late Pleistocene from 10,000 to 12,000 years ago.[55]

---

[51]*Palmyra Herald*, 19 February 1823, quoted in Dan Vogel, *Indian Origins and the Book of Mormon: Religious Solutions from Columbus to Joseph Smith* (Salt Lake City: Signature Books, 1986), 47.

[52]Björn Kurtén and Elaine Anderson, *Pleistocene Mammals of North America* (New York: Columbia University Press, 1980), 357.

[53]T. Douglas Price, "The View from Europe: Concepts and Questions about Terminal Pleistocene Societies," in *The First Americans: Search and Research*, ed. Tom D. Dillehay and David J. Meltzer (Boca Raton, FL: CRC Press, 1991), 196.

[54]Adrian Lister and Paul Bahn, *Mammoths* (New York: Macmillan, 1994), 31, indicated that the range of woolly mammoth (*Mammuthus primigenius*) was limited to Alaska, Canada, and northern United States. John M. Harris and Shelley M. Cox, "Rancho La Brea Mammoths," *Current Research in the Pleistocene* 10 (1993): 97, pointed out that earlier authorities concluded that both the imperial mammoth (*Mammuthus imperator*) and the Columbian mammoth were found at the La Brea tar pits, while more recently scholars have identified these remains as either the imperial mammoth or the Columbian mammoth, adding the probability favors the single species being the latter.

[55]Gary Haynes, *Mammoths, Mastodonts, and Elephants: Biology, Behavior, and the Fossil Record* (Cambridge, England: Cambridge University Press, 1991), 198, 264. Hugh Nibley, *Since Cumorah: The Book of Mormon in the Modern World*, 2d ed., The Collected Works of Hugh Nibley, ed. John W. Welch (Salt Lake City: Deseret Book Co., 1988; Provo, UT: Foun-

In the last four decades numerous refinements in carbon-14 dating have shown that not all radiocarbon dates are equally valid. Since their accuracy varies according to type of material being dated and the possibilities of contamination, Donald K. Grayson, professor of archaeology at the University of Washington, analyzed the thirty-eight genera of mammals that supposedly became extinct during the late Pleistocene period and found that only seven genera have the very best radiocarbon dates. Two of these seven are the mammoth and the mastodon, with twenty-five good dates ranging from 10,395 ± 100 years ago back to more than 33,000 years ago, scattered over thirteen different archaeological sites.[56] In 1993 three Russian scientists announced that Old World woolly mammoths (*Mammuthus primigenius*), which were stranded on Wrangel Island in the East Siberian Sea off northeastern Siberia, evolved into midget mammoths only four to six feet high and survived until about 3,700 years ago.[57] However, the evidence that neither the mammoth nor the mastodon of North America survived the last Ice Age is strong. Accordingly, these animals had been extinct thousands of years before the Jaredites, the earliest Book of Mormon people, lived in the New World.

Horses in the Book of Mormon

Several references to horses are scattered throughout the Book of Mormon. First of all, after leaving Jerusalem, living in

---

dation for Ancient Research and Mormon Studies, 1988), 7:225, overstated the period during which archaeologists date the extinction of the mammoth and the mastodon in North America: "The guesses of the scientists range all the way from hundreds of thousands to mere hundreds of years ago."

[56]Donald K. Grayson, "The Chronology of North American Late Pleistocene Extinctions." *Journal of Archaeological Science* 16 (March 1989): 158-59.

[57]S. L. Vartanyan, V. E. Garutt, and A. V. Sher, "Holocene Dwarf Mammoths from Wrangel Island in the Siberian Arctic," *Nature* 362 (25 March 1993): 337-40.

the wilderness for eight years, and sailing across the ocean, Nephi described what wild animals their small colony encountered as they arrived in the New World:

> And it came to pass that we did find upon the land of promise, as we journeyed in the wilderness, that there were beasts in the forests of every kind, both the cow and the ox, and the ass and the horse, and the goat and the wild goat, and all manner of wild animals, which were for the use of men (1 Ne. 18:25).

These indigenous animals were found—not brought—by the Nephites.[58] In the first century B.C. the Lamanite King Lamoni gave orders to his servants to prepare "his horses and chariots" (Alma 18:9; 20:6) for two trips. Under the direction of Lachoneus, their governor, and Gidgiddoni, the chief captain of their army, in A.D. 17 the Nephites gathered "their horses, and their chariots, and their cattle, and all their flocks and their herds" (3 Ne. 3:22) into the lands of Zarahemla and Bountiful in defense against the Gadianton robbers. The Nephite plan was to assemble enough "provisions, and horses and cattle, and flocks of every kind that they might subsist" (3 Ne. 4:4) for seven years. A possible interpretation of this verse is that they ate horse meat during this period.[59] However, nine years later there were still horses alive among the people, for in A.D. 26 the Nephites returned to their original lands, "every man, with his family, his flocks and his herds, his horses and his cattle" (3 Ne. 6:1). The Jaredites, who date from the third millennium B.C.,

---

[58]In spite of the statement that the Nephites "found" animals in the New World, Hamblin, "Basic Methodological Problems," 193, explained the absence of archaeological evidence for such animals by suggesting that "a species may have existed only in small numbers—introduced by, and limited to the civilizations of the Nephites—which subsequently became extinct."

[59]Diane E. Wirth, *A Challenge to the Critics: of Scholarly Evidences of the Book of Mormon* (Bountiful, UT: Horizon Publishers, 1988), 56. However, D. G. Matheny, "Does the Shoe Fit?" 303-304, pointed out that if the Nephites were living the Mosaic dietary laws, they would not be allowed to eat horses, since they "divide not the hoof."

also had horses (Ether 9:19).

Several species of horses existed in prehistoric America, including the Pleistocene horse, *Equus scotti*.[60] At least 130 individuals of *Equus occidentalis* were trapped in the La Brea tar pits.[61] B. H. Roberts warned that these Pleistocene finds at Rancho La Brea cannot be used to sustain the Book of Mormon claim concerning horses, since there is "positive and well nigh universal testimony about the absence of the horse from America within historic times."[62] More recently Bruce J. MacFadden, curator of the Florida Museum of Natural History at the University of Florida, stated that the extinction of the horse in the Americas occurred about 11,000 years ago at the close of the Pleistocene era.[63] This is supported by fifteen good radiocarbon dates, with the youngest being 10,370 ± 350 years ago.[64] The extinction of the horse before the growth of

---

[60]Chester Stock, *Rancho La Brea: A Record of Pleistocene Life in California*, 7th ed., rev. by John M. Harris, Science Series, no. 37 (Los Angeles: Natural History Museum of Los Angeles County, 1992), 39.

[61]John M. Harris and George J. Jefferson, *Rancho La Brea: Treasures of the Tar Pits*, Science Series, no. 31 (Los Angeles: Natural History Museum of Los Angeles County, 1985), 32.

[62]Roberts, "Difficulties," chap. ii, 18, in Roberts Collection; Roberts, *Studies of the Book of Mormon*, 104.

[63]Bruce J. MacFadden, *Fossil Horses: Systematics, Paleobiology, and Evolution of the Family Equidae* (Cambridge, England: Cambridge University Press, 1992), 3. MacFadden added: "In a minority view, Clutton-Brock . . . believes that they may have persisted into historical times." In fairness one must clarify that Juliet Clutton-Brock, *Domesticated Animals from Early Times* (Austin, TX: University of Texas Press, 1981; London: British Museum, 1981), 81, did not take that position, but simply referred to others who did: "In America the horse may have been extinct 8,000 years ago although some people believe it lingered on until the post-Columbian period." In the reprint eight years later Juliet Clutton-Brock, *A Natural History of Domesticated Animals* (Austin, TX: University of Texas Press, 1989), 81, deleted the last eleven words.

[64]Grayson, "Chronology," 158. Hamblin, "Basic Methodological Problems," 194, stated that the horse is "generally thought to have been extinct by the end of Pre-Classic times (before A.D. 300)." Hamblin confused the generally accepted period for the extinction of the horse on the American

civilization in Mesoamerica is also supported by the fact that no depictions of the horse occur in any pre-Columbian art.[65]

Ferguson was aware that there was no support for the existence of the horse during Book of Mormon times.[66] Just as the discredited Jean Frédéric Waldeck saw elephants depicted in Mayan ruins, so Milton R. Hunter, an LDS General Authority in the First Council of Seventy, saw horses; and in his *Archaeology and the Book of Mormon* he displayed a photograph of a carved stone showing a bearded man standing by a horse on the Temple of Wall Panels in Chichén Itzá.[67] However, this reputed "horse" reaches only to the height of a man's waist, and John L. Sorenson rightly suggested that Hunter's animal is probably a deer.[68]

Sorenson, in an effort to support his position that the horse might have survived into Book of Mormon times, stated the following:

> Archaeologist Paul S. Martin, for example, saw no theoretical reason why "pockets" of horses and other Pleistocene fauna could not have survived as late as 2,000 B.C. Dr. Ripley Bullen thought horses could have lasted until 3,000 B.C. in Florida, and J. J. Hester granted a possible 4,000 B.C. survival date.[69]

---

continents, missing the date by over 8,000 years.

[65]Millard Sheets, *The Horse in Folk Art* (La Jolla, CA: Mingei International Museum of World Folk Art, 1984), 12.

[66]Ferguson, letter to Chris B. Hartshorn, 18 April 1962, in Thomas Stuart Ferguson Collection, Manuscript 1549, Special Collections and Manuscripts, Harold B. Lee Library, Brigham Young University, Provo, UT; hereafter abbreviated to Ferguson Collection, BYU.

[67]Milton R. Hunter, *Archaeology and the Book of Mormon* (Salt Lake City: Deseret Book Co., 1956), 6.

[68]Sorenson, *Animals,* 15.

[69]John L. Sorenson, "Once More: The Horse," in *Reexploring the Book of Mormon: The F.A.R.M.S. Updates,* ed. John W. Welch (Salt Lake City: Deseret Book Co., 1992; Provo, UT: Foundation for Ancient Research and Mormon Studies, 1992), 98-99. Daniel C. Peterson, "Book of Mormon Economy and Technology," in *Encyclopedia of Mormonism,* ed. Daniel H.

Let us examine Sorenson's three assertions. (1) Paul S. Martin, professor of geosciences at the University of Arizona, was quoted out of context, for after expressing the theoretical possibility that Sorenson referred to, Martin then made the following strong statement: "But in the past two decades concordant stratigraphic, palynological [relating to the study of pollen], archaeological, and radiocarbon evidence to demonstrate beyond doubt the post-glacial survival of an extinct large mammal has been confined to extinct species of *Bison*."[70] (2) Ripley Bullen spoke in general of the extinction of mammals in Florida and not specifically of the horse as Sorenson asserted.[71] (3) James J. Hester, professor of anthropology at the University of Colorado, did not suggest that the horse survived until 4,000 B.C., but rather used a date more than two thousand years earlier.[72] Hester's date of 8,240 years before the present (with a variance of ± 960 years) was published in 1976, but the validity of the radiocarbon dating for these horse remains at Whitewater Draw, Arizona, has been questioned. The next youngest horse date of 10,370 ± 350 years ago has a better quality of material being dated and stronger association between the

---

Ludlow (New York: MacMillan Publishing Co., 1992), 1:173, referred to Sorenson's argument about the survival of the horse into the Book of Mormon period. Hugh Nibley, *Teachings of the Book of Mormon* (Provo, UT: Foundation for Ancient Research and Mormon Studies, 1993), 4:1-3, stated that the absence of the horse "is the strongest argument, supposedly, that has been raised against the Book of Mormon," and then answered the problem by simply asserting that the horse never became extinct in North America.

[70]Paul S. Martin, "The Discovery of America," *Science* 179 (9 March 1973): 974n3.

[71]Robert A. Martin and S. David Webb, "Late Pleistocene Mammals from the Devil's Den Fauna, Levy County," in *Pleistocene Mammals of Florida*, ed. S. David Webb (Gainesville, FL: University Presses of Florida, 1974), 144, quoting Ripley Bullen.

[72]James J. Hester, "The Agency of Man in Animal Extinctions," in *Pleistocene Extinctions: The Search for a Cause*, ed. Paul S. Martin and H. E. Wright (New Haven, CT: Yale University Press, 1967), 183.

material actually being tested and the extinct genus.[73] Clearly, Sorenson's three arguments for a late survival of the horse do not hold up under scrutiny.[74] Certain now-extinct species may have survived in particular areas after the Ice Age. For example, one scholar recently stated that "in one locality in Alberta, *Equus conversidens* [a short-legged, small horse] may still have been in existence about 8,000 B.P. [before present]."[75] While there may have been small "pockets" of horses surviving after the Late Pleistocene extinctions, the time period for such survivals would still be long before the earliest Jaredites of the Book of Mormon.

John W. Welch, a professor of law at BYU, referred to the find in Mayapán of horse remains which were "considered by the zoologist studying them to be pre-Columbian."[76] Examination of Welch's citation reveals that he misrepresented the evi-

---

[73]Jim I. Mead and David J. Meltzer, "North American Late Quaternary Extinctions and Radiocarbon Record," in *Quaternary Extinctions: A Prehistoric Revolution*, ed. Paul S. Martin and Richard G. Klein (Tucson, AZ: University of Arizona Press, 1984), 446. Mead and Meltzer, ibid., 447, explained: "When one considers only those genera for which we have demonstrably reliable dates . . . that are not derived from bone collagen (*Camelops, Equus, Mammut, Mammuthus, Nothrotheriops, Panthera*), a familiar pattern appears. These reliable dates . . . indicate that late Pleistocene extinctions lasted no later than 10,000 yr B.P. [before present] and possibly were complete by 10,800 yr B.P."

[74]Sorenson, *Ancient American Setting*, 395n63, asserted that one scholar discovered "horse remains in southwest Yucatán caves in association with artifacts." Examining Sorenson's source reveals that Henry C. Mercer, *The Hill-Caves of Yucatán: A Search for Evidence of Man's Antiquity in the Caverns of Central America* (Philadelphia: J. B. Lippincott Co., 1896), 40, 69, 170, 172, found in the Sayab cave two horse teeth which "had probably worked down from the surface in recent time," in Chekt-a-leh cave he found a horse phalanx which "must have been modern and Spanish," and in Lara cave he also found bones of the European horse, *Equus caballus*, which had been imported into the Americas since the fifteenth century. Consequently, Sorenson's implication of finding a pre-Columbian horse is not supported.

[75]Björn Kurtén, *Before the Indians* (New York: Columbia University Press 1988), 98.

[76]Welch, *Finding Answers*, 8.

dence, which does not date to pre-Columbian times (and hence potentially to the Book of Mormon period) but rather to prehistoric Pleistocene times. This find at Cenote Ch'en Mul consists of one complete horse tooth and fragments of three others, which were found six feet below the surface in black earth and were "heavily mineralized [fossilized], unlike any other material in the collections."[77] Thousands of bones and teeth were examined at Mayapán, which is a Late Post-Classic site established in the thirteenth century A.D., but these four horse teeth were the only ones fossilized. The reporting scholar did not suggest that the Mayan people had ever seen a pre-Columbian horse, but that in Pleistocene times horses lived in Yucatán, and that "the tooth fragments reported here could have been transported in fossil condition" by the Maya as curiosities.[78] Thus, Welch's assertion about pre-Columbian horses must be corrected to refer to ancient Pleistocene horses, since these fossilized horse teeth at Mayapán date to thousands of years before the Jaredites.

Faced with strong evidence of the prehistoric extinction of the horse in the New World at the end of the last Ice Age, Sorenson sidestepped the issue by suggesting that Joseph Smith used the term "horse" to translate a word on the plates for either a tapir or a deer.[79] Deanne Matheny responded to this suggestion:

---

[77]Harry E. D. Pollock and Clayton E. Ray, "Notes on Vertebrate Animal Remains from Mayapán," *Current Reports* (Carnegie Institution), no. 41 (August 1957): 638.

[78]Clayton E. Ray, "Pre-Columbian Horses from Yucatán," *Journal of Mammalogy* 38 (May 1957): 278. The horses lived during the Pleistocene period and by Mayan times their teeth were already fossils.

[79]Sorenson, *Ancient American Setting.* 293-96. Sorenson, ibid., 299, suggested a known native American animal for various Book of Mormon animals, proposing that the brocket is either the Book of Mormon cow or goat, the bison is either the cow or ox, the deer is either the cow, horse, or goat, the tapir is either the horse, ox, or ass, while the llama and alpaca are either the cow, ox, ass, or sheep.

It seems unlikely that both Jaredites and Nephites, who were well-acquainted with horses, would have mistaken a deer or a tapir for a horse. Their experience in the Old World should have led them to categorize the small New World deer and the squat stout tapir as animals considerably different from the horse.[80]

The endangered Baird's tapir, ranging in the wild from Mexico to Ecucador, is "well suited for movement through the dense vegetation along the banks of rivers and the edges of forests, which are favorite grazing areas."[81] This rarely-seen tapir seems an unlikely candidate for the Book of Mormon horse. Ferguson had earlier rejected the possibility of identifying the horse with the tapir.[82] When the Maya first saw the European horse or cow, they called it by the name of the largest animal they knew—the tapir. Glenna Neilsen Grimm, who received her Ph.D. in anthropology at the University of Utah, contrasted the differing naming techniques of the Maya and the Spaniards:

> They [the Maya] did not have a word for the horse. They didn't have a word for the cow. They weren't familiar with these animals. However, the Spaniards who knew what a horse looked like and what a cow looked like, when they saw the tapir . . . they called it a pig. Now they were familiar with pigs from the Old World and they were familiar with horses, so they didn't call it a horse—it doesn't look like a horse—and being a nocturnal animal I don't know that it [the tapir] could ever fulfill the usage that people put horses to.[83]

---

[80]D. G. Matheny, "Does the Shoe Fit?" 306.

[81]John F. Eisenberg, Colin P. Groves, and Kathy MacKinnon, "Tapirs," in *Grzimek's Encyclopedia of Mammals.* ed. Sybil P. Parker (New York: McGraw-Hill Publishing Co., 1990), 4:599.

[82]Milton R. Hunter and Thomas Stuart Ferguson, *Ancient America and the Book of Mormon* (Oakland, CA: Kolob Book Co., 1950), 309.

[83]Glenna Nielsen Grimm, "The Material Culture of the Book of Mormon," audio tape, 13 May 1992, Sunstone Book of Mormon Lecture, in the Sunstone Foundation Records, Accession A0370, Manuscripts Division, J. Willard Marriott Library, University of Utah, Salt Lake City.

When people confront a previously unknown animal, they often name it according to a characteristic feature or similarity to another animal. However, the Book of Mormon does not say "like a horse" or "similar to a cow," so there is no evidence that the names of animals refer merely to similar animals.[84]

Sorenson has dropped his advocacy of the tapir as the animal that the Nephites and Jaredites called the "horse" and in 1994 focused on the deer, suggesting the possibility that the deer may have been ridden in Mesoamerica. Sorenson pointed out that, when first seeing Spanish horses, the Aztecs called them "the deer-which-carried-men-upon-their-backs." Sorenson concluded that "such information shows that there is nothing inherently implausible in the idea" of Mesoamerican men riding deer.[85] However, Stephen E. Thompson, an LDS Egyptologist at Brown University, questioned Sorenson's logic, saying that "if this is the way Aztecs referred to horses, then obviously the major difference between deer and horses was that horses carried men, while deer did not.[86] Also, the Mesoamerican subspecies of the white tailed deer, which rarely weighs more than 110 pounds, is much smaller than those found further north in North America.[87]

As further support for understanding the Book of Mormon horse as a deer, Sorenson stated that in the Quiché Maya language the word *keh* means "deer or horse" and the related

---

[84]The transliteration of the usual animal names "cumoms" and "cureloms" (Ether 9:19) suggests that Joseph Smith normally translated the names of animals (such as the horse, cow, sheep, goat, etc.) as long as a close equivalent was available.

[85]Sorenson, "Viva Zapato!" 347.

[86]Stephen E. Thompson, "'Critical' Book of Mormon Scholarship," review of *New Approaches to the Book of Mormon,* ed. Brent Metcalfe, and *Review of Books on the Book of Mormon,* ed. Daniel Peterson, in *Dialogue: A Journal of Mormon Thought* 27 (Winter 1994): 204.

[87]Valerius Geist, "White-tailed or Mule Deer (Genus *Odocoileus*)," in *Grzimek's Encyclopedia,* 5:215.

word *kieh* means "horse."[88]   However, Sorenson misused his source, the *Quiché-English Dictionary,* for it specifies that the term *kieh* is the twentieth-century word for the modern horse in the central and western area of native Quiché speakers, while the term *keh* indicates the native white-tailed deer during all time periods and also refers to the European horse introduced by the Spaniards in the sixteenth century.[89] The pre-Columbian Quiché term *keh* did not mean horse because there were no horses to provide names for. Raymond Matheny suggested that proposing various substitute terms is "a weak way to try to explain the presence of these names in the Book of Mormon."[90]

It was an assumption by common people in early nineteenth-century America that horses—as well as asses, oxen, cows, sheep, goats, and swine—were native to America, though serious scholars were aware that these animals had been imported by the Europeans.[91] After surveying the most up-to-date evidence, Deanne Matheny concluded that "at this point then there is no convincing evidence that the horse survived until the period of the Mesoamerican civilizations."[92]   B. H. Roberts referred to the difficulty of establishing the existence of the horse in America during historic times as one of "our

---

[88]Sorenson, *Ancient American Setting,* 296, 395n67.

[89]Munro S. Edmonson, *Quiche-English Dictionary* (New Orleans, LA: Tulane University of Louisiana, 1965), 57-58. Munro S. Edmonson, letter to author, 18 September 1994, in author's possession, explained: "The word *keh* meant 'deer' until the arrival of Spanish horses in Guatemala in 1524. ... At a later date some dialects changed the pronunciation of the original word to *kieh,* which means 'deer,' 'horse,' or sometimes merely 'animal.' The form *keh* meaning 'deer' does go back to at least the eighth century A.D., but has nothing to do with horses. The super-Mormons [*sic*] are again, alas, wrong."

[90]R. T. Matheny, "Book of Mormon Archaeology," 30.

[91]Vogel, *Indian Origins,* 46, 91n67.

[92]D. G. Matheny, "Does the Shoe Fit?" 306.

embarrassing problem."[93] The absence of support for Book of Mormon animals—at the same time as there exists clear evidence of what the Mesoamerican animals actually were—constitutes a serious obstacle to the books's historicity.

No. 3—The Metallurgy Test of the Book of Mormon

In the "Metallurgy Test" Ferguson quoted numerous passages from the Book of Mormon that refer to bellows, brass, breastplates, chains, copper, engravings, gold, hilts, iron, ore, plowshares, silver, steel, and swords, and then repeated each metal, object used in the metallurgical process, or metallic product, with the added comment that there is no evidence for that item. He then remarked:

> Metallurgy does not appear in the region under discussion until about the ninth century A.D. None of the foregoing technical demands are met by the archaeology of the region proposed as Book of Mormon lands and places. I regard this as a major weakness in the armor of our proponents and friends. (It is just as troublesome to the authors of the other correlations—those [who] have gone before—including Tom Ferguson.)
>   I doubt that the proponents will be very convincing, if they contend that evidence of metallurgy is difficult to find and a rarity in archaeology. Where mining was practiced—as in the Old Testament world—mountains of ore and tailings have been found. Artifacts of metal have been found. Art portrays the existence of metallurgical products. Again, the score is zero. In view of the magnitude of metallurgical skills and usage in the Book of Mormon, . . . plenty of evidence should have turned up by now in the regions pointed to in the primary papers of this symposium, if our friends have things pinpointed.[94]

---

[93]Roberts, "Difficulties," chap. ii, 22, in Roberts Collection; Roberts, *Studies of the Book of Mormon*, 107.

[94]Ferguson, "Written Symposium," 20-21, in Ferguson Collection, UU.

William J. Hamblin, professor of history at BYU, criticized those who see "large-scale metal 'industries'" among Book of Mormon peoples, affirming that the text "claims only that certain metals were known to the Nephites."[95] However, the Book of Mormon attributes advanced metallurgical skills to both Jaredites and Nephites, and John E. Clark, professor of anthropology at BYU, admitted that the Book of Mormon peoples had metallurgy.[96] Also, Glenna Nielsen Grimm said that "sophisticated metallurgical processes were engaged in that involved the mining and refining of both ferrous [i.e., iron] and non-ferrous ores."[97] Consider the impressive description of metallurgical technology during the time of Kish, a Jaredite king about 1,500 B.C.:[98]

> And they did work all manner of ore, and they did make gold, and silver, and iron, and brass, and all manner of metals; and they did dig it out of the earth; wherefore, they did cast up mighty heaps of earth to get ore, of gold, and of silver, and of iron, and of copper. And they did work all manner of fine work (Ether 10:23).

One must keep in mind the important distinction between mere metalworking and true metallurgy. Metalworking means the cold hammering and shaping of metal,[99] while metallurgy

---

[95]Hamblin, "Basic Methodological Problems," 191. Hamblin continued: "Thus it is only [Luke] Wilson's *interpretation* of the Book of Mormon claiming the existence of widespread iron *industries* in Pre-Classic Mesoamerica which cannot be reconciled with the archaeological record," with emphasis in original. Hamblin can only understand the Book of Mormon as not having metallurgy by ignoring—or reinterpreting—the passages that indicate such advanced skills.

[96]John E. Clark, "Book of Mormon Geography," in *Encyclopedia of Mormonism*, ed. Daniel H. Ludlow (New York: Macmillan Publishing Co., 1992), 1:178.

[97]Grimm, "Material Culture," in Sunstone Foundation Records.

[98]Sorenson, *Ancient American Setting,* 118.

[99]David A. Palmer, *In Search of Cumorah: New Evidences for the Book of Mormon from Ancient Mexico* (Bountiful, UT: Horizon Publishers, 1981), 114, incorrectly used the term "metallurgy," since his examples

requires temperatures of 700° to 800° C and involves some or all of the following technological processes: smelting, casting, gilding, annealing, soldering, and alloying.[100] The Book of Mormon does specify the practice of smelting among the Jaredites, for Ether explained that Shule "did molten out of the hill, and made swords out of steel" (Ether 7:9). It also refers to refining ore (Hel. 6:11).

Raymond Matheny described the metallurgical technology needed to produce iron objects:

> A ferrous industry is a whole system of doing something. It's just not an esoteric process that a few people are involved in, but ferrous industry—that means mining iron ores and then processing these ores and casting these ores into irons and then making steels and so forth —this is a process that's very complicated. . . . In other words, society would have to be organized at a certain level before ferrous industry would be feasible.
> The technology of mining is problematical for the Book of Mormon. Where do you find iron ores in sufficient quantity to create an industry? . . . No evidence has been found in the New World for ferrous metallurgical industry dating to pre-Columbian times. And so this is a king-size kind of problem, it seems to me, for so-called Book of Mormon archaeology. This evidence is absent.[101]

Matheny also pointed out that the extraction of iron from ore needs high temperatures and various fluxing substances which produce slag, which in turn become indestructible rock forms. In the 1920s B. H. Roberts summarized the situtation,

---

related to metalworking skills; cf. D. G. Matheny, "Does the Shoe Fit?" 289.

[100]Karen O. Bruhns, "The Crucible: Sociological and Technological Factors in the Delayed Diffusion of Metallurgy to Mesoamerica," in *New Frontiers in Archaeology of the Pacific Coast of Southern Mesoamerica*, ed. Frederick Bove and Lynette Heller (Tempe, AZ: Arizona State University, 1989), 224.

[101]R. T. Matheny, "Book of Moormon Archaeology," 22-23.

saying that "there is nothing on which the later investigators of our American antiquities are more unanimously agreed upon than the matter of the absence of the knowledge of, and hence the non-use of, iron or steel among the natives of America."[102] This condition concerning the complete absence of iron still exists today. The metalsmiths in Peru—not Mesoamerica—developed skills in gold and silver by 1,000 B.C., with copper working appearing about A.D. 500, but no pre-Columbian iron metallurgy developed anywhere in the New World.[103]

Historical and comparative linguistics of various Mesoamerican languages sometimes suggests the existence of a word for metal during the period from ca. 2,500 B.C. to A.D. 400.[104] Citing a study which proposed a word for metal in the reconstructed Proto-Mixtecan language, Sorenson said that "the researchers were puzzled by the fact that a word for 'metal' seemed to have existed in the protolanguage at about 1,000 B.C."[105] Sorensen misrepresented his source, since the linguists, Robert E. Longacre and René Millon, actually said:

---

[102]Roberts, "Book of Mormon Study," chap. viii, 7, in Box 9, Book 2, Roberts Collection; Roberts, *Studies of the Book of Mormon*, 198. Roberts wondered if Smith's error about the existence of iron in the Book of Mormon was perhaps due to Ethan Smith: "Could it be that Ethan Smith, influenced and misled by the reported discovery of the evidence of iron and its uses among the native Americans in ancient times, was innocently followed into this error by the author of the Book of Mormon?"

[103]Robert Raymond, *Out of the Fiery Furnace: The Impact of Metals on the History of Mankind* (University Park, PA: Pennsylvania State University Press, 1986), 22. The hammering of unsmelted meteoric iron is metalworking, not metallurgy.

[104]Roberto Escalante, "El vocabulario cultural de las lenguas de Mesoamérica," in *La validez teórica del concepto Mesoamérica*, X1X Mesa Redonda (Mexico City: Instituto Nacional de Antropología e Historia and Sociedad Mexicana de Anthropología, 1990), 156-61, concerning the reconstructed Proto-Mayan, Proto-Havean, and Proto-Otomanguean languages. Lyle Campbell and Terrence Kaufman, "A Linguistic Look at the Olmecs," *American Antiquity* 41 (January 1976): 85, 87-88, concerning the reconstructed Proto-Mixe-Zoquean language of about 1,500 B.C. Both of these sources quoted in Sorenson, "Viva Zapato!" 320.

[105]Sorenson, *Ancient American Setting*, 279.

The linguistic evaluation of a set provides the framework for its cultural evaluation, but however strong it may be linguistically this does not provide proof that the specific aspect of Proto-Mixtecan or Proto-Amuzgo-Mixtecan life it represents actually existed on that horizon. . . . For example, one set, linguistically evaluated as solid, reconstructs in Proto-Mixtecan with the meaning *bell* or perhaps *metal*. . . . The existence of metal or metal bells at this early date is highly improbable on the basis of existing archaeological evidence. Examination of the set suggests that the original meaning may have been *rattle* but it is impossible to be certain of this.[106]

Longacre and Millon explained that greater certainty is obtained when a group of related vocabulary terms describing a specific cultural practice is reconstructed for the protolanguage. The likelihood of the same "semantic shifts" having occurred in all of the words associated with such a practice is highly improbable. Longacre and Millon discussed six strong complexes of related terms: the Maize Complex, the Maguey Complex, the Agricultural Complex, the Masa Preparation Complex, the Weaving Complex, and the Palm Complex, but they referred again to the conjectured word for "metal" in a list of six terms excluded for various reasons.[107] This effort to determine vocabulary items in the Proto-Mixtecan language brought forth merely a conjectured word for either metal, or a bell, or a rattle, and not a group of related metallurgical terms. This certainly does not reveal names for many different kinds of metal, such as the numerous metals required by the Book of Mormon—(1) gold, (2) silver, (3) iron, (4) steel, (5) copper, (6) brass, and (7) an unknown substance named "ziff."

Sorenson suggested possible instances of early metal in Mesoamerica. The earliest copper known consists of a piece of

---

[106]Robert E. Longacre and René Millon, "Proto-Mixtecan and Proto-Amuzgo-Mixtecan Vocabularies: A Preliminary Cultural Analysis," *Anthropological Linguistics* 3 (April 1961): 22.

[107]Ibid., 24-25, 29.

sheeting from Cuicuilco in the valley of Mexico, which according to Sorenson probably dates to about the first century B.C.[108] However, Emil W. Haury, one of the archaeologists on the original project but not the one who actually removed the copper artifact from the ground, believed that "the Cuicuilco copper is assignable to the late period of Aztec dominance of the Valley of Mexico," as hinted by a mingling of Aztec pottery with Preclassic pottery on the mound, as well as the fact that copper sheeting and copper nails indicate later developments in metallurgy.[109]

In his annotated bibliography on the Book of Mormon metals, Sorenson classified each instance of metal in one of five groups as to the certainty of the identification, analysis, and dating.[110] These range from an "A" category, in which the item was uncovered by a professional archaeologist in a datable context, successively down to a fifth category, in which incomplete information made a reliable assessment difficult. Only two examples in Sorenson's "A" category fall within Book of Mormon times. The first find, which contains iron and copper, is described as "a metal-resembling substance, small, irregular shaped pieces."[111] It was found at Teotihuacán and is dated from A.D. 300 to 400. The second instance is a claw-shaped bead of the gold-copper alloy known as tumbaga, which was excavated at Altun Ha in northern Belize.[112] David M. Pendergast, archaeologist at the Royal Ontario Museum at Toronto, dated

---

[108]Sorenson, *Ancient American Setting*, 278.

[109]Emil W. Haury, "Cuicuilco in Retrospect," *The Kiva* 41 (Winter 1975): 199, quoted in D. G. Matheny, "Does the Shoe Fit?" 288.

[110]John L. Sorenson, *Metals and Metallurgy relating to the Book of Mormon Text* (Provo, UT: Foundation for Ancient Research and Mormon Studies, 1992), passim.

[111]Linné, *Mexican Highland Cultures*, 132.

[112]David M. Pendergast, "Tumbaga Object from the Early Classic Period, Found at Altun Ha, British Honduras (Belize)," *Science* 168 (3 April 1970): 117.

this metallic animal claw to "somewhat before A.D. 500," which would place it after the Book of Mormon, but Sorenson initially stretched this to include the hundred year period from A.D. 400 to 500, and then lowered it further to A.D. 350 to 450.[113] Both of these examples were found outside the area which Sorenson has proposed as Book of Mormon lands.

Deanne Matheny remarked concerning Sorenson's bibliographic study on metals:

> The question that has again not been considered [by Sorenson] is whether the specimens were of local manufacture or represent trade pieces from lower Central America. The majority of the specimens date to Late Classic times falling outside of the Book of Mormon period. The few that are genuinely Early Classic or slightly earlier seem to be trade pieces not produced in the area. We are still left with virtually the entire span of time covered by Book of Mormon events with no metallurgy in the area chosen by Sorenson.[114]

When metallurgy began in Mesoamerica during the Terminal Classic Period about the ninth century A.D., the tools and techniques were borrowed from Costa Rica and the Isthmus of Panama and ultimately from Andean South America.[115] From the third century A.D. onwards various metal objects were imported as trade goods into Mesoamerica from this southeastern place of manufacture. There is no evidence of pre-Columbian metallurgical production in Mesoamerica before the ninth century A.D.[116] Even though the use of metal is usually considered to be an important aspect in the growth of culture, all the civilizations in Mesoamerica developed with-

---

[113]Cf. variant dates in Sorenson, *Metals and Metallurgy*, 40, 69.

[114]D. G. Matheny, "Does the Shoe Fit?" 291.

[115]Bruhns, "Crucible," 221.

[116]Dorothy Hosler, *The Sounds and Colors of Power: The Sacred Metallurgical Technology of Ancient West Mexico* (Cambridge, MA: The Massachusetts Institute of Technology, 1994), 12.

out the use of metal.[117] By the time metal appeared the culture was beginning to decline.[118]

Metal Swords in the Book of Mormon

Because of the absence of metal swords in Mesoamerica, William J. Hamblin and the late A. Brent Merrill, who served as a major in the U.S. Air Force, proposed that "the most likely candidate for the Book of Mormon sword is the weapon known in Nahuatl as the *macuahuitl* or *macana*."[119] Hamblin and Merrill presented a number of parallels between the wooden *macuahuitl* and Book of Mormon swords, but they attempted to explain away specific statements that the latter swords were made of steel.[120] The Book of Mormon makes numerous references to swords, but most of these are ambiguous in the sense that they do not indicate the material from which the swords were made. The critical question is the type

---

[117]Dorothy Hosler, "Archaeometallurgy: The Development of Ancient Mesoamerican Metallurgy," *JOM [Journal of Minerals, Metals, and Materials Society]* 42 (May 1990): 44.

[118]Welch, *Finding Answers*, 9, who would like to have metallurgy in Mesoamerica during Book of Mormon times, misrepresented an article in *Scientific American*, referring to "the degree of sophistication now observable in the craftsmanship of ancient Mesoamerican metallurgists." However, Heather Lechtman, "Pre-Columbian Surface Metallurgy," *Scientific American* 250 (June 1984): 56-63, said nothing about Mesoamerican metallurgy, but rather dealt exclusively with the Chavin, the Moche, and the Chimú cultures of Andean South America

[119]William J. Hamblin and A. Brent Merrill, "Swords in the Book of Mormon," in *Warfare in the Book of Mormon*, ed. Stephen D. Ricks and William J. Hamblin (Salt Lake City: Deseret Book Co., 1990; Provo, UT: Foundation for Ancient Research and Mormon Studies, 1990), 338. Cf. D. G. Matheny, "Does the Shoe Fit?" 292-97.

[120]Hamblin and Merrill, "Swords," 342-43, also misinterpreted a metaphorical reference at Alma 24:12, which works perfectly well with steel swords, concerning the stains of sin being removed by God. James White, "Of Cities and Swords: The Impossible Task of Mormon Apologetics," *Christian Research Journal* (Summer 1996): 35, criticized Hamblin and Merrill for an "egregious redefinition of terms."

of material used for the sword—not whether the Aztec *macuahuitl* is defined as a sword, a broad-sword, or a club.[121] Early in Nephite history one of the original colonizers, Nephi, described his own sword-making activities and instructed his relatives and descendants how to work in various metals, including steel:

> And I, Nephi, did take the sword of Laban, and after the manner of it did make many swords, lest by any means the people who were called Lamanites should come upon us and destroy us. . . . And I did teach my people to build buildings, and to work in all manner of wood, and of iron, and of copper, and of brass, and of steel, and of gold, and of silver, and of precious ores, which were in great abundance (2 Ne. 5:14-15).

Thus, Nephite weapons included metal swords fashioned after Laban's sword. It is fortunate that there exists a detailed description of that sword:

> And I [Nephi] beheld his [Laban's] sword, and I drew it forth from the sheath thereof; and the hilt thereof was of pure gold, and the workmanship thereof was exceeding fine, and I saw that the blade thereof was of the most precious steel (1 Ne. 4:9).[122]

---

[121]William J. Hamblin, "An Apologist for the Critics: Brent Lee Metcalfe's Assumptions and Methodologies," review of "Apologetic and Critical Assumptions about the Book of Mormon Historicity," by Brent Lee Metcalfe, in *Review of Books on the Book of Mormon* 6, no. 1 (1994): 481-83. Summarizing Hamblin's research, Daniel C. Peterson, "LDS Scholars Refute Attacks on the Book of Mormon," *This People* 15 (Summer 1994): 31, sidestepped the issue of the metal swords of the Book of Mormon.

[122]Hamblin and Merrill, "Swords," 343, suggested that "a possible difficulty with interpreting the *macuahuitl* as the Book of Mormon sword concerns the five references in the Book of Mormon to drawing a sword." The passage of 1 Ne. 4:9 specifically mentions that the sword was drawn from its sheath, but Hamblin and Merrill discounted its applicability since reference is being made to Laban's sword from the Near East. The four other Book of Mormon passages have the wording "drew his sword" and for these cases they argued that "these references could describe grasping or brandishing a sword before combat rather than actually 'drawing' it from a sheath." Since it was published just one year before the Book of Mormon

Both the sharpness and the relative shortness of this steel-bladed sword is demonstrated by Nephi's grabbing the hair of Laban's head with one hand and decapitating him with his other hand wielding the sword (1 Ne. 4:18). Laban's early-sixth-century steel sword is consistent with what is known about the technology in the Near East, where carburizing and quenching iron was practiced to produce steel since about 800 B.C.[123] Jarom, though only a great-grandson of Lehi, lived at least until 238 years after Lehi had departed from Jerusalem. Jarom provided a description of the cultural achievements of his people in the fourth century B.C.:

> And we [the Nephites] multiplied exceedingly, and spread upon the face of the land, and became exceeding rich in gold, and in silver, and in precious things, and in fine workmanship of wood, in buildings, and in machinery, and also in iron and copper, and brass and steel, making all manner of tools of every kind to till the ground, and weapons of war—yea, the sharp pointed arrow, and the quiver, and the dart, and the javelin, and all preparations for war (Jarom 1:8).

The much earlier account of the Jaredites is recorded in the Book of Ether. Jared, one of the original colonists, had a great-grandson named Shule, whose time period has been estimated at ca. 2,800 B.C., which is much earlier than the Iron Age in the Old World. Ether indicated the metallurgical skills during this era:

> Wherefore, he [Shule] came to the hill Ephraim, and he did molten out of the hill, and made swords out of steel

---

was dictated, Noah Webster, *An American Dictionary of the English Language* (New York: S. Converse, 1828), provides a good indication of contemporary meanings. Webster gave as one of his forty definitions of the transitive verb "draw" the following: "to pull out, as to *draw* a sword or dagger from its sheath; to unsheathe," but not the meaning of brandishing a sword.

[123]Kenneth C. Barraclough, *Steelmaking before Bessemer* (London: Metals Society, 1984), 1:13.

for those whom he had drawn away with him; and after he had armed them with swords he returned to the city Nehor, and gave battle unto his brother Corihor, by which means he obtained the kingdom and restored it unto his father Kib (Ether 7:9).

Shule smelted suitable ore to make steel swords, so there is no rational way to interpret this passage as referring to wooden swords.[124] That Jaredite swords over two thousand years later at the end of their history were still made of metal blades is confirmed by an account elsewhere in the Book of Mormon. An exploratory party of forty-three Nephites discovered the remains of the Jaredites in the early second century B.C. King Limhi described what they found:

> And for testimony that the things that they had said are true they have brought twenty-four plates which are filled with engravings, and they are of pure gold. And behold, also, they have brought breastplates, which are large, and they are of brass and of copper, and are perfectly sound. And again, they have brought swords, the hilts thereof have perished, and the blades thereof were cankered with rust (Mosiah 8:9-11).

These Nephites discovered the land where more than two million Jaredites over a period of years lost their lives (Ether 15:1). In the end, only the historian Ether survived to write the story. Consequently, this description of the discovered remains of their armor and weapons provides a glimpse into the

---

[124]Hamblin and Merrill, "Swords," 347, suggested that one might "equate this Jaredite steel with the 'steel' of the King James translation of the Old Testament, which actually refers to the Hebrew word for 'bronze.'" According to Ludwig Koehler and Walter Baumgartner, *Hebräisches und aramäisches Lexikon zum Alten Testament*, ed. Johann J. Stamm, 3d ed. (Leiden: E. J. Brill, 1974), 3:647-48, 653, the Hebrew words *nᵉchûshᵃh* and *nᵉchosheth* mean copper, bronze, or brass. It is not clear why the KJV mistranslation would justify Joseph Smith mistranslating in the same way. Cf. Mark D. Thomas "Swords Cankered with Rust," review of *Warfare in the Book of Mormon*, ed. Stephen D. Ricks and William J. Hamblin, in *Sunstone* 15 (September 1991): 55, and William J. Hamblin, "Sharper Than a Two-Edged Sword," *Sunstone* 15 (December 1991): 54-55.

level of their technology near the end of their civilization. The handles of their swords, presumably made of wood, had disintegrated, but the metal blades had merely rusted. Thus, whether these Jaredite blades were made of iron, steel, or copper, metal swords were used among the Jaredites from about 2,800 B.C. to the end of their civilization.[125]   B. H. Roberts observed that "the Book of Mormon thoroughly commits us to the fact of the use of iron and steel among Book of Mormon peoples."[126]

The Maya in Mesoamerica were Stone Age people with offensive weapons such as knives, spears, lances, javelins, broadswords, battle-axes, war-clubs, and even a combination mace-dagger. The points or blades for these weapons were manufactured either from flint found in limestone beds or from obsidian located in volcanic lava flows. The weapons used by Mayan warriors can be documented from stone monuments, artwork on vases, ceramic statuettes, and surviving artifacts. The Mayan broadswords, which by the later Aztecs were called *macuahuitls*, were a "long and heavy double-edged flint-swords apparently designed to be held with two hands to be applied in close combat."[127]   The small flint or obsidian blades were inserted into groves on opposite sides of the wooden club, which in battle could be as deadly as a metal sword.   The Aztec oak

---

[125]D. G. Matheny, "Does the Shoe Fit?" 285, assumed that the blades of the Jaredite swords were made "of ferrous metal." Sorenson, "Viva Zapato!" 324, countered Matheny, correctly pointing out that the blades "could just as well have been copper, which also rusts."

[126]Roberts, "Difficulties," chap. ii, 22, in Roberts Collection; Roberts, *Studies of the Book of Mormon*, 107. The use of metal swords does not imply that the Book of Mormon peoples did not also have wooden weapons, for clubs are mentioned—probably made of wood. Both Nephites and Lamanites used clubs: Zeniff used them against the Lamanites (Mosiah 9:16), certain Lamanite prisoners employed clubs in an escape attempt (Alma 57:14), and some Lamanite robbers used clubs (Alma 17:36-37).

[127]Francis Robicsek, "The Weapons of the Ancient Maya," in *Circumpacifica*, ed. Bruno Illius and Matthias Laubscher (Frankfurt am Main: Peter Lang, 1990), 372.

broad sword (*macuahuitl*), which was two feet eight inches long, most likely was developed in the mid-fourteenth century.[128] When a Spanish conquistador armed with his steel sword fought an Aztec warrior with his wooden *macuahuitl* the similarity was immediately noticed and "the Aztec term *tepuz-macuahuitl* ('metal macuahuitl') was soon applied to the import."[129]

After examination of both the physical evidence in Mesoamerican archaeology and the textual evidence in the Book of Mormon, Deanne Matheny commented:

> [Prescott] Follett notes in his study of Maya weapons that what he classifies as the standard type of Maya *macuahuitl* is "more in the nature of a war-club or mace than the true broad-sword type of *macuahuitl*." ... I am aware of no evidence presently available suggesting the existence of the sword type of *macuahuitl* during the period covered by the Book of Mormon.
> ... There is never any indication in the Book of Mormon that the metal swords are not being referred to, and metal swords are the only type ever specifically mentioned.[130]

Accordingly, Ferguson's statement in his "Metallurgy Test" that the archaeology of Mesoamerica does not support the presence of metal implements during the Book of Mormon era still stands. The absence of Mesoamerican copper/bronze/brass metallurgy during Book of Mormon times and the complete absence of Mesoamerican iron metallurgy during any pre-Columbian time period constitute a major problem for the historicity of the Book of Mormon. This is especially the case

---

[128]Ross Hassig, *Mexico and the Spanish Conquest*, Modern Wars in Perspective (London and New York: Longman, 1994), 25. Cf. Ross Hassig, *War and Society in Ancient Mesoamerica* (Berkeley and Los Angeles and Oxford: University of California Press, 1992), 112, 231*n*27.

[129]Michael D. Coe, "Pre-Conquest America," in *Swords and Hilt Weapons*, ed. Anne Cope (London: Multimedia Books, 1993), 222.

[130]D. G. Matheny, "Does the Shoe Fit?" 296-97.

since it is known what kinds of stone weapons were used in Preclassic Mesoamerica.

No. 4—The Script Test of the Book of Mormon

The last major test—the "Script Test"—involves the identification of translatable inscriptions of a people. This is a crucial test, since a developed writing system is a hallmark of civilization. Ferguson felt that the "Script Test" was "the most exacting and definitive and precise of all,"[131] and suggested that New World inscriptions ought to be found in cuneiform (for the Jaredites) and Hebrew and Egyptian (for the Nephites). Nephi made the following statement at the beginning of the Book of Mormon:

> Yea, I make a record in the language of my father, which consists of the learning of the Jews and the language of the Egyptians. And I know that the record which I make is true; and I make it with mine own hand; and I make it according to my knowledge (1 Ne. 1:2-3).

Two divergent interpretations of this statement have been made by LDS scholars. Hugh Nibley, professor of history and religion at BYU, understood it to mean that the Nephite record was kept in the Egyptian language,[132] while John L. Sorenson interpreted it to indicate that the records were kept in the Hebrew language using Egyptian characters.[133] In the early fifth century A.D. Moroni explained about the records kept:

---

[131]Ferguson, "Written Symposium," 26, in Ferguson Collection, UU.

[132]Hugh Nibley, *Lehi in the Desert and the World of the Jaredites* (Salt Lake City: Bookcraft, 1952), 13-20; reprinted in *Lehi in the Desert, The World of the Jaredites, There Were Jaredites,* The Collected Works of Hugh Nibley, ed. John W. Welch (Salt Lake City: Deseret Book Co., 1988; Provo UT: Foundation for Ancient Research and Mormon Studies, 1988), 5:13-19.

[133]Sorenson, *Ancient American Setting,* 74-81.

And now, behold, we have written this record according to our knowledge, in the characters which are called among us the reformed Egyptian, being handed down and altered by us, according to our manner of speech. And if our plates had been sufficiently large we should have written in Hebrew; but the Hebrew hath been altered by us also; and if we could have written in Hebrew, behold, ye would have had no imperfection in our record (Morm. 9:32-33).

In 1971 Ferguson felt that a friend of his had succeeded in deciphering the Mayan hieroglyphs as a result of comparisons with the cuneiform texts of the ancient Assyrian language, but this premature finding was not confirmed by further research.[134] No cuneiform inscriptions have ever been discovered anywhere in the Americas.[135]

Ferguson discussed the evidence for Hebrew mentioned in a letter from George F. Carter, professor of geography at Texas A&M University: "A seal found at Tlatilco, a suburb of Mexico City, bears the Hebrew name, *Hiram*, apparently in Egyptian script! . . . A cylinder found at Tlatilco, Mexico, bearing a Hebrew name, *Hiram!* Wow!"[136] Ferguson accepted the Tlatilco seal as having Hebrew inscriptions, but there are serious problems in reading it as a Hebrew text. Carter quoted in his letter to Ferguson the entire proposed translation of the Tlatilco roller stamp as made by the maverick scholar Barry Fell: "Seal of King Shishak Hiram. Forgers will be decapi-

---

[134]Ferguson, letter to J. Willard Marriott, 30 March 1971, in the John Willard and Alice Sheets Marriott Collection, Manuscript 164, Box 17, Fd 15, Manuscripts Division, J. Willard Marriott Library, University of Utah, Salt Lake City.

[135]For Jean Frederic Waldeck's artistic creation of cuneiform markings, see the bottom-right glyph in fig. 30 of the author's *Quest for the Gold Plates*, 185.

[136]Ferguson, "Written Symposium," 24, with emphasis in original, in Ferguson Collection, UU.

tated."[137] Fell's identification and supposed translation have not passed the scrutiny of other scholars.[138] Though Carter originally accepted Fell's translation, he changed his mind and in 1989 affirmed that the Tlatilco seal did not contain the Hebrew word "Hiram."[139] Consequently, the purported evidence from Tlatilco must be ignored. By 1982 even Ferguson had concluded that there is no evidence of Hebrew in pre-Columbian America.[140]

Ferguson next discussed Egyptian inscriptions:

> Three glyphs on a three-inch cylinder seal, found at Chiapa de Corzo, state of Chiapas, Mexico, by the New

---

[137]George F. Carter, letter to Ferguson, 6 March 1975, in Ferguson Collection, UU. One's confidence in Fell's ability must plummet since he claimed to have translated the first line of a new version of the Anthon transcript (this version was "discovered" in 1980, but was later revealed to be a forgery of Mark Hofmann), as follows: "Revelation of Nefi: I have written these things , I, Nefi, a son born to sagacious parents." Cf. 1 Ne. 1:1 with Barry Fell, "An Enciphered Ancient Moorish Text," typescript, 1980, in the H. Michael Marquardt Collection, Accession 900, Box 105, Fd 6, Manuscripts Division, J. Willard Marriott Library, University of Utah, Salt Lake City; hereafter abbreviated to Marquardt Collection.

[138]Michael D. Coe, letter to author, 26 April 1988, in author's possession, said concerning Fell's translation: "As for the Tlatilco 'seal' (i.e., roller stamp), no reputable archaeologist believes that it has the name 'Hiram' on it—nor do they have any faith in any of Barry Fell's other dubious claims."

[139]George F. Carter, "Mexican Sellos: Writing in America, or the Growth of an Idea," in *Diffusion and Migration: Their Roles in Cultural Development*, ed. P. G. Duke et alia (Calgary: Chacmool, University of Calgary Archaeological Association, 1978), 187, 192, 201. George F. Carter, letter to author, 3 July 1989, in author's possession.

[140]Ferguson, letter to Robert M. Carmack, 7 January 1982, in Ferguson Collection, UU. William J. Hamblin, review of *Archaeology and the Book of Mormon*, by Jerald Tanner and Sandra Tanner, in *Review of Books on the Book of Mormon* 5 (1993): 260, 270-71, overstated the case when he claimed that "the Bat Creek inscription is now widely accepted as a Hebrew text." For the controversy concerning the authenticity of this A.D. 100 to 200 Hebrew inscription in Tennessee, see J. Huston McCulloch, "The Bat Creek Inscription: Did Judean Refugees Escape to Tennessee?" *Biblical Archaeology Review* 19 (July-August 1993): 46-53, 82-83; and P. Kyle McCarter, Jr., "Let's Be Serious about the Bat Creek Stone," *Biblical Archaeology Review* 19 (July-August 1993): 54-55, 83.

World Archaeological Foundation. Identified as Egyptian by only one great scholar, William Foxwell Albright (now deceased). Identification seriously questioned by other great scholars—because of the limited number of glyphs in the find. (Probably the biggest strike so far in support of our proponents—and the *only one* in this technical and demanding testing of their hypotheses).[141]

Ferguson admitted that this identification of Egyptian hieroglyphs in Mesoamerica is strongly questioned by other scholars.

Calendar Dates and Hieroglyphics Deciphered

In 1841 the American explorer John Lloyd Stephens said concerning the ruins of one of the Mayan cities:

One thing I believe, that its history is graven on its monuments. No Champollion has yet brought to them the energies of his enquiring mind. Who shall read them?[142]

After years of intense study of the fourteenth-century Codex Dresden, the clue written by a native Mayan scribe in the margin of the *Book of Chilam Balam of Mani* that a bar was the number five and a dot was the number one, and Alfred P. Maudslay's accurate drawings of the Copán stelae, the German scholar, Ernst W. Förstemann, first decoded complex Mayan calendrical texts in the 1880s. In 1905 J. Thomas Goodman proposed a correlation of Mayan dates to the European

---

[141]Ferguson, "Written Symposium," 24, with emphasis in original, in Ferguson Collection, UU. For the opinions of Matthew W. Stirling, J. Alden Mason, and David H. Kelley concerning this roller stamp, see the author's *Quest for the Gold Plates*, 61-62.

[142]John Lloyd Stephens, *Incidents of Travel in Central America, Chiapas, and Yucatan* (New York: Harper and Brothers, 1841), 1:159-60.

calendar.[143] For decades there were several competing theories concerning how the two dating systems should be aligned to each other.[144] However, the Goodman-Martínez-Thompson correlation, which was slightly revised from Goodman's original correlation, has won general acceptance since it has been independently confirmed by the latest refinement in radiocarbon dating.[145] In the Mayan system of bar-and-dot arithmetic, the numbers were indicated using three symbols: the dot for one, the bar for five, and a stylized shell for zero.

The Mayan had two systems of counting days. The *haab* or vague year consists of eighteen named months of twenty days each, with five extra days added at the end to make a 365-day year. The *tzolkin* or Sacred Round consists of twenty named days associated with thirteen consecutive numbers or a

---

[143]J. Thomas Goodman, "Maya Dates," *American Anthropologist 7* (October-November 1905): 642-47.

[144]Sharer, *Ancient Maya,* 575, pointed out that Herbert Spinden reduced all Mayan dates of the Goodman-Martínez-Thompson correlation by 256 years, George Vaillant added 256 years to such dates, and several correlations were based on the almanac in the Dresden Codex.

[145]A correlation problem of a different sort confronts students of the Book of Mormon. John L. Sorenson, "The Book of Mormon as a Mesoamerican Codex," *Newsletter and Proceedings of the S.E.H.A.,* no. 139 (December 1976): 8n55, explained the problem: "Nephite record allots just over '600 years' for the span in secular time from 597/6 B.C., Zedekiah's first regnal year, to 6/5 B.C., probably Christ's birth. If 600 360-day (Maya) tuns (i.e., one and one-half baktuns) is meant, the 591.36 sidereal years is covered quite precisely. If not, the chronology is inexplicable." However, the Mayan "tun" of the eighteen twenty-day months does not fit the Book of Mormon pattern of months within a year, since at Alma 49:1, 29, the eleventh month is near the end of the year, indicating a twelve-month year not an eighteen-month year. In order to cover the period from leaving Jerusalem in 587 (not 597) B.C. to the birth of Jesus in 5 B.C., Randall P. Spackman, *Introduction to Book of Mormon Chronology: The Principal Prophecies, Calendars, and Dates* (Provo, UT: Foundation for Ancient Research and Mormon Studies, 1993), 4, 15, 17, 28, 30, proposed that Lehi's prophecy of 600 years refers to twelve-moon years of 354 days each, reducing the period to 582 years. Spackman, ibid., 61, then suggested that from the birth of Jesus they used a 365-day solar year. Spackman's 354-day year has no parallel in Mesoamerica.

260-day cycle. Meshing the vague year with the Sacred Round produced the Calendar Round. Since there are 18,980 possible combinations between the two systems, the same sequence did not return until every fifty-two years. The basic unit in the Mayan Long Count (also called the Initial Series) was the day or *kin*. The multiples of days is as follows:

20 *kins*	=	1 *uinal* (20 days)
18 *uinals*	=	1 *tun* (360 days)
20 *tuns*	=	1 *katun* (7200 days)
20 *katuns*	=	1 *baktun* (144,000 days)

A Long Count date included these five divisions, along with the position in the Calendar Round when the date ended. The calendrical dates on Mayan monuments can be confidently read and correlated to our calendar.[146] The Mayan calendar can indicate extremely large numbers. For example, on Stela 1 at the ruins of Cobá in Quintana Roo appears the rare expanded date for the Mayan creation, which is so phenomenally large that 40,000,000,000,000,000,000,000,000,000,000 years—that is 40 octillion years—would have to pass away before the cycle would come around again![147]

Förstemann's solving of the Mayan calendar system was the first stage in breaking the code of the Mayan hieroglyphics. By the mid-twentieth century several discoveries moved studies

---

[146]Munro S. Edmonson, *The Book of the Year: Middle American Calendrical Systems* (Salt Lake City: University of Utah Press, 1988), 27, gave the earliest Long Count date as 36 B.C., which was discovered by Gareth Lowe at Chiapa de Corzo. Sharer, *Ancient Maya*, 622, indicated that the earliest known lowland Mayan inscription is the Tikal Stela 29 date of 292 B.C., but this is a typographical error for A.D. 292.

[147]George E. Stuart, "The Calendar," in Gene S. Stuart and George E. Stuart, *Lost Kingdoms of the Maya* (Washington, D.C.: National Geographic Society, 1993), 177. Stuart provided an analogy to help understand this huge span of years: "The interval is approximately equal to the fifteen-billion-year span that separates us from the cosmic "big bang" multiplied almost 3,000,000,000,000,000,000 times!"

dramatically forward. In the early 1950s Yuri V. Knorosov, a Russian epigrapher, began to decipher Mayan hieroglyphs when he discovered that the hieroglyphs were mixed with both words and syllables.[148] In 1958 Heinrich Berlin, a German epigrapher, discovered what he called "emblem glyphs" or hieroglyphic symbols indicating the names of particular cities or possibly the dynastic family ruling them for several generations.[149] Each emblem glyph functions similar to the way an image of the space needle identifies the city of Seattle in American culture since the 1960s. Emblem glyphs have been identified for a number of Mesoamerican sites.[150] In 1960 Tatiana Proskouria-koff, another Russian scholar, revealed the historical content of the Mayan inscriptions at Piedras Negras to such an extent that it can now be stated that "the figures which appear in Classic reliefs are not gods and priests but dynastic autocrats and their spouses, children, and subordinates."[151] In a very real sense carved representations which formerly were considered to be gods and underworld lords were transformed into actual people who had a place in Mayan history. In December 1973 the First Palenque Round Table became a landmark Mayan conference, due to the unique chemistry resulting from bringing traditional dirt archaeologists together with epigraphers, art historians,

---

[148] [Michael West, ed.,] "Knorosov in Mexico," *Institute of Maya Studies Newsletter* 24 (October 1995): 6.

[149] Charles Gallenkamp, *Maya: The Riddle and Rediscovery of a Lost Civilization*, 3d rev. ed. (New York: Viking, 1985), 118-19.

[150] Peter Mathews, *The Proceedings of the Maya Hieroglyphic Weekend, October 27-28, 1990, Cleveland State University*, ed. Phil Wanyerka (Austin, TX: Maya Hieroglyphic Weekend, 1991), 85-86, listed emblem glyphs for thirty-five sites.

[151] Michael D. Coe, *The Maya*, 5th ed., fully rev. and exp., Ancient Peoples and Places (London: Thames and Hudson, 1993), 196. See Tatiana Proskouriakoff, *Maya History*, ed. Rosemary A. Joyce (Austin, TX: University of Texas Press, 1993).

LAMAR PETERSEN

and astronomers at the very site of Mayan ruins.[152] At this conference Linda Schele and Peter Mathews announced that they had identified the dynastic successions of all Palenque rulers extending back to A.D. 465. With these important developments in deciphering Mayan hieroglyphics—not just calendar dates—year by year more glyphs are being translated.[153]

In his "Book of Mormon Difficulties" B. H. Roberts quoted Frederick S. Dellenbaugh to the effect that "no authentic trace of any Old World language thus far has been found on this [the American] continent.[154] In comparing Mesoamerican hieroglyphic writing with Egyptian hieroglyphs Linda Miller Van Blerkom of the anthropology department at the University of Colorado stated that "all six classes of signs which are found in word-syllabic writing systems [such as Egyptian] can be demonstrated for the Maya."[155] Such a comparison did not imply that the two languages are in any way related. Likewise, Joyce Marcus compared Egyptian writing and Mesoamerican writing merely "in its format and in its function"—but not as related writing systems.[156] Scholars today see no linguistic relationship

---

[152]Michael D. Coe, *Breaking the Maya Code* (New York: Thames and Hudson, 1992), 196.

[153]Linda Schele and Nikolai Grube, *The Proceedings of the Maya Hieroglyphic Workshop [on] Late Classic and Terminal Classic Warfare, March 11-12, 1995*, ed. Phil Wanyerka (Austin, TX: Maya Hieroglyphic Workshop, 1995).

[154]Roberts, "Difficulties," chap. i, 45, in Roberts Collection; Roberts, *Studies of the Book of Mormon*, 87. Welch, *Finding Answers*, 7, countered Roberts's statement by mentioning the research of Brian Stubbs in comparing Hebrew and Uto-Aztecan languages. Brian Stubbs, *Elements of Hebrew in Uto-Aztecan: A Summary of the Data* (Provo, UT: Foundation for Ancient Research and Mormon Studies, 1988), found a few unrelated correlations among thousands of grammatical possibilities.

[155]Linda Miller Van Blerkom, "A Comparison of Maya and Egyptian Hieroglyphics," *Katunob* 11, no. 3 (August 1979): 6.

[156]Joyce Marcus, *Mesoamerican Writing Systems: Propaganda, Myth, and History in Four Ancient Civilizations* (Princeton, NJ: Princeton University Press, 1992), 19.

between any native American language or script and "ancient Egyptian, Sumarian/Akkadian, or Hebrew languages or writing systems."[157] Gordon R. Willey, formerly on the board of directors of the New World Archaeological Foundation, stated that no relationships have been established between a native American Indian language and any Old World language.[158]

The four main Mesoamerican writing systems are the Aztec, Mixtec, Zapotec, and Maya. However, both the Mixtec and Aztec developed in the Post-Classic Period, dating from the tenth century A.D.[159] The origins of the Mayan hieroglyphic system are unclear but it is often considered the most significant cultural achievement in the New World. The hieroglyphs inscribed on stone monuments are a later development of inscriptions on other media. There are indications that an ancient place name has survived up to the present.[160] However, no personal or place names in the Book of Mormon have been discovered or deciphered—except biblical names discovered in Old World sites. Especially now that the Mayan writing system can be understood to a great degree, this lack of confirmation has become a serious problem for the Book of Mormon.

---

[157]Edward H. Ashment, "'A Record in the Language of My Father': Evidence of Ancient Egyptian and Hebrew in the Book of Mormon," in *New Approaches to the Book of Mormon: Explorations in Critical Methodology*, ed Brent Lee Metcalfe (Salt Lake City: Signature Books, 1993), 341.

[158]Gordon R. Willey, *An Introduction to American Archaeology* (Englewood Cliffs, NJ: Prentice-Hall, 1966), 1:17. Willey, ibid., 1:25n20, added in an endnote that the sole exception to this statement is the Eskimo language, which "is the same in America and Siberia." Joseph H. Greenberg, *Language in the Americas* (Stanford, CA: Stanford University Press, 1987), 331, also argued for the genetic unity of New World languages, except for the Na-Dene and Eskimo-Aleut families.

[159]Marcus, *Mesoamerican Writing Systems*, 29.

[160]David Stuart, *The Yaxhá Emblem Glyph as Yax-ha* (Washington, D.C: Center for Maya Research, 1985), 4, said: "I therefore propose that the place name Yaxha was used during the Classic Period, probably in reference to both the site and the lake which go by this same name today." See David Stuart and Stephen D. Houston, *Classic Maya Place Names* (Washington, D.C: Dumbarton Oaks Research Library, 1994).

Ferguson's Dilemma about the Book of Mormon

Ferguson's 1975 listing of problems remains unanswered twenty-three years later. Thus, these points still stand as serious obstacles to authenticating the Book of Mormon. In his study Ferguson remarked that no one, "from Joseph Smith to the present day, has put his finger on a single point of terrain that was a Book of Mormon geographical place."[161]

Hugh Nibley explained concerning the Book of Mormon:

> We can never prove absolutely that the Book of Mormon is what it claims to be; but any serious proven fault in the work would at once condemn it. If I assume the Book of Mormon to be fraudulent, then whatever is correct in it is merely a lucky coincidence, devoid of any real significance. But if I assume that it is true, then any suspicious passage is highly significant and casts suspicion on the whole thing, no matter how much of it is right.[162]

---

[161]Ferguson, "Written Symposium," 4, in Ferguson Collection, UU. T. Michael Smith, "A New Discovery and Caution," *Ancient America Foundation Newsletter*, no. 3 (December 1994): 4, also stated: "We don't yet have a verified first-ever 'Mesoamerican site to Book of Mormon text site' correspondence." For an RLDS perspective on the Book of Mormon, see the articles in Raymond C. Treat, ed., *Recent Book of Mormon Developments: Articles from the Zarahemla Record* (Independence, MO: Zarahemla Research Foundation, 1992). However, compare Alison V. P. Coutts, "Earnestly Seeking," review of *Recent Book of Mormon Developments*, by Raymond Treat, in *Review of Books on the Book of Mormon* 7, no. 2 (1995): 253-55.

[162]Hugh Nibley, "New Approaches to Book of Mormon Study: Part I, Some Standard Tests," *The Improvement Era* 56 (November 1953): 831. The text quotes Nibley's words as expressed in 1953, but most of these words were intentionally deleted and replaced in the 1989 F.A.R.M.S. reprint, *The Prophetic Book of Mormon*, The Collected Works of Hugh Nibley, ed. John W. Welch (Salt Lake City: Deseret Book Co., 1989; Provo UT: Foundation for Ancient Research and Mormon Studies, 1989), 8:56, by the revised wording: "Thus, while we can never prove absolutely that the Book of Mormon is what it claims to be, we are justified at the outset in assuming that it is what it claims to be. If one assumes that it is true, its features at least become testable." The reprint also eliminated the following analogy by Nibley concerning a counterfeit dollar bill: "The reader cannot

In establishing the ambitious program for the New World Archaeological Foundation, Ferguson essentially followed the procedure outlined by Nibley, in which one began with the assumption that the Book of Mormon was true.[163]

Ferguson concluded his study for this written symposium with the remark that the meager amount of specific support for the Book of Mormon left him in a real dilemma. Ferguson then referred to Dee F. Green, assistant professor of anthropology at Weber State College, who made the following declaration:

> The first myth we need to eliminate is that Book of Mormon archaeology exists. Titles on books full of archaeological half-truths, dilettanti on the peripheries of American archaeology calling themselves Book of Mormon archaeologists regardless of their education, and a Department of Archaeology at BYU devoted to the production of Book of Mormon archaeologists do not insure that Book of Mormon archaeology really exists. The Book of Mormon is really there so we *can* have Book of Mormon studies, and archaeology is really there so we can study archaeology, but the two are not wed. *At least they are not wed in reality since no Book of Mormon location is known with reference to topography.*[164]

Concerning this statement about there being no real archaeology of the Book of Mormon, Ferguson wishfully remarked: "I,

---

produce absolute proof that the dollar bill in his pocket is genuine; it may look all right even to the trained eye and still contain minute evidence of counterfeiting which escape[s] the expert; but if there is anything obviously wrong with it, we then have absolute proof that it is counterfeit."

[163]Ferguson's intense belief in the Book of Mormon during the 1930s, 1940s, 1950s, and early 1960s contrasts sharply with the early skepticism of Fawn M. Brodie and Dale L. Morgan. See Gary F. Novak, "Naturalistic Assumptions and the Book of Mormon," *Brigham Young University Studies* 30 (Summer 1990): 24-30.

[164]Dee F. Green, "Book of Mormon Archaeology: The Myths and the Alternatives," *Dialogue: A Journal of Mormon Thought* 4 (Summer 1969): 77, with emphasis in original.

for one, would be happy if Dee were wrong."[165]

Ferguson told Ronald O. Barney, an employee of the LDS Church's Historical Department, about the following episode which occurred during a board meeting of the New World Archaeological Foundation sometime after 1967, and probably after Ferguson had prepared his 1975 archaeological study. In Barney's words:

> Ferguson felt that he really made a point in telling me about his experience with the New World Archaeological Foundation after rejecting the Book of Mormon. He said that at one of their professional meetings he presented a list of some claims that the Book of Mormon made concerning the material culture that ought to have remained if there really was a Book of Mormon people in Central or South America. . . . He said that the leading men there could offer no explanation as to why these things did not exist in archaeological digs. The lack of these artifacts was a very important evidence to him that the Book of Mormon was a fanciful attempt at creating the divine here on the earth.[166]

Along with his 1976 letter to Harold W. Lawrence, Ferguson sent a copy of his 1975 "Written Symposium on Book of Mormon Geography," and explained concerning the Book of Mormon that "what is in the ground [archaeologically] will never conform to what is in the book" because it is fiction produced by Joseph Smith.[167]

---

[165]Ferguson, "Written Symposium," 29, in Ferguson Collection, UU.

[166]Ronald O. Barney, interview with Ferguson, 4 January 1983, typed on 19 April 1984, in Box 77, Fd 13, Marquardt Collection.

[167]Ferguson, letter to Mr. and Mrs. Harold W. Lawrence, 20 February 1976, in Ferguson Collection, UU. Recently some have not considered the antiquity or modernity of the Book of Mormon as an either/or issue. For example, Blake T. Ostler, "The Book of Mormon as a Modern Expansion of an Ancient Source," *Dialogue: A Journal of Mormon Thought* 20 (Spring 1987): 66-123, argued a middle-of-the-road position that the Book of Mormon contains both translations of ancient texts and nineteenth-century "expansions" authored by Joseph Smith. For responses to Ostler, see Stephen E. Robinson, "The 'Expanded' Book of Mormon?" in *The Book of*

John L. Sorenson, who did not indicate whether or not he was referring specifically to Ferguson's 1975 analysis, expressed his opinion concerning Ferguson:

> He was not one whose careful "study" led him to see greater light, light that would free him from Latter-day Saint dogma, as [Charles M.] Larson represents. Instead he was just a layman, initially enthusiastic and hopeful but eventually trapped by his unjustified expectations, flawed logic, limited information, perhaps offended pride, and lack of faith in the tedious research that real scholarship requires. The negative arguments he used against the Latter-day Saint scriptures in his last years display all these weaknesses.[168]

Sorenson's rather harsh indictment of Ferguson's efforts requires some comment. True, Ferguson was not a professional archaeologist, but he was convinced that his expectations were justified. Also, Ferguson would disagree vehemently with Sorenson's criticism about his lacking "faith in the tedious research that real scholarship requires," since it was Ferguson's strong belief in the value of the careful research carried out by competent scholars that helped him form his arguments concerning the archaeological problems of the Book of Mormon.

Sorenson's characterization ignored Ferguson's deep-seated desire to follow the truth wherever it led him—even if it took him far from the fervent convictions of his youth. On the other hand, Jerald and Sandra Tanner overstated the case when they asserted that "Ferguson believed that archaeology

---

Mormon: Second Nephi, the Doctrinal Structure, ed. Monte S. Nyman and Charles D. Tate, Jr. (Provo, UT: Religious Studies Center, Brigham Young University, 1989), 391-414; and Robert L. Millet, "The Book of Mormon, Historicity, and Faith," *Journal of Book of Mormon Studies* 2 (Fall 1993): 4, reprinted in Robert L. Millet, *The Power of the Word: Saving Doctrines from the Book of Mormon* (Salt Lake City: Deseret Book Co., 1994), 292-93.

[168]John L. Sorenson, "Addendum," to John Gee's review of *By His Own Hand upon Papyrus: A New Look at the Joseph Smith Papyri,* by Charles M. Larson, in *Review of Books on the Book of Mormon* 4 (1992): 119.

disproved the Book of Mormon."[169] For Ferguson, when asked if it was really true that he had found no evidence for the Book of Mormon, responded by saying that the question was too general, since "some [archaeological] findings tend to support —some tend to contradict" the Book of Mormon and "archaeology casts grave doubt on Bk. of Abraham and some doubt on Bk. of Mormon."[170] So, while the absence of archaeological evidence can never disprove the Book of Mormon, it does cast some suspicion on it, especially since the plant, animal, technological, and literary evidence during the Preclassic time period in Mesoamerica paints a clearer picture year by year.

Sorenson classified his own Book of Mormon geography as sometimes being "probable," and then added "if the shoe fits, wear it."[171] Deanne Matheny concluded her critique of Sorenson:

> For me these models [by Hauck and Sorenson] require too many changes and arbitrary interpretations, too many deviations from the plain meaning of the words in the text of the Book of Mormon, for either of them to achieve even a partial fit with the geographical and archaeological evidence. . . .
> Does the shoe fit for the current Limited Tehuántepec theory models? Rather than a comfortable "Cinderella" fit, it is more like a "step-sister" mismatch, requiring considerable remodeling of shoe and foot.[172]

Likewise, Ferguson responded to Sorenson's earlier geo-

---

[169]Jerald Tanner and Sandra Tanner, "Ferguson's Two Faces: Mormon Scholar's 'Spoof' Lives on after His Death," *Salt Lake City Messenger*, no. 69 (September 1988): 7, with emphasis in original.

[170]Ferguson, handwritten response on letter of J. Don Cerchione to Ferguson, 21 July 1976, in Ferguson Collection, UU.

[171]Sorenson, *Ancient American Setting*, 188.

[172]D. G. Matheny, "Does the Shoe Fit?" 321-22. Sorenson, "Viva Zapato!" 301, remained unconvinced by D. G. Matheny's review and answered her by saying, "Yes, the shoe fits—a little stiffly but about as well as most new shoes that need getting used to."

graphical study—which was titled with the question "Where in the World?"—by answering that Book of Mormon geography exists nowhere in the real world. Describing his own 1975 study, Ferguson divulged that "the real implication of the paper is that you can't set Book of Mormon geography down any-where—because it is fictional and will never meet the require-ments of the dirt-archaeology." [173] In his view the Book of Mormon is not a translated account of historical peoples, but a fictional story concocted by Joseph Smith, perhaps with the assistance of one or two others. In what is essentially a response to Ferguson's skepticism, David A. Palmer said: "To say that there is no Book of Mormon geography is to me absurd. There is a geography. I believe that the Book of Mormon history occurred in real time and space."[174] Sorenson was also aware of Ferguson's liberal position and expressed the options as follows: "Either the Book of Mormon promised land was in some portion of Mesoamerica or it was nowhere."[175]

At the Sunstone Symposium in 1984 Raymond Matheny summarized the Book of Mormon problem in a way very much like Ferguson's assessment:

> All these [Book of Mormon cultural traits] paint a scene that seems to be quite foreign to what I am familiar with in the archaeological record of the New World.... And the terminologies and the language used and the meth-ods of explaining and putting things down are nine-teenth century literary concepts and cultural experi-ences one would expect Joseph Smith and his colleagues

---

[173]Ferguson, letter to Lawrences, 20 February 1976, in Ferguson Col-lection, UU.

[174]David A. Palmer, "Symposium on Book of Mormon Geography: Re-sponse of David A. Palmer to Papers by V. G. Norman and J. L. Sorenson," typescript, April 1975, 13, in Tolman Collection.

[175]John L. Sorenson, quoted in Bergera and Priddis, *Brigham Young University*, 85. In a similar manner Sorenson, *Ancient American Setting*, 31, stated: "One point needs to be emphasized: the Book of Mormon account actually did take place *some*where," with emphasis in original.

would experience. . . . If I were doing this cold like John Carlson is here, I would say in evaluating the Book of Mormon that it had no place in the New World whatsoever. . . . It seems like these are anachronisms. It seems like the items are out of time and place, in trying to put them into the New World. And I think there's a great difficulty here for we Mormons in understanding what this book [of Mormon] is all about.[176]

B. H. Roberts, after demonstrating in the Book of Mormon the similarity of the character traits of the three anti-Christs named Sherem, Nehor, and Korihor, reluctantly stated:

They are all of one breed and brand; so nearly alike that one mind is the author of them, and that a young and undeveloped, but piously inclined mind. The evidence I sorrowfully submit, points to Joseph Smith as their creator. It is difficult to believe that they are the product of history, that they come upon the scene separated by long periods of time, and among a race which was the ancestral race of the red man of America.[177]

---

[176]R. T. Matheny, "Book of Mormon Archaeology," 25-26, 30-31. The typescript has "and trying to put them into the New World," but to make sense the "and" has been changed to an "in." R. T. Matheny, in a 1992 letter quoted in Hamblin, "Basic Methodological Problems," 190, explained that "the question [to which he was asked to respond at the 1984 Sunstone Symposium] dealt with how does a non-Mormon archaeologist evaluate the Book of Mormon in terms of its cultural content and claims. My answer to the question was an *ad hoc* response where I tried to put myself in a non-Mormon's professional shoes and talked about the nature of the problems that the Book of Mormon poses for the archaeologist."

[177]Roberts, "Book of Mormon Study," part II, chap. iii, 13-14, in Roberts Collection; Roberts, *Studies of the Book of Mormon*, 271. For a reproduction of a page from Roberts's "Book of Mormon Study," see fig. 27 of the author's *Quest for the Gold Plates*, 148. A little later, after comparing the final battles of the Jaredites and Nephites, B. H. Roberts, "Book of Mormon Study," part II, chap. iv, 17; Roberts, *Studies of the Book of Mormon*, 283, asked: "Is all this sober history inspired written and true, representing things that actually happened? Or is it a wonder-tale of an immature mind, unconscious of what a test he is laying on human credulity when asking men to accept his narrative as a solemn history?"

Michael D. Coe, professor of anthropology at Yale University, offered some suggestions to Mormons:

> Forget the so-far fruitless quest for the Jaredites, Nephites, Mulekites, and the lands of Zarahemla and Bountiful: there is no more chance of finding them than of discovering the ruins of the bottomless pit described in the book of Revelation. . . . Continue the praiseworthy excavations in Mexico, remembering that little or nothing pertaining to the Book of Mormon will ever result from them.[178]

Likewise, Ferguson found that the known archaeology of Mesoamerica does not fit the requirements of the Book of Mormon. This raised for him serious questions about the antiquity of the volume. From his youth he had assumed that the Book of Mormon was historical—and had believed in it intensely—but during the last thirteen years of his life Ferguson maintained that that assumption was wrong and the best explanation was found in Joseph Smith and his nineteenth century environment.[179]

The Contributions of Tom Ferguson

Ferguson's odyssey was an attempt at verification of the historical claims of the Book of Mormon. His early faith concerning the Book of Mormon is exemplified in a 1957 assessment addressed to the LDS First Presidency: "To me, the Book

---

[178]Michael D. Coe, "Mormons and Archaeology: An Outside View," *Dialogue: A Journal of Mormon Thought* 8, no. 2 (1973): 48, with Coe's plural "Revelations" having been corrected. For an explanation of the methods and theory of archaeology, see Wendy Ashmore and Robert J. Sharer, *Discovering Our Past: A Brief Introduction to Archaeology*, 2d ed. (Mountain View, CA: Mayfield Publishing Co., 1996).

[179]For a criticism of an environmental explanation of the Book of Mormon, see Gary F. Novak, "Examining the Environmental Explanation of the Book of Mormon," review of *Joseph Smith's Response to Skepticism*, by Robert N. Hullinger, in *Review of Books on the Book of Mormon* 7, no. 1 (1995): 139-54.

of Mormon is like a sleeping volcano, ready to burst forth with knowledge of greatest import for the whole world."[180] This book was the love of his life—second only to his family. Providing archaeological support for the Book of Mormon, Ferguson explained, was his own "magnificent obsession" in life.[181]

Fred W. Nelson, Jr., radiation safety officer at Brigham Young University, described Ferguson's effect on how Mormons relate Mesoamerican cultures with the Book of Mormon:

> It would be fair to say that his books, along with the many lectures he gave throughout his life, have had a great influence on the general membership of the LDS Church with regard to how they relate to the Book of Mormon and archaeology.[182]

Ferguson possessed a dynamic personality and an enthusiasm that was contagious among the people with whom he worked. Though he was only an amateur archaeologist, he was an independent thinker who plunged seriously into his cause. Ferguson was the indispensable force behind the founding of the New World Archaeological Foundation in 1952.[183] In spite of the fact, as one Mormon scholar said, that "there have been no spectacular finds (from the Book of Mormon point of view), no Zarahemlas discovered, no gold plates brought to light, no horses uncovered, and King Benjamin's tomb remains

---

[180]Ferguson, letter to the First Presidency, 22 November 1957, in Ferguson Collection, BYU.

[181]Ferguson, letter to Allie [Alice] Marriott, 7 September 1954, in Ferguson Collection, BYU, alluding to the 1954 Universal motion picture, based on Lloyd C. Douglas's novel, *Magnificent Obsession*.

[182]Fred W. Nelson, Jr., "In Honor of Thomas Stuart Ferguson," *Newsletter and Proceedings of the S.E.H.A.*, no. 161 (May 1987): 2.

[183]For a bibliography of publications of the New World Archaeological Foundation, see Thomas A. Lee, Jr., *New World Archaeological Foundation Obra, 1952-1980* (Provo UT, and San Cristóbal de las Casas, Chiapas: New World Archaeological Foundation, 1981).

unexcavated,"[184] still Ferguson's key involvement with the New World Archaeological Foundation will be his lasting accomplishment, for it became a major force in the Preclassic archaeology of Mesoamerica. The non-Mormon archaeologist Michael D. Coe expressed admiration concerning the role that Ferguson played:

> While the guiding light of this [NWAF] endeavor, Ferguson, was also an Iron Rod, from the beginning everything was put on what non-Mormons would consider a scholarly underpinning.... There can be no question that the New World Archaeological Foundation's program has been an unqualified success.... Credit for this goes to the foresight of Ferguson and the original directors....[185]

The professional archaeological investigations of the now essentially-defunct New World Archaeological Foundation into the origins of Mesoamerican civilization owe much to the work of Ferguson. It is unfortunate that—just because archaeological confirmation of the Book of Mormon has not come forth as anticipated by both Ferguson and the Mormon Church leaders who funded the foundation—the Church has decided to reduce the New World Archaeological Foundation to a token organization.

Ferguson's Resolution of the Dilemma

Ferguson's quest did not follow a straight course. He lived his life as a dedicated Latter-day Saint, expecting with the certainty of the true believer that he would find archaeological proof of the historical authenticity of the Book of Mormon. However, the physical evidence he looked so diligently for did

---

[184]Green, "Book of Mormon Archaeology," 77. The horses which have been discovered are either Pleistocene fossils or post-Conquest bones, but not during the Book of Mormon time span.

[185]Coe, "Mormons and Archaeology," 45-46.

not come forth. In the end, Ferguson was theologically ship-
wrecked less by the failure to find persuasive archaeological
support for the Book of Mormon than by his encounter with
independent translations of the Joseph Smith Egyptian papyri.
Though his ship ran aground, it did not sink, and he managed
to salvage what he felt were its essentials. Ferguson himself
used nautical imagery, saying that he wanted "to stay aboard
the good ship, Mormonism—for various reasons that I think
valid."[186]

Ferguson's odyssey traversed the whole gamut of firm
faith, exciting exploration, devastating doubt, and calm con-
tentment. Garth N. Jones, speaking at the 1989 Sunstone
Symposium held at the University of Utah, summarized
Ferguson's point of view near the end of his life:

> Ferguson experienced an odyssey with all of its seren-
> dipitous beauties and qualities. He died a wise and
> tolerant person, understanding the importance of myth
> in human affairs.... Ferguson understood and appreci-
> ated the good qualities of the LDS Church and its
> community of believers.[187]

Throughout the last thirteen years of his life Ferguson
was a broad-minded humanist. In the most-recent Ferguson
letter to have been discovered, he explained his position:

> Now that my eyes have been opened. . . , I see more
> clearly into many other conflicts and problems the
> Prophet [Joseph Smith] had, and have conviction that
> he was a phony with lots of meritorious ideas. I have
> decided not to attack him openly—in my opinion, now,
> all religions are man-made, and most of them do more

---

[186]Ferguson, letter to Lawrences, 9 February 1976, in Ferguson Collection, UU.

[187]Garth N. Jones, response to the author's "Odyssey of Thomas Stuart
Ferguson," typescript, 1989, 2-3, in the Garth N. Jones Collection, Acces-
sion 1557, Manuscripts Division, J. Willard Marriott Library, University of
Utah, Salt Lake City.

228

good than harm—so let them be.[188]

If one were a satisfied, active Mormon, Ferguson would not want that person to change. If one decided that the Book of Mormon was composed by Joseph Smith, he counseled him/her to stay in the LDS Church and keep quiet, in order to enjoy the benefits of being a member. If one could not follow this path but felt the need to leave the LDS Church, he encouraged that person to do so. If one were happy as an orthodox Christian, his advice was, stay that way. The bottom line of Ferguson's position was that whatever works for a person and gives meaning to life was, by definition, good for that person.

One may feel that Ferguson's ideas are completely mistaken, or one may feel that his reconciliation of the conflict between faith and reason is a worthwhile solution. Given Ferguson's own disillusionment, one must give him credit for having resolved the dilemma to his personal satisfaction, for he was at peace with himself and often spoke of the need to consider the Big Picture. However, it would be unfair to Ferguson to say that he completely lost faith in Mormonism. He continued his church activity and he justified his sometimes waffling behavior on various social and cultural grounds. He saw many beneficial things in the religions of mankind, and Mormonism was to him the most useful—but not ultimately true.

Though Ferguson doubted that Joseph Smith could translate Egyptian texts, though he repudiated the antiquity of the Book of Abraham, though he rejected the authenticity of the Book of Mormon, though he questioned that Joseph Smith or anyone else was a true prophet of God—still he considered the LDS Church to be a wonderful fraternity, valued church activity and fellowship, sang in his ward choir, appreciated the moral principles of the Book of Mormon, developed a more

---

[188]Ferguson, letter to George F. Carter, 24 May 1977, in Ferguson Collection, UU, which letter was donated in January 1996.

tolerant attitude about the opinions of others, felt that religion served a genuine need in human life, found relaxation in working in the garden, and enjoyed life immensely. In fact Thomas Stuart Ferguson was playing tennis when a massive heart attack brought immediate death on 16 March 1983 at the age of sixty-seven.[189] His legacy is a commitment to the search for truth.

---

[189]His death certificate gave the cause of death as "arteriosclerotic heart disease and hypertension."

Selected
Bibliography

Allen, James B. "Eight Contemporary Accounts of Joseph Smith's First Vision: What Do We Learn from Them?" *The Improvement Era* 73 (April 1970): 4-13.

Anderson, Richard L. *Investigating the Book of Mormon Witnesses*. Salt Lake City: Deseret Book Co., 1981.

_____. "Personal Writings of the Book of Mormon Witnesses." In *Book of Mormon Authorship Revisited: The Evidence for Ancient Origins*, ed. Noel B. Reynolds, 40-60. Provo, UT: Foundation for Ancient Research and Mormon Studies, 1997.

Anderson, Rodger I. *Joseph Smith's New York Reputation Reexamined*. Salt Lake City: Signature Books, 1990.

Arrington, Leonard J. "Joseph Fielding Smith: Faithful Historian." *Dialogue: A Journal of Mormon Thought* 7 (Spring 1972): 21-24.

Ashment, Edward H. "'A Record in the Language of My Father': Evidence of Ancient Egyptian and Hebrew in the Book of Mormon." In *New Approaches to the Book of Mormon: Explorations in Critical Methodology*, ed. Brent Lee Metcalfe, 329-93. Salt Lake City: Signature Books, 1993.

Ashmore, Wendy, and Robert J. Sharer. *Discovering Our Past: A Brief Introduction to Archaeology*. 2d ed. Mountain View, CA: Mayfield Publishing Co., 1996.

Austin, Emily M. *Mormonism; or, Life among the Mormons,*

Being an Autobiographical Sketch, Including an Experience of Fourteen Years of Mormon Life. Madison, WI: M. J. Cantwell, 1882.

Bacheler, Origen. *Mormonism Exposed, Internally and Externally*. New York, 1838.

Backman, Milton. V., Jr. *Joseph Smith's First Vision: Confirming Evidences and Contemporary Accounts*. 2d ed., rev. and enl. Salt Lake City: Bookcraft, 1980.

Bacon, Francis. *Essays*. Ed. Michael J. Hawkins. London: Everyman, 1994.

Bean, Willard. *A. B. C. History of Palmyra and the Beginning of "Mormonism."* Palmyra, NY: Palmyra Courier Co., 1938.

B[enton], A[bram] W. "Mormonites." *Evangelical Magazine and Gospel Advocate* 2 (9 April 1831): 120.

Bergera, Gary James, and Ronald Priddis. *Brigham Young University: A House of Faith*. Salt Lake City: Signature Books, 1985.

Best, Karl F. "Changes in the Revelations, 1833-1835." *Dialogue: A Journal of Mormon Thought* 25 (Spring 1992): 87-112.

Birrell, Verla L. *The Book of Mormon Guide Book*. Salt Lake City, 1948.

Blanton, Richard E. et alia. *Ancient Mesoamerica: A Comparison of Change in Three Regions*. 2d ed. Cambridge, England: Cambridge University Press, 1993.

Bloom, Harold. *The American Religion: The Emergence of the Post-Christian Nation*. New York: Simon and Schuster, 1992.

Bove, Frederick, and Lynette Heller. *New Frontiers in Archaeology of the Pacific Coast of Southern Mesoamerica*. Tempe, AZ: Arizona State University, 1989.

Bowen, Albert E. *Constancy amid Change*. Salt Lake City: The Deseret News Press, 1944.

Braden, Clark, and E. L. Kelly. *Public Discussion of the Issues between the Reorganized Church of Jesus Christ of Latter*

Day Saints and the Church of Christ (Disciples), held in Kirtland, Ohio. St. Louis, MO: Christian Publishing Co, 1884; reprint, Rosemead, CA: Old Paths Book Club, 1955.

Brodie, Fawn M. *No Man Knows My History: The Life of Joseph Smith, The Mormon Prophet.* 2d ed., rev. and enl. New York: Vintage Books, a division of Random House, Inc., 1995.

Brooks, Juanita, ed. *On the Mormon Frontier: The Diary of Hosea Stout, 1844-1861.* 2 vols. Salt Lake City: University of Utah Press and Utah State Historical Society, 1982.

Bush, Lester E., Jr. "The Spaulding Theory Then and Now." *Dialogue: A Journal of Mormon Thought* 10 (Autumn 1977): 40-69.

Bushman, Richard L. *Joseph Smith and the Beginnings of Mormonism.* Urbana, IL: University of Illinois Press, 1984.

_____. "The Visionary World of Joseph Smith." *Brigham Young University Studies* 37, no. 1 (1997-1998): 183-204.

Call, Lamoni. *2000 Changes in the Book of Mormon.* Bountiful, UT, 1898.

_____. *Mormon Inspiration.* Salt Lake City, 1928.

Campbell, Alexander. *Delusions: An Analysis of the Book of Mormon.* Boston: B. H. Green, 1831.

Canning, Ray R. *My Continuing Quest: Sociological Perspectives on Mormonism.* Salt Lake City: Freethinker Press, 1996.

Cannon, Donald Q., and Lyndon W. Cook, ed. *Far West Record: Minutes of The Church of Jesus Christ of Latter-day Saints, 1830-1844.* Salt Lake City: Deseret Book Co., 1983.

Caswall, Henry. *The City of the Mormons; or, Three Days at Nauvoo, in 1842.* London: J. G. F. and J. Rivington, 1842.

Charles, Melodie Moench. "Book of Mormon Christology."

In *New Approaches to the Book of Mormon: Explorations in Critical Methodology,* ed. Brent Lee Metcalfe, 81-114. Salt Lake City: Signature Books, 1993.

Cheesman, Paul R. *The Keystone of Mormonism: Early Vision of the Prophet Joseph Smith.* Provo, UT: Eagle Systems International, 1988.

Clark, J. Reuben, Jr. *On the Way to Immortality and Eternal Life.* Salt Lake City: Deseret Book Co., 1949.

Clark, John A. *Gleanings by the Way.* Philadelphia: W. J. and K. Simon, 1842.

Clark, John E. "Book of Mormon Geography." In *Encyclopedia of Mormonism,* ed. Daniel H. Ludlow, 1:176-79. New York: Macmillan Publishing Co., 1992.

Coe, Michael D. "Mormons and Archaeology: An Outside View." *Dialogue: A Journal of Mormon Thought* 8, no. 2 (1973): 40-48.

_____. *Breaking the Maya Code.* New York: Thames and Hudson, 1992.

_____ *The Maya.* 5th ed., fully rev. and exp. Ancient Peoples and Places. London: Thames and Hudson, 1993.

Compton, Todd. *In Sacred Loneliness: The Plural Wives of Joseph Smith.* Salt Lake City: Signature Books, 1997.

Cook, Lyndon W. *The Revelations of the Prophet Joseph Smith: A Historical and Biographical Commentary of the Doctrine and Covenants.* Salt Lake City: Deseret Book, 1985.

_____, ed. *David Whitmer Interviews: A Restoration Witness.* Orem, UT: Grandin Book Co., 1991.

_____. *William Law: Biographical Essay, Nauvoo Diary, Correspondence, Interview.* Orem, UT: Grandin Book Co., 1994.

Cope, Anne. *Swords and Hilt Weapons.* London: Multimedia Books, 1993.

Coutts, Alison V. P. "Earnestly Seeking." Review of *Recent Book of Mormon Developments,* by Raymond Treat. In

Review of Books on the Book of Mormon 7, no. 2 (1995): 253-55.

Cowdery, Oliver. Letter III to W. W. Phelps. *Latter Day Saints' Messenger and Advocate* 1 (December 1834): 41-43.

_____. Letter IV to W. W. Phelps. *Latter Day Saints' Messenger and Advocate* 1 (February 1835): 77-80.

_____. Letter to William Frye, *Latter Day Saints' Messenger and Advocate* 2 (December 1835): 234-37.

Crary, Christopher G. *Pioneer and Personal Reminiscences.* Marshalltown, IA: Marshall Printing Co., 1893.

Dickinson, Ellen E. *New Light on Mormonism.* New York: Funk and Wagnalls, 1885.

Dillehay, Tom D., and David J. Meltzer, eds. *The First Americans: Search and Research.* Boca Raton, FL: CRC Press, 1991.

Embry, Jessie L. *Black Saints in a White Church: Contemporary African American Mormons.* Salt Lake City: Signature Books, 1994.

Ericksen, E. E. *Psychological and Ethical Aspects of Mormon Group Life.* Salt Lake City: University of Utah Press, 1975.

Evans, Richard C. *Forty Years in the Mormon Church: Why I Left It!* Toronto, Canada, 1920.

Faulring, Scott H., ed. *An American Prophet's Record: The Diaries and Journals of Joseph Smith.* 2d ed. Salt Lake City: Signature Books in association with Smith Research Associates, 1989.

Firmage, Edwin B., ed. *An Abundant Life: The Memoirs of Hugh B. Brown.* Salt Lake City: Signature Books, 1988.

Gibbons, Francis M. *Joseph Smith: Martyr, Prophet of God.* Salt Lake City: Deseret Book Co., 1977.

Green, Dee F. "Book of Mormon Archaeology: The Myths and the Alternatives." *Dialogue: A Journal of Mormon Thought* 4 (Summer 1969): 49-55.

BIBLIOGRAPHY

Griffith, Michael T. *Refuting the Critics: Evidences of the Book of Mormon's Authenticity.* Bountiful, UT: Horizon Publishers, 1993.

Gunn, Stanley. *Oliver Cowdery: Second Elder and Scribe.* Salt Lake City: Bookcraft, 1962.

Hamblin, William J. "Sharper Than a Two-Edged Sword." *Sunstone* 15 (December 1991): 54-55.

_____. Review of *Archaeology and the Book of Mormon,* by Jerald Tanner and Sandra Tanner. In *Review of Books on the Book of Mormon* 5 (1993): 250-72.

_____. "Basic Methodological Problems with the Anti-Mormon Approach to the geography and Archaeology of the Book of Mormon." *Journal of Book of Mormon Studies* 2 (Spring 1993): 161-97.

_____. "An Apologist for the Critics: Brent Lee Metcalfe's Assumptions and Methodologies." Review of "Apologetic and Critical Assumptions about the Book of Mormon Historicity," by Brent Lee Metcalfe. In *Review of Books on the Book of Mormon* 6, no. 1 (1994): 434-523.

Hamblin, William J., and A. Brent Merrill. "Swords in the Book of Mormon." In *Warfare in the Book of Mormon,* ed. Stephen D. Ricks and William J. Hamblin, 329-51. Salt Lake City: Deseret Book Co., 1990; Provo, UT: Foundation for Ancient Research and Mormon Studies, 1990.

Harris, Martin. Interview conducted by Joel Tiffany, published in "Mormonism—No. II," *Tiffany's Monthly* 5, no. 4 (August 1859): 163-70.

Hassig, Ross. *War and Society in Ancient Mesoamerica.* Berkeley and Los Angeles and Oxford: University of California Press, 1992.

_____. *Mexico and the Spanish Conquest.* Modern Wars in Perspective. London and New York: Longman, 1994.

Haynes, Gary. *Mammoths, Mastodonts, and Elephants: Biology, Behavior, and the Fossil Record.* Cambridge, England:

Cambridge University Press, 1991.

Hickman, Josiah E. *The Romance of the Book of Mormon.* Salt Lake City: Deseret News Press, 1937.

Hill, Donna. *Joseph Smith: The First Mormon.* Garden City, NY: Doubleday and Co., 1977.

Hill, Marvin S. "Cultural Crisis in the Mormon Kingdom: A Reconsideration of the Causes of Kirtland Dissent." *Church History* 49 (September 1980): 286-97.

_____. "The First Vision Controversy: A Critique and Reconciliation." *Dialogue: A Journal of Mormon Thought* 15 (Summer 1982): 31-46.

_____. *Quest for Refuge: The Mormon Flight from American Pluralism.* Salt Lake City: Signature Books, 1989.

_____. "Afterword." *Brigham Young University Studies* 30 (Fall 1990): 117-24.

Hinckley, Bryant S. *Doctrine and Covenants Studies.* Salt Lake City: Deseret Sunday School Union Board, 1948.

Hinckley, Gordon B. *Be Thou an Example.* Salt Lake City: Deseret Book Co., 1981.

_____. *Teachings of Gordon B. Hinckley.* Salt Lake City: Deseret Book Co., 1997.

Holland, Jeffrey R. *Christ and the New Covenant: The Messianic Message of the Book of Mormon.* Salt Lake City: Deseret Book Co., 1997.

Homer, William H. "The Passing of Martin Harris." *Improvement Era* 29 (March 1926): 468-72.

Hosler, Dorothy. *The Sounds and Colors of Power: The Sacred Metallurgical Technology of Ancient West Mexico* (Cambridge, MA: The Massachusetts Institute of Technology, 1994.

Howard, Richard P. "An Analysis of Six Contemporary Accounts Touching Joseph Smith's First Vision." In *Restoration Studies I: Sesquicentennial Edition*, ed. Maurice L. Draper. Independence, MO: Herald Publishing House, 1980.

BIBLIOGRAPHY

Howe, Eber D. *Mormonism Unvailed; or, A Faithful Account of that Singular Imposition and Delusion, from Its Rise to the Present Time.* Painesville, OH, 1834.

Hubbard, Elbert. *Little Journeys to the Homes of Great Philosophers.* 2 vols. East Aurora, NY: The Roycrofters, 1904.

Hunt, James H. *Mormonism, Embracing the Origin, Rise, and Progress of the Sect, with an Examination of the Book of Mormon, also Their Troubles in Missouri, and Final Expulsion from the State.* St. Louis: Ustick and Davies, 1844.

Hutchinson, Anthony A. "The Word of God is Enough: The Book of Mormon as Nineteenth-Century Scripture." In *New Approaches to the Book of Mormon: Explorations in Critical Methodology,* ed. Brent Lee Metcalfe, 1-19. Salt Lake City: Signature Books, 1993.

Jenson, Andrew. "The Eight Witnesses." *The Historical Record* 7 (October 1888): 609-22.

Jessee, Dean C. "How Lovely was the Morning." Review of *Joseph Smith's First Vision* by Milton V. Backman. In *Dialogue: A Journal of Mormon Thought* 6 (Spring 1971): 85-88.

_____. "Joseph Knight's Recollection of Early Mormon History." *Brigham Young University Studies* 17 (Autumn 1976): 29-39.

_____, ed. *The Papers of Joseph Smith.* 2 vols. Salt Lake City: Deseret Book Co., 1989-1992.

Johnson, Joel H. Poem. *Times and Seasons* 2 (15 July 1841): 482.

Kelley, William H. "The Hill Cumorah, and the Book of Mormon." *The Saints' Herald* 28 (1 June 1881): 161-68.

Kenney, Scott G., ed. *Wilford Woodruff's Journal:1833-1898, Typescript.* 9 vols. Midvale, Utah: Signature Books, 1983-1985.

Kipling, Rudyard. *From Sea to Sea: Letters of Travel.* 2 vols. New York: Doubleday and McClure Co., 1899.

Kirkham, Francis W. *A New Witness for Christ in America: The*

Book of Mormon. 2 vols. Enl. 3d ed. Salt Lake City: Utah Printing Co., 1959-1960.

Kunich, John C. "Multiply Exceedingly: Book of Mormon Population Sizes." In *New Approaches to the Book of Mormon: Explorations in Critical Methodology*, ed. Brent Lee Metcalfe, 231-67. Salt Lake City: Signature Books, 1993.

Lamb, Martin T. *The Golden Bible; or, The Book of Mormon. Is It from God?* New York: Ward and Drummond, 1886.

Larson, Stan. *Quest for the Gold Plates: Thomas Stuart Ferguson's Archaeological Search for the Book of Mormon.* Salt Lake City: Freethinker Press in association with Smith Research Associates, 1996.

Lister, Adrian, and Paul Bahn. *Mammoths.* New York: Macmillan, 1994.

Lundwall, Nels B., comp. *Assorted Gems of Priceless Value.* Salt Lake City, 1944.

MacFadden, Bruce J. *Fossil Horses: Systematics, Paleobiology, and Evolution of the Family Equidae.* Cambridge, England: Cambridge University Press, 1992.

Madsen, Brigham D. "Reflections on LDS Disbelief in the Book of Mormon as History." *Dialogue: A Journal of Mormon Thought* 30 (Fall 1997): 87-97.

Madsen, Gordon A. "Joseph Smith's 1826 Trial: The Legal Setting." *Brigham Young University Studies* 30 (Spring 1990): 91-108.

Marcus, Joyce. *Mesoamerican Writing Systems: Propaganda, Myth, and History in Four Ancient Civilizations.* Princeton, NJ: Princeton University Press, 1992.

Marquardt, H. Michael, and Wesley P. Walters. *Inventing Mormonism: Tradition and the Historical Record.* 2d ed. [Salt Lake City]: Smith Research Associates, 1998.

Martin, Stuart. *The Mystery of Mormonism.* New York: E. P. Dutton and Co., 1920.

Matheny, Deanne G. "Does the Shoe Fit? A Critique of the

Limited Tehuantepec Geography." In *New Approaches to the Book of Mormon: Explorations in Critical Methodology*, ed. Brent Lee Metcalfe, 269-328. Salt Lake City: Signature Books, 1993.

Mathews, Peter. *The Proceedings of the Maya Hieroglyphic Weekend, October 27-28, 1990, Cleveland State University*. Ed. Phil Wanyerka. Austin, TX: Maya Hieroglyphic Weekend, 1991.

McCarter, P. Kyle, Jr. "Let's Be Serious about the Bat Creek Stone." *Biblical Archaeology Review* 19 (July-August 1993): 54-55, 83.

McCulloch, J. Huston. "The Bat Creek Inscription: Did Judean Refugees Escape to Tennessee?" *Biblical Archaeology Review* 19 (July-August 1993): 46-53, 82-83.

McGavin, E. Cecil. *An Apology for the Book of Mormon*. Salt Lake City: Deseret News Press, 1930.

_____. *Cumorah's "Gold Bible."* 2d ed. Salt Lake City: Bookcraft, 1948.

_____. *The Historical Background of the Doctrine and Covenants*. Salt Lake City: Paragon Printing Co., 1949.

Merrill, Joseph F. "The Place the Book of Mormon along with Cardinal Teachings Holds in the Lives of Latter-day Saints." *Deseret News*, 19 January 1929, Church Department, sect. 3, p. 6.

Metcalf, Anthony. *Ten Years before the Mast*. Malad City, ID, 1888.

Metcalfe, Brent Lee. "The Priority of Mosiah: A Prelude to Book of Mormon Exegesis." In *New Approaches to the Book of Mormon: Explorations in Critical Methodology*, ed. Brent Lee Metcalfe, 395-444. Salt Lake City: Signature Books, 1993.

_____. "Apologetic and Critical Assumptions about Book of Mormon Historicity." *Dialogue: A Journal of Mormon Thought* 26 (Fall 1993): 153-84.

Millet, Robert L. "The Book of Mormon, Historicity, and

Faith." *Journal of Book of Mormon Studies* 2 (Fall 1993): 1-13.

_____. *The Power of the Word: Saving Doctrines from the Book of Mormon.* Salt Lake City: Deseret Book Co., 1994.

Morton, William A. *Why I Believe the Book of Mormon to Be the Word of God.* Salt Lake City: Deseret News Press, 1966.

Mulder, William. "Mormonism and Literature." *The Western Humanities Review* 9 (Winter 1954-1955): 85-89.

Nelson, Nels L. *Scientific Aspects of Mormonism; or, Religion in Terms of Life.* New York: G. P. Putnam's Sons, 1904.

_____. "Human Side of the Book of Mormon." *The Mormon Point-of-View: A Quarterly Magazine* 1 (1 April 1904): 105-56.

Nibley, Hugh. *Since Cumorah: The Book of Mormon in the Modern World.* 2d ed. The Collected Works of Hugh Nibley: Volume 7, ed. John W. Welch. Salt Lake City: Deseret Book Co., 1988; Provo, UT: Foundation for Ancient Research and Mormon Studies, 1988.

_____. *Lehi in the Desert, The World of the Jaredites, There Were Jaredites.* The Collected Works of Hugh Nibley: Volume 5, ed. John W. Welch. Salt Lake City: Deseret Book Co., 1988; Provo UT: Foundation for Ancient Research and Mormon Studies, 1988.

_____. *The Prophetic Book of Mormon.* The Collected Works of Hugh Nibley: Volume 8, ed. John W. Welch. Salt Lake City: Deseret Book Co., 1989; Provo UT: Foundation for Ancient Research and Mormon Studies, 1989.

_____. *Tinkling Cymbals and Sounding Brass: The Art of Telling Tales about Joseph Smith and Brigham Young.* The Collected Works of Hugh Nibley: Volume 11, ed. David J. Whittaker. Salt Lake City: Deseret Book Co., 1991; Provo, UT: Foundation for Ancient Research and Mormon Studies, 1991.

_____. *Teachings of the Book of Mormon.* 4 vols. Provo, UT:

Foundation for Ancient Research and Mormon Studies, 1993.

Novak, Gary F. "Naturalistic Assumptions and the Book of Mormon." *Brigham Young University Studies* 30 (Summer 1990): 23-40.

_____. "Examining the Environmental Explanation of the Book of Mormon." Review of *Joseph Smith's Response to Skepticism*, by Robert N. Hullinger. In *Review of Books on the Book of Mormon* 7, no. 1 (1995): 139-54.

Nutting, John D. *Mormonism Proclaiming Itself a Fraud.* Cleveland, OH: Utah Gospel Mission, 1901.

Ostler, Blake T. "The Book of Mormon as a Modern Expansion of an Ancient Source." *Dialogue: A Journal of Mormon Thought* 20 (Spring 1987): 66-123.

Parker, Sybil P., ed. *Grzimek's Encyclopedia of Mammals.* 5 vols. New York: McGraw-Hill Publishing Co., 1990.

Petersen, LaMar. *Problems in Mormon Text.* Salt Lake City, 1957.

_____. *Hearts Made Glad: The Charges of Intemperance against Joseph Smith the Mormon Prophet (and Folkes that Dronken ben of Ale).* Salt Lake City, 1975.

Peterson, Daniel C. "Book of Mormon Economy and Technology." In *Encyclopedia of Mormonism*, ed. Daniel H. Ludlow, 1:172-75. New York: MacMillan Publishing Co., 1992.

_____. "LDS Scholars Refute Attacks on the Book of Mormon." *This People* 15 (Summer 1994): 29-33.

_____. "Is the Book of Mormon True? Notes on the Debate." In *Book of Mormon Authorship Revisited: The Evidence for Ancient Origins*, ed. Noel B. Reynolds, 141-77. Provo, UT: Foundation for Ancient Research and Mormon Studies, 1997.

Peterson, Jeanette Favrot. *Precolumbian Flora and Fauna: Continuity of Plant and Animal Themes in Mesoamerican Art.* San Diego: Mingei International Museum of World

Folk Art, 1990.

Pratt, Orson. *An Interesting Account of Several Remarkable Visions and of the Late Discovery of Ancient American Records.* Edinburgh: Ballantyne and Hughes, 1840.

_____. *Divine Authenticity of the Book of Mormon.* Liverpool, England: R. James, 1850.

_____. "The Pre-existence of Man." *The Seer* 1 (February-September 1853): 17-24, 37-41, 49-57, 65-72, 81-89, 97-104, 113-21, 129-35.

_____. "Repentance." *The Seer* 2 (March 1854): 233-40.

Priest, Josiah. *American Antiquities and Discoveries in the West.* Albany, NY: Hoffman and White, 1833.

Prince, Gregory A. *Power from on High: The Development of Mormon Priesthood.* Salt Lake City: Signature Books, 1995.

Proskouriakoff, Tatiana. *Maya History.* Ed. Rosemary A. Joyce. Austin, TX: University of Texas Press, 1993.

Quinn, D. Michael, trans. and ed. "The First Months of Mormonism: A Contemporary View by Rev. Diedrich Willers." *New York History* 54 (1973): 317-33.

_____. *Early Mormonism and the Magic World View.* Salt Lake City: Signature Books, 1987.

_____. "150 Years of Truth and Consequences about Mormon History. *Sunstone* 16 (February 1992): 12-14.

_____. *The Mormon Hierarchy: Origins of Power.* Salt Lake City: Signature Books, 1994.

_____. *The Mormon Hierarchy: Extensions of Power.* Salt Lake City: Signature Books, 1997.

Remy, Jules. *A Journey to Great-Salt-Lake City.* 2 vols. London: W. Jeffs, 1861.

Reynolds, George. *The Myth of the "Manuscript Found," or the Absurdities of the "Spaulding Story."* Salt Lake City: Juvenile Instructor Office, 1883.

_____. "History of the Book of Mormon." *The Contributor* 5 (June-August 1884): 321-26, 361-67, 401-408.

BIBLIOGRAPHY

Ricks, Joel. "Urim and Thummim." *Improvement Era* 18 (May 1915): 611-15.

Ricks, Stephen D. "Book of Mormon Studies." In *Encyclopedia of Mormonism*, ed. Daniel H. Ludlow, 1:205-209. 5 vols. New York: Macmillan Publishing Co., 1992.

Riley, I. Woodbridge. *The Founder of Mormonism: A Psychological Study of Joseph Smith, Jr.* New York: Dodd, Mead and Co., 1902.

Roberts, B. H. "Book of Mormon Translation: Interesting Correspondence on the Subject of the Manual Theory." *Improvement Era* 9 (July 1906): 706-713.

_____. *Defense of the Faith and the Saints.* 2 vols. Salt Lake City: The Deseret News, 1907-1912.

_____, ed. *History of the Church of Jesus Christ of Latter-day Saints, Period I: History of Joseph Smith, the Prophet by Himself.* 6 vols. Salt Lake City: Deseret Book Co., 1902-1912.

_____ "Book of Mormon Difficulties: A Study." Typescript, 1921, in the B. H. Roberts Collection, Manuscript 106, Box 9, Book 1, Manuscripts Division, J. Willard Marriott Library, University of Utah, Salt Lake City.

_____. "A Book of Mormon Study." Typescript, 1922, in Box 9, Books 2-3, Roberts Collection.

_____. "A Parallel." Typescript, 1927, in Box 16, Fd 3, Roberts Collection.

_____. *A Comprehensive History of The Church of Jesus Christ of Latter-day Saints, Century I.* 6 vols. Salt Lake City: The Church of Jesus Christ of Latter-day Saints, 1930.

_____. *Studies of the Book of Mormon.* Ed. Brigham D. Madsen. 2d ed. Salt Lake City: Signature Books, 1992.

Robicsek, Francis. "The Weapons of the Ancient Maya." In *Circumpacifica*, ed. Bruno Illius and Matthias Laubscher. Frankfurt am Main: Peter Lang, 1990.

Robinson, Stephen E. "The 'Expanded' Book of Mormon?" In *The Book of Mormon: Second Nephi, the Doctrinal Struc-*

ture, ed. Monte S. Nyman and Charles D. Tate, Jr., 391-414. Provo, UT: Religious Studies Center, Brigham Young University, 1989.

Sabloff, Jeremy A. *The New Archaeology and the Ancient Maya*. New York: Scientific American Library, 1990.

Schele, Linda, and David Freidel. *A Forest of Kings: The Untold Story of the Ancient Maya*. New York: William Morrow, 1990.

Schele, Linda, and Nikolai Grube. *The Proceedings of the Maya Hieroglyphic Workshop [on] Late Classic and Terminal Classic Warfare, March 11-12, 1995*. Ed. Phil Wanyerka. Austin, TX: Maya Hieroglyphic Workshop, 1995.

Sharer, Robert J. *The Ancient Maya*. 5th ed. Stanford, CA: Stanford University Press, 1994.

Sheldon, William. *Mormonism Examined; or, Was Joseph Smith a Divinely Inspired Prophet?* Broadhead, WI, [1876].

Shook, Charles A. *The True Origin of the Book of Mormon*. Cincinnati, OH: The Standard Publishing Co., 1914.

Sjodahl, Janne M. *An Introduction to the Study of the Book of Mormon*. Salt Lake City: Deseret News Press, 1927.

Skousen, Royal. "Book of Mormon Manuscripts." In *Encyclopedia of Mormonism*, ed. Daniel H. Ludlow, 1:185-86. 5 vols. New York: Macmillan Publishing Co., 1992.

_____. "Translating the Book of Mormon: Evidence from the Original Manuscript." In *Book of Mormon Authorship Revisited: The Evidence for Ancient Origins*, ed. Noel B. Reynolds, 62-93. Provo, UT: Foundation for Ancient Research and Mormon Studies, 1997.

Smith, George D., ed. *An Intimate Chronicle: The Journals of William Clayton*. Salt Lake City: Signature Books in association with Smith Research Associates, 1995.

Smith, James E. "How Many Nephites? The Book of Mormon at the Bar of Demography." In *Book of Mormon Authorship Revisited: The Evidence for Ancient Origins*, ed. Noel B. Reynolds, 255-93. Provo, UT: Foundation for Ancient Research and Mormon Studies, 1997.

Smith, Joseph. "Church History." *Times and Seasons* 3 (1 March 1842): 706-10.

Smith, Joseph, III. "Last Testimony of Sister Emma [Smith]." *The Saints' Herald* 26 (1 October 1879): 289-90.

Smith, Joseph, III, and Heman C. Smith. *History of the Church of Jesus Christ of Latter Day Saints*. 4 vols. Lamoni, IA: Board of Publication of the Reorganized Church of Jesus Christ of Latter Day Saints, 1897-1903.

Smith, Joseph Fielding. *Church History and Modern Revelation*. 2 vols. Salt Lake City: The Council of the Twelve Apostles of the Church of Jesus Christ of Latter-day Saints, 1953.

_____. "Urim and Thummim." *The Improvement Era* 57 (June 1954): 382-83.

Smith, Lucy Mack. "Preliminary Manuscript." A photocopy of this manuscript is located in Accession 989, Manuscripts Division, J. Willard Marriott Library, University of Utah, Salt Lake City.

_____. *Biographical Sketches of Joseph Smith the Prophet, and His Progenitors for Many Generations*. Liverpool, England: Published for Orson Pratt by S. W. Richards, 1853.

Smith, William. *William Smith on Mormonism*. Lamoni, IA: Herald Steam Book and Job Office, 1883.

Sorenson, John L. *An Ancient American Setting for the Book of Mormon*. Salt Lake City: Deseret Book Co., 1985; Provo, UT: Foundation for Ancient Research and Mormon Studies, 1985.

_____. *Animals in the Book of Mormon: An Annotated Bibliography*. Provo, UT: Foundation for Ancient Research and Mormon Studies, 1992.

_____. *Metals and Metallurgy relating to the Book of Mormon Text*. Provo, UT: Foundation for Ancient Research and Mormon Studies, 1992.

_____. "Once More: The Horse." In *Reexploring the Book of*

Mormon: The F.A.R.M.S. Updates, ed. John W. Welch, 98-100. Salt Lake City: Deseret Book Co., 1992; Provo, UT: Foundation for Ancient Research and Mormon Studies, 1992.

_____. "Viva Zapato! Hurray for the Shoe!" Review of "Does the Shoe Fit?" by Deanne G. Matheny, in *Review of Books on the Book of Mormon* 6, no. 1 (1994): 297-361.

_____. "The Book of Mormon as a Mesoamerican Record." In *Book of Mormon Authorship Revisited: The Evidence for Ancient Origins,* ed. Noel B. Reynolds, 391-521. Provo, UT: Foundation for Ancient Research and Mormon Studies, 1997.

Spackman, Randall P. *Introduction to Book of Mormon Chronology: The Principal Prophecies, Calendars, and Dates.* Provo, UT: Foundation for Ancient Research and Mormon Studies, 1993.

Spalding, Franklin S. *Joseph Smith, Jr., as a Translator.* Salt Lake City: The Arrow Press, 1912.

Sperry, Sidney B. *Problems of the Book of Mormon.* Salt Lake City: Bookcraft, 1964.

_____. *Answers to Book of Mormon Questions (formerly Problems of the Book of Mormon).* Salt Lake City: Bookcraft, 1967.

Stevenson, Edward. "The Three Witnesses to the Book of Mormon." *The Latter-day Saints' Millennial Star* 48 (21 June 1886): 389-91.

_____. *Reminiscences of Joseph, the Prophet, and the Coming Forth of the Book of Mormon.* Salt Lake City, 1893.

Stock, Chester. *Rancho La Brea: A Record of Pleistocene Life in California.* 7th ed., rev. by John M. Harris. Science Series, no. 37. Los Angeles: Natural History Museum of Los Angeles County, 1992.

Stuart, Gene S., and George E. Stuart. *Lost Kingdoms of the Maya.* Washington, D.C.: National Geographic Society, 1993.

Stubbs, Brian. *Elements of Hebrew in Uto-Aztecan: A Summary of the Data.* Provo, UT: Foundation for Ancient Research and Mormon Studies, 1988.

Sumner, William Graham. *The Folkways: A Study of the Sociological Importance of Usages, Manners, Customs, Mores, and Morals.* Boston: Ginn and Co., 1940.

Talmage, James E. *Jesus the Christ: A Study of the Messiah and His Mission according to Holy Scriptures both Ancient and Modern.* Salt Lake City: The Deseret News, 1915.

Tanner, Jerald, and Sandra Tanner, eds. *Roberts' Manuscripts Revealed: A Photographic Reproduction of Mormon Historian B. H. Roberts' Secret Studies on the Book of Mormon.* Salt Lake City: Modern Microfilm Co., 1980.

_____. *Mormonism: Shadow or Reality.* 5th ed. Salt Lake City: Utah Lighthouse Ministry, 1987.

_____. "Ferguson's Two Faces: Mormon Scholar's 'Spoof' Lives on after His Death." *Salt Lake City Messenger,* no. 69 (September 1988): 1-10.

_____, eds. *Ferguson's Manuscript Unveiled.* Salt Lake City: Utah Lighthouse Ministry, 1988.

Taylor, John. *The Government of God.* Liverpool, England: S. W. Richards, 1852.

Thomas, Mark D. "Swords Cankered with Rust." Review of *Warfare in the Book of Mormon,* ed. Stephen D. Ricks and William J. Hamblin. In *Sunstone* 15 (September 1991): 55.

Thompson, Charles. *Evidences in Proof of the Book of Mormon.* Batavia, NY: D. D. Waite, 1841.

Thompson, Stephen E. "'Critical' Book of Mormon Scholarship." Review of *New Approaches to the Book of Mormon,* ed. Brent Metcalfe, and *Review of Books on the Book of Mormon,* ed. Daniel Peterson. In *Dialogue: A Journal of Mormon Thought* 27 (Winter 1994): 197-206.

Time-Life Books. *The Magnificent Maya.* Lost Civilizations. Alexandria, VA: Time-Life Books, 1993.

Traum, Samuel W. *Mormonism against Itself*. Cincinnati, OH: Standard Publishing Co., 1910.

Tucker, Pomeroy. *Origin, Rise, and Progress of Mormonism: Biography of Its Founders and History of Its Church*. New York: D. Appleton and Co., 1867.

Turner, Jonathan B. *Mormonism in All Ages; or, The Rise, Progress, and Causes of Mormonism, with the Biography of Its Author and Founder, Joseph Smith, Junior*. New York: Platt and Peters, 1842.

Twain, Mark, pseud. [Samuel Langhorne Clemens]. *Roughing It*. Hartford, CT: American Publishing Co., 1872.

Van Wagoner, Richard S., and Steven C. Walker. "Joseph Smith: 'The Gift of Seeing.'" *Dialogue: A Journal of Mormon Thought* 15 (Summer 1982): 49-68.

Vogel, Dan. *Indian Origins and the Book of Mormon: Religious Solutions from Columbus to Joseph Smith*. Salt Lake City: Signature Books, 1986.

_____, comp. and ed. *Early Mormon Documents*. Salt Lake City: Signature Books, 1996.

Walker, John Phillip, ed. *Dale Morgan on Early Mormonism: Correspondence and a New History*. Salt Lake City: Signature Books, 1986.

Walker, Ronald W. "Martin Harris: Mormonism's Early Convert." *Dialogue: A Journal of Mormon Thought* 19 (Winter 1986): 29-43.

Ward, Artemus. *Artemus Ward: His Travels*. New York: Carleton, 1865.

Wardle, James D. "Shall We Improve the Book of Mormon?" *The Saints' Herald* 102 (21 March 1955): 9-10.

Watson, Elden Jay, ed. *Manuscript History of Brigham Young, 1801-1844*. Salt Lake City, 1968.

Weed, Thurlow. *Autobiography of Thurlow Weed*. Ed. Harriet A. Weed. Boston: Houghton, Mifflin and Co., 1883.

Welch, John W. Finding Answers to B. H. Roberts' Questions and "An Unparallel." Provo, UT: Foundation for Ancient Research and Mormon Studies, 1985.

White, James. "Of Cities and Swords: The Impossible Task of Mormon Apologetics." *Christian Research Journal* (Summer 1996): 29-35.

Whitmer, David. *An Address to All Believers in Christ*. Richmond, MO, 1887.

Whitney, Orson F. *Life of Heber C. Kimball, an Apostle, the Father and Founder of the British Mission*. Salt Lake City: The Kimball Family, 1888.

Whittaker, David J. "Substituted Names in the Published Revelations of Joseph Smith." *Brigham Young University Studies* 23 (Winter 1983): 103-12.

Widtsoe, John A. "The Folly of Astrology." *Improvement Era* 4 (February 1901): 289-95.

_____. *Gospel Interpretations: Aids to Faith in a Modern Day*. Salt Lake City: Bookcraft, 1947.

_____. *Discourses of Brigham Young*. Salt Lake City: Deseret Book Co., 1973.

Widtsoe, John A., and Franklin S. Harris, Jr. *Seven Claims of the Book of Mormon: A Collection of Evidences*. Independence, MO: Zion's Printing Co., 1937.

Wirth, Diane E. *The Challenge to the Critics: Scholarly Evidences of the Book of Mormon*. Bountiful, UT: Horizon Publishers, 1988.

Wood, Wilford C., ed. *Joseph Smith Begins His Work*. 2 vols. Salt Lake City: Deseret News Press, 1958.

Wright, David P. "'In Plain Terms That We May Understand': Joseph Smith's Transformation of Hebrews in Alma 12-13." In *New Approaches to the Book of Mormon: Explorations in Critical Methodology*, ed. Brent Lee Metcalfe, 165-229. Salt Lake City: Signature Books, 1993.

Wyl, W., pseud. [Wilhelm Ritter von Wymetal]. *Mormon Portraits; or, The Truth about Mormon Leaders from 1830 to 1886*. Salt Lake City: Tribune Printing and Publishing Co., 1886.

Index

INDEX

Cannon, Tracy Y., xi
Carter, George F., 210
Caswall, Henry, 37, 79
Chase, Clark, 26
Chase, Mason, 27, 132, 138
Chase, Willard: found stone in well, 26; Joseph Smith wished to obtain stone, 27; money digging business, 26; stone borrowed by Hyrum Smith, 27
Christensen, B. Keith, 170
Clark, J. Reuben, Jr., xii, 123-24
Clark, John Alonzo, 75, 89
Clark, John E., 197
Clayton, William, 42
Cobb, James T., 56
Coe, Michael D., 225, 227
Cole, Abner (alias Obadiah Dogberry), 21, 48, 54
Cowdery, Oliver, xiv, 31, 34, 39, 48, 80-81, 82, 83; narrative in form of letters, 11-13; priesthood restoration, 141-45; role of Rev. Lane, 17; witness to Book of Mormon, 84-86
Cowdery, Warren, 85
Crary, Christopher G., 92

D

Dellenbaugh, Frederick S., 216
Dickinson, Ellen, 53

E

Ephraim, blood of, xv
Ericksen, E. E., xx

Evans, Richard C., 98-99
Evans, Richard L., xii

F

Fell, Barry, 210-11
Ferguson, Thomas Stuart, 30-31, 169-75, 179-80, 193, 196, 208, 209-212, 218-30
First Vision, xii, 1-10
Flinders, Comfort E. Godfrey, 90
Forstemann, Ernst W., 212, 214
Fulghum, Robert, xxiv

G

Gatschet, Albert S., 184
Gibbons, Francis M., 52
Gilbert, John H., 34, 90-91
Golden Plates, xiv, 63, 79-80, 84
Goodman, J. Thomas, 212
Goodson, John, 111
Grant, Heber J., 121-22
Grant, Jedediah M., 161
Grayson, Donald K., 186
Green, Dee F., 219
Grimm, Glenna Neilsen, 193, 197

H

Hale, Alvah, 139
Hale, Emma. *See* Smith, Emma Hale
Hale, Isaac, 52, 78, 133; on translation of plates, 26
Hamblin, William J., 197, 203

252

INDEX

Tolman, Calvin D., 170
Townsend, Jesse, 55
Traum, Samuel W., 115-16
Treasures, hidden, 57, 59
Tucker, Pomeroy, 114-15
Turner, Jonathan B., 113-14
Tuttle, Daniel S., 30, 31
Twain, Mark, 105
Two stones, 38, 134

U

Urim and Thummim, xiv, 24, 25, 36-47

V

Van Blerkom, Linda Miller, 216

W

Waldeck, Jean Frédéric, 183, 189
Wallace, Henry A., 104
Ward, Artemus, 114
Warren, Bruce W., 170
Washburn, J. Nile, 170
Weed, Thurlow, 34
Welch, John W., 191, 192
Wentworth, John, 7
Whitmer, David, 24, 26, 39, 41, 83, 92, 147, 150-51; heard stories that Joseph Smith has plates, 65-66; Joseph Smith did not use the plates in the translation, 95; Joseph Smith placed stone in hat, 36; on translation process, 96; saw plates in a vision or in the spirit,

76; witness to Book of Mormon, 86-88
Widtsoe, John A., xi, xii, xvii, 52, 84
Willey, Gordon R., 217
Wirthlin, Joseph, xii
Witnesses: condition of faith in viewing the plates, 77; three witnesses, 75; to Book of Mormon, 73
Woodruff, Wilford: saw Urim and Thummim (seer stone), 44; who God is, 157
Wright, David P., 119

Y

Young, Brigham, xix, 58, 79, 120, 161; competition to obtain the plates, 66-67; exhibited seer stone, 36; on returning plates to Hill Cumorah, 82-83; on treasures in the earth, 53; on Urim and Thummim, 43; saw seer stone, 43
Young, Levi Edgar, xi; visit with, xii

About the Author

LaMar Petersen was born in Ogden, Utah, on 23 December 1910—exactly 105 years after the day of Joseph Smith's birth. As he grew older he became intrigued with the wonder tales of angels, visions, and pronouncements from heaven as proclaimed by Joseph Smith, the Prophet of Palmyra.

As Mr. Petersen studied he also began to write: *Problems in Mormon Text*, and *Hearts Made Glad*, as well as articles on Mormon history. He was a member of the Advisory Board of Editors for the *Utah Historical Quarterly* for eighteen years. Though he was an aspiring historian, his first love and profession was music. He directed the Mozart School of Music for thirty years and has been for seventy years a professional organist in Salt Lake churches. He still serves in this capacity at age eighty-seven.